Previous page: Northern Lights, Jökulsárlón (p142) Above: Flateyri (p207)

Contents

Best Experiences 6
Calendar 26
Trip Builders 34
7 Things to Know
About Iceland 44
Read, Listen,
Watch & Follow 46

Reykjavík 48

Eat Reykjavík 54
Into the Night 62
Culture Night 68
A Capital of Culture 72
Urban Hiking 78
Listings 80

The Golden Circle 84

Þingvellir
National Park 88
Water Works 94
Get Outside 96
Listings 98

Southwest Iceland & Reykjanes Peninsula 100

The Blue Lagoon 104
Not the Blue Lagoon 108
Eruptions & Lava 110
Listings 114

Vestmannaeyjar Side Trip 116

South Coast & Southern Highlands 118

Chasing Waterfalls 122
Coast Road Trip to Vík ... 124
Trekking in Þórsmörk 126
Landmannalaugar
Hiking 128
Listings 130

The East & Southeast 132

Exploring Skaftafell 136
Jökulsárlón Jaunt 142
Eastern Villages 146
Eastern Escape 148
Hallormsstaður Forest .. 152
Borgarfjörður Eystri 154
Listings 156

Akureyri 158

Adventure in
Eyjafjörður 162
Playing in the Snow 164
Cultural Curiosities 166
Listings 168

North Iceland 170

Heavenly
Showstopper 176
Arctic Coast Way 182
Flippers & Feathers 184
Journey Through
Stories 188
Island Explorations 192
Icelandic Horse
Culture 194
Listings 198

The Westfjords 200

Westfjords on Water 206
Road-Tripping Nirvana .. 210
Hornstrandir Hikes 214
Listings 216

West Iceland 218

Into the Earth 224
On the Saga Trail 226
Hiking in the West 232
Listings 234

Black-sand beach near Vík (p125)

Practicalities	236
Arriving	238
Getting Around	240
Safe Travel	242
Money	243
Accommodation	244
Responsible Travel	246
Essentials	248
Language	250

ESSAYS

A New Icelandic Cuisine	60
A Brief Take on Icelandic Craft Beer	66
A Path to Musical Excellence?	76
The History of Iceland	90
Pool Etiquette	106
Volcanoes	112
Skaftafell on Foot	140
Glaciers	144
Looking Skyward	180
Modern Legends	190
Tölting Through Time	196
Westfjords Way of Life	208
Sagaland	228

VISUAL GUIDES

Icelandic Food	58
Astronomical Iceland	178
Wild Things	186
Fjords & Landscapes	212
Wildlife of the West	230

SKIES ALIGHT

Green, pink, purple, red, white and even yellow Northern Lights (aurora borealis) can be seen dancing across clear dark skies. The colourful winter sunrises in late morning and early sunsets are also a spectacle. If you're visiting during the bright summers, stay up to watch the midnight sun barely set – and then rise again – or make the most of the long days and go for an evening hike.

→ CELESTIAL OFFERINGS

The Northern Lights get all the attention, but they share the sky with bright stars, meteor showers and the midnight sun.

▶ Learn more on p176 and p178

Left Northern Lights, Jökulsárlón glacier lagoon (p142) **Right** The Milky Way **Below** Winter evening, Reykjavik (p48)

ENDLESS DAYS

In midsummer, the Earth is more tilted towards the sun resulting in 24hr daylight in parts of Iceland around summer solstice. The further north, the brighter the nights.

↑ LIGHT & DARK

Some visitors find the long days disorienting. The bright nights can interfere with your sleep, so bring an eye mask in case you're camping or on the off chance your accommodation doesn't have blackout curtains. Likewise, the long winter days can make you feel sluggish. Locals take vitamin D–rich cod-liver oil to compensate for the lack of light.

Best Viewing Experiences

▶ **Go in search of the Northern Lights along the Arctic Coast Way.** (p182)

▶ **Gaze up at the stars and spot the constellations.** (p178)

▶ **Summit Snæfellsjökull glacier on a midnight-sun hike.** (p224)

▶ **Celebrate the summer solstice on Grímsey island on the Arctic Circle.** (p193)

▶ **Hike up Húsavíkurfjall for stupendous scenery and a celestial show.** (p177)

ARTS & **HERITAGE**

Culture and history buffs visiting Iceland won't be disappointed. Festivals and concerts are held around the country and beyond the grand galleries in Reykjavík, there are small quirky museums in even the smallest of settlements. Unique ways to immerse yourself in the sagas await, like taking a dip in Grettislaug pool and going to battle via a VR exhibition.

Left Turf houses, Icelandic Folk and Outsider Art Museum **Right** Statue of Leifur Eiríksson by Alexander Stirling Calder, Reykjavík **Below** Reykjavík Art Museum, Hafnarhús

→ VIKING DISCOVERIES

According to the sagas, Leifur Eiríksson arrived in America 500 years before Columbus.

▶ Visit the Leif Eiriksson Center (p227) in Búðardalur to learn more

IN FOCUS

Scenes from a number of blockbusters and popular TV series have been shot in Iceland, including *Game of Thrones*, *Eurovision Song Contest: The Story of Fire Saga*, *Fast and Furious 8*, *Prometheus*, and *Rogue One: A Star Wars Story*.

▶ Read more on p190

↑ MUST VISIT

The Reykjavík Art Museum, hosted at three locations and exhibiting local and international modern and contemporary artists, is a real gem. The museum also houses the collections of three of Iceland's most famous artists: Erró, Kjarval and Ásmundur Sveinsson.

▶ Find out more on p73

Best History & Culture Experiences

▶ **Visit the Alþingi, site of Iceland's first parliament.** (p88)

▶ **Explore saga sites in West Iceland.** (p226)

▶ **Observe colourful and curious exhibitions at the Icelandic Folk and Outsider Art Museum outside Akureyri.** (p166)

▶ **Become a warrior in Sauðárkrókur and take part in a virtual-reality Battle of Iceland.** (p189)

▶ **Immerse yourself in the favourite retreat of Iceland's artists in Seyðisfjörður.** (p147)

HOT-WATER
HEALING

Icelanders have been harnessing the power of geothermal heat for centuries. Today, almost every town has a heated swimming pool with hot-pots. More recently, spas and geothermal baths have been popping up in stunning locations all over the country, offering next-level luxury. Visiting natural hot springs, however, remains a unique experience.

→ SPA VS SPRING

Spa lovers are spoilt for choice with baths overlooking the ocean, lakes and mountains. But the no-fuss natural hot springs remain authentic and free.

▶ Discover more on p217 and p234

Left Natural hot springs, Landmannalaugar (p129) **Right** Blue Lagoon (p104) **Below** Sea swimming

POOL ETIQUETTE

To maintain hygiene and keep chlorine levels low, pool guests must first shower naked. Communal showering is part of the pool culture, so do your best to fit in.

▶ Read more on p45 and p106

↑ NEW BEGINNINGS

Sea swimming exploded in popularity during Covid-19. Join the annual New Year's Day dip at Nauthólsvík, followed by a catch-up in the hot tub.

Best Soaking Experiences

▶ Find out what all the hype is about in the waters of the Blue Lagoon. (p104)

▶ Discover natural hot springs and pools in unforgettable settings along the Westfjords Way. (p211)

▶ Sweat it out in the steam room at a local swimming pool in Reykjavík. (p82)

▶ Gaze out onto the fjord from Hofsós Swimming Pool. (p199)

▶ Architecture meets stunning thermal baths out east at Vök Baths. (p147)

CULINARY
CREATIONS

Eating out in Iceland certainly isn't cheap, but choose wisely and you may end up enjoying some of the best food experiences of your life. Innovative chefs are spotlighting local ingredients and modernising traditional cuisine into a feast. Seafood and lamb feature heavily, but vegetarian and vegan options are widely available.

★ FROZEN FAVOURITE

Icelanders love ice cream, even on the coldest of days. Ice-cream parlours are all over the country. For something fancy, try Omnom Chocolate (p57) in Reykjavík.

Left Langoustines ('Icelandic lobster')
Right Restaurant ice cream **Below** Picnicking, Landmannalaugar (p128)

MUST TRY

A family-run restaurant on Vestmannaeyjar, Slippurinn uses only local produce and follows the philosophies of New Nordic and Slow Food.
▶ Read about Vestmannaeyjar on p114

↑ PACK A PICNIC

Prepare your favourite snacks, find a bench or throw down a blanket and dine in nature.

Best Food Experiences

▶ **Dine out at some of Reykjavík's top-notch eateries.** (p54)

▶ **Savour hyper-local flavours on a trip to Flatey island in Breiðafjörður.** (p43)

▶ **Catch your own fish off the North Iceland village of Hauganes.** (p182)

▶ **Sample the increasing selection of Icelandic craft beers.** (p66)

▶ **Treat yourself to some 'Icelandic lobster', a speciality of the town of Höfn.** (p157)

HIDDEN
WONDERS

While checking off your list of big attractions, keep an eye out for unexpected discoveries. Beyond the top sites are lesser-known gems worth the extra mile. Ask locals for tips as you travel around the island. If you're lucky, they might share their secrets – or you'll uncover your own!

Left Stórurð **Right** Kvernufoss
Below Flatey island

→ **QUIET NEIGHBOUR**

Want a tip for another spectacular waterfall? **Kvernufoss** is a must-visit, hidden not far from its more famous neighbour, Skógafoss.
▶ Read about the falls on p123

ROCK & WATER

Accessible on a day hike, the vibrant blue-green lagoon at Stórurð is surrounded by giant boulders and sits atop a mountain ridge in East Iceland.
▶ Learn more about Stórurð on p155

↑ **ESCAPE INTO TIMELESSNESS**

Just like the West Iceland island of the same name, the Flatey of the north seems light years away from the busyness of modern daily life.
▶ Discover this private paradise on p193

Best Surprise Experiences

▶ Drive the Arctic Coast Way, passing oceanic vistas, remote natural gems and coastal villages. (p182)

▶ Walk through Iceland's largest forest at Hallormsstaður. (p152)

▶ Uncover the East Fjords' artist hub of Seyðisfjörður. (p147)

▶ Photograph tucked-away waterfalls along the South Coast. (p233)

▶ Paddle to Vigur island, a birdwatcher's paradise. (p207)

FIRE & ICE

It's hard to avoid the fire and ice cliché because it describes Iceland's elemental geology so well. Glaciers cover around 10% of the area of the country and volcanic activity is a fact of life. The lava flows from the recent Fagradalsfjall eruption exemplify the island's ever-changing landscape.

→ THE BIG MELT

Iceland's glaciers have been rapidly retreating. At risk of disappearing by mid-century, Snæfellsjökull is a reminder of what the planet stands to lose due to climate change.

▶ Learn more about Snæfellsjökull on p224

Left Fagradalsfjall erupting, 2021 **Right** Snæfellsjökull **Below** Snorkelling, Þingvellir National Park

LAVA LAND

Spend a couple of hours walking around the giant jagged lava field of Dimmuborgir ('Dark Castles'). It is believed that Dimmuborgir's strange pillars and crags were created in an eruption 2000 years ago when the lava formed a lake over marshland. The marsh water started to boil and steam jets rose through the molten lava, cooling it and creating the pillars.

▶ Explore more of the Mývatn area on p198

↑ TOP EXPERIENCE

When visiting Þingvellir National Park, dive where the two continents meet.

▶ Discover Þingvellir National Park on p88

Best Active Experiences

▶ **Hike towards Fagradalsfjall** to witness the site of Iceland's 2021 eruption. (p111)

▶ **Descend deep into the dormant volcano** of Þríhnúkagígur. (p111)

▶ **Go snowmobiling on top of Langjökull glacier.** (p97)

▶ **Visit Heimaey island** in Vestmannaeyjar, evacuated – and since resettled – during the 1973 eruption. (p116)

▶ **Ski Snæfellsjökull**, the glacier-topped stratovolcano on Snæfellsnes Peninsula. (p224)

↘ RING ROAD

- ▶ 1332km
- ▶ Mostly one lane in either direction
- ▶ Usually accessible year-round
- ▶ Dipped headlights must be on at all times when driving in Iceland
- ▶ Speed limit on sealed roads is 90 km/h

EPIC ROAD TRIP

Iceland's Ring Rd (Rte 1) encircles the island, connecting most of its inhabited regions. A road trip along the 1332km national highway takes you past jagged coastline, secluded fishing villages, glistening glaciers and waterfall after dazzling waterfall. There are plenty of options for detours along the way too.

Best Driving Experiences

▶ Drive the Ring Rd between Reykjavík and Vík, passing waterfalls, glaciers and black beaches. (p36)

▶ Continue past Vík along the south coast to Jökulsárlón for its iceberg-filled lagoon. (p142)

▶ Check out the Arctic Coast Way and Westfjords Way. (p182 and p210)

BUDGET ICELAND

As one of the most expensive countries on the planet, Iceland and affordable in the same sentence may seem like an oxymoron. But there are ways to keep costs down without sacrificing your trip. Shrink car-rental costs, for example, by using public transport, staying in one location or cycling.

→ BATHING HEAVEN

A quintessential Iceland experience is soaking in the hot tubs of a geothermally heated swimming pool. Admission is cheap and pools are located across the country.

▶ Discover some of the best on p109

Best Affordable Experiences

▶ **Explore Reykjavík on foot and discover some of its unique and quirky sites.** (p78)

▶ **Rent a bike and pedal around Reykjavík.** (p52)

▶ **Escape the city, heading east to hike in Skaftafell National Park.** (p136)

▶ **Unwind in the free Guðlaug Baths geothermal pool at the beach in Akranes.** (p234)

★ MEAL PLANNING

To save, pick up a cool box to store your snacks and picnic lunches on the road. Plan your meals out to a few select recommended spots.

▶ Find out more about how to keep costs down on p243

Above left Cyclist, Reykjavík
Left Forest Lagoon (p163), Akureyri

LET IT SNOW

Long and dark winters don't mean locals stay indoors for half the year. Stay active with outdoor activities year-round and make the most of the snow when it shows. There are ski resorts and backcountry skiing options across the country. For non-skiers, try sledding, snowshoeing or snowmobiling.

→ HIT THE SLOPES

Explore near-uncharted territory on a multiday ski-to-sailboat expedition from Ísafjörður.
▶ Find out more on p206

Left Snowmobiling, Vatnajökull glacier (p136) **Right** Sailboat cruising, Ísafjörður **Below** Cross-country skiing near Ólafsfjörður

ADRENALINE FIX

Race across the wintery landscapes on a snowmobiling tour.
▶ Discover where on p97

↑ SNOW TIME

Cross-country skiing really took off during the Covid-19 pandemic. Book a course in Ólafsfjörður or Siglufjörður.
▶ Find out more on p165

Best Snow Experiences

▶ Journey to remote backcountry skiing locations in the Westfjords and North Iceland. (p216 and p164)

▶ Warm up in the hot tub in the Westfjords as snowflakes fall from the sky. (p211)

▶ Ski under the Northern Lights in Akureyri. (p164)

▶ Enjoy winter sports at festivals in North Iceland. (p165)

▶ Go beneath the glaciers and into an ice cave near Skaftafell. (p136)

THE GREAT OUTDOORS

Pristine nature is really what Iceland is all about. Traverse mountain slopes and wade highland rivers, or ride an Icelandic horse along wild coastlines or past lava landscapes. Once you're done, choose between countless other activities, including kayaking, sailing, skiing, glacier climbing and much, much more. There's always more to do in Iceland.

→ **WAY TO THE WATERFALL**

Iceland has countless waterfalls. Some, like **Glymur**, can only be reached on foot – the ultimate reward on your hike.

▶ *For more waterfalls, see p122*

Left Landscape along the Laugavegur trail (p129) **Right** Glymur
Below Camper at Skógar (p123)

PITCH YOUR TENT

Experience sleeping outdoors in the midnight sun at some of the country's beautifully situated campsites. Þórsmörk in the Southern Highlands is a local favourite and also has great hikes. If considering camping offsite, first look up 'where you can camp' on ust.is for the latest laws.

▶ Read about hiking and staying overnight in Þórsmörk on p126

↑ TRAVEL SAFETY & CODE

To stay out of trouble, before setting off on your outdoor adventure, even if it's just a short hike, make sure you've done your research (safetravel.is), checked the forecast and have the right gear. And remember to leave the area as you found it – or better still do some plogging along the way.

▶ Find out more about plogging on p246

Best Outdoor Experiences

▶ **Trek the 54km Laugavegur trail between Landmannalaugar and Þórsmörk.** (p129)

▶ **Take a trip to West Iceland for its hiking trails, such as the trail to Glymur.** (p233)

▶ **Get close to nature and explore the countryside on horseback.** (p97)

▶ **Sail to Hornstrandir for a guided hike in wilderness.** (p214)

▶ **Lace up your boots and head to Borgarfjörður Eystri for more sublime hiking.** (p154)

WATER **WORLD**

▬ Staggering glaciers carved with deep crevasses and hidden ice caves. Coastal fjords rising above colourful fishing villages. Highland rivers journeying to the great blue sea. Iceland is blessed with rich water resources essential for life on the island but also providing a natural playground full of opportunities for discovery.

→ BOUNTY OF THE SEA

Learn about how the ocean sustains life in the Westfjords community of Suðureyri on the Seafood Trail guided walk.
▶ Read more about coastal communities on p209

Left Whale diving near Húsavík (p184)
Right Fishing boats, Suðureyri
Below Vök Baths

WEIGHTLESS WELLNESS

Many of the country's geothermal pools offer regular relaxation floating sessions using Flothetta, a specially designed floating cap and support for use in water therapy. @samflotfyriralla, @flothetta

↑ DON'T MISS

Relax in Vök Baths floating pools on East Iceland's lake Urriðavatn – and take a dip in the chilly lake.
▶ Learn about the Vök Baths on p147

Best Marine Experiences

▶ Sail in search of the giants of the deep and visit the whale museum in Húsavík. (p185)

▶ Venture to remote northern islands where small communities still live year-round. (p192)

▶ Kick your adrenaline into action on a river-rafting trip in Skagafjörður. (p199)

▶ Get a glimpse of the deep with some cold-water diving. (p169 and p207)

▶ Fish for arctic char in volcanic lakes around Landmannalaugar. (p129)

↓ National Day

Iceland's National Day marks the country's gaining of independence from Denmark in 1944, and is celebrated on 17 June with parades, live music, street theatre and more.

← Highland Trails

Highland mountain 4WD roads and hiking trails usually open mid- to late June – sometimes as late as July – and the prime hiking season begins.

→ Summer Solstice

The midnight sun peaks around 21 June, the longest day of the year, when the sky never goes completely dark. It's best enjoyed with an evening hike.

Puffins in Residence

Puffins visit Ingólfshöfði, Vestmannaeyjar and elsewhere from May to early August. Everywhere along this stretch of Ring Rd is crowded.

JUNE — Average daytime max: 13°C / Days of rainfall: 9.3 (Reykjavík) — **JULY**

Iceland in SUMMER

The first weekend of August – with the Monday being a public holiday – is the biggest travel weekend of the year with outdoor festivals of all sorts.

↘ Reykjavík Festivals

Reykjavík goes festival crazy in August, with Innipúkinn Festival (indie music), Reykjavík Pride and Reykjavík Jazz Festival.

Demand for accommodation peaks during summer. Book tours, flights and insurance in advance.

↓ Berry Picking

Pick wild blueberries, bilberries and crowberries in late August. In the capital area, try Heiðmörk Conservation Area.

AUGUST

Average daytime max: 14.9°C
Days of rainfall: 10.3

Average daytime max: 14.1°C
Days of rainfall: 11.6

📦 Packing Notes

Blackout curtains are common, but to block out the bright summer nights pack an eye mask too.

Iceland in AUTUMN

SEPTEMBER — **OCTOBER**

Average daytime max: 11.4°C
Days of rainfall: 15 (Reykjavík)

Expect smaller crowds but cooler temperatures, with sudden changes in conditions possible. Changing foliage in September and October.

You might be able to travel one or more of the highland routes in September, but no guarantees, and they're closed by October.

Boat trips on Jökulsárlón run from May to October. Interior F roads close in September or October and won't open again until June.

Days are still long, but the Northern Lights start to become visible around the autumn equinox. Some services and attractions are closed.

↓ Imagine Peace Tower

Yoko Ono's artwork lights up the sky each year from 9 October, John Lennon's birthday. Located on Viðey island.

JOANNE WASTCHAK/SHUTTERSTOCK, KATRINASA/SHUTTERSTOCK, CREATIVE STOCK PHOTO/SHUTTERSTOCK, ZUMA PRESS, INC./ALAMY.

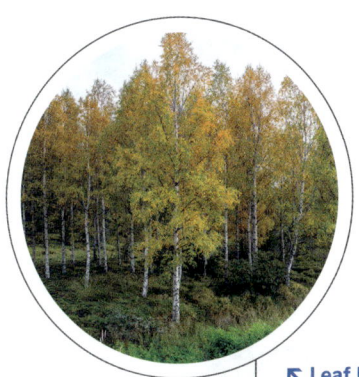

↘ Iceland Airwaves Music Festival

Reykjavík comes alive with music performances by local and international acts – both emerging and established.

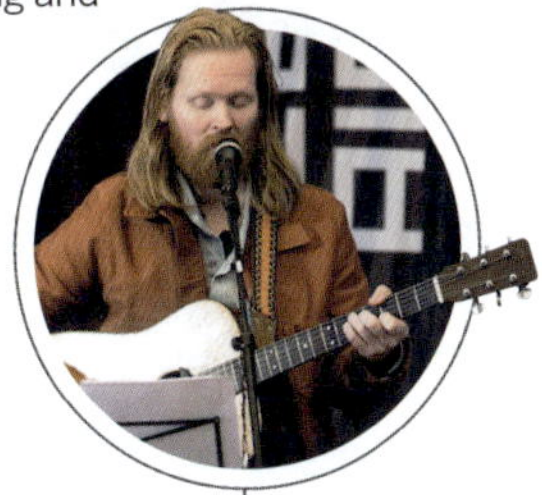

↖ Leaf Peeping

Stunning autumn foliage in Hallormsstaðaskógur out in East Iceland, and elsewhere.

Although storms and bad weather can shake things up, heavy snowfall is rare. Catch the end of the season, with bargain hotel prices.

NOVEMBER

Average daytime max: 7.6°C
Days of rainfall: 13.1

Average daytime max: 4.7°C
Days of rainfall: 13.7

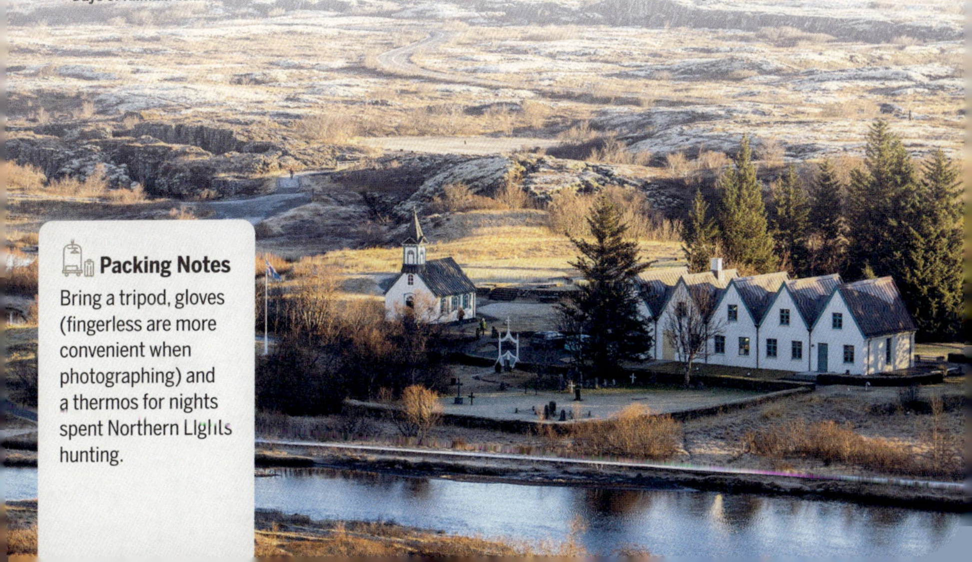

Packing Notes

Bring a tripod, gloves (fingerless are more convenient when photographing) and a thermos for nights spent Northern Lights hunting.

← Winter Solstice
The shortest day of the year is around 21 December with four hours of daylight in Reykjavík, and even less the further north you go.

It's safe to access most natural ice caves only from November to March when cool temperatures mean they stop melting. Visit only with a certified tour operator.

Winter is the best time to see the Northern Lights. Ice caves are accessible. Ski resorts nationwide are usually open from winter to spring.

→ New Year's Eve
The bonfires and fireworks in Reykjavík have become a visitor attraction. Good viewpoints are in front of Perlan and Hallgrímskirkja church.

DECEMBER   Average daytime max: 3.3°C   **JANUARY**
Days of rainfall: 14.6 (Reykjavík)

Iceland in
WINTER

→ Christmas in the North

Iceland's Christmas spirit lights the snow-covered north, with twinkling lights, Christmas displays and the Yule Lads annual bath (p165) at lake Mývatn.

JENNYWONDERLAND/SHUTTERSTOCK, JANE RIX/SHUTTERSTOCK, MARTIBSTOCK/SHUTTERSTOCK, ROBERTO LA ROSA/SHUTTERSTOCK, PALMI GUDMUNDSSON/SHUTTERSTOCK, WILDSNAP/SHUTTERSTOCK, YASSMIN PHOTO/SHUTTERSTOCK

↓ The Sun Returns

In Ísafjörður, in the Westfjords, the first rays of sun rise above the mountain ridge and touch parts of town after weeks of absence.

← Midwinter Feast

Þorrablót is an old festival in January and February. A buffet of traditional Icelandic food is washed down with Brennivín (Icelandic schnapps). Many restaurants offer a Þorrablót menu.

FEBRUARY

Average daytime max: 3.2°C
Days of rainfall: 15.3

Average daytime max: 3.3°C
Days of rainfall: 15

←Explore the Highlands

The harshest possible winter backdrop is ideal for guided tours by snowmobile, ski or super-Jeep, driven by local professionals.

🧳 Packing Notes

Bring your warm, windproof clothes. Also sunglasses: snow and the low winter sun can be blinding, especially when driving.

Iceland awakes from winter. Mountain roads slowly become passable again across the country, and puffins arrive in May.

← Aldrei fór ég suður
Held during the Easter long weekend in Ísafjörður, the Westfjords, this music festival is a local favourite.

↓ DesignMarch
March is lots of fun in Reykjavík, with DesignMarch, covering fashion to architecture, and the Food & Fun culinary festival.

Mývatn Winter Festival
Early March brings the Mývatn Winter Festival, with ice fishing, dog sledding, and sports and family events, plus peak off-piste skiing around Tröllaskagi.

↗ AK Extreme
Held on Hlíðarfjall and in downtown Akureyri, North Iceland, this snowboarding and music festival peaks with the big jump contest.

MARCH

Average daytime max: 4.2°C
Days of rainfall: 14.2 (Reykjavík)

APRIL

Iceland in
SPRING

Expect improving weather, and fewer crowds and lower prices than summer. Road conditions make it a good time to travel the South Coast or the Ring Rd.

↘ Whale-Watching Season

The first boats head out in March to look for humpbacks, blue whales and other marine life off Iceland's northern coast.

↑ Time for Wizards

Out in the Westfjords in May, don't miss the Icelandic Sorcery Festival, with music and more in Holmavik.

MAY

Average daytime max: 6.9°C
Days of rainfall: 12

Average daytime max: 10.1°C
Days of rainfall: 10.8

Packing Notes

Layered clothing is key in changeable spring weather. Don't forget a waterproof and breathable outer layer.

REYKJAVÍK
Trip Builder

TAKE YOUR PICK OF MUST-SEES AND HIDDEN GEMS

From a grim, seemingly endless night in winter to incomprehensibly bright nights in summer. A chill and laid-back mood during daytime to a dynamic party scene at night. Reykjavík is a big city in a tiny package next door to nature.

Trip Notes

Hub town Reykjavík

How long Allow one week, including day trips from the capital

Getting around Many places can be visited on foot or with rental scooters and bikes. Bus transport is decent, but car rental may be a good choice too.

Tips Depending on your style of travel, renting a car and exploring on your own may be a cheaper option than going on guided tours.

Grótta
Stroll on the beach at the tip of the Reykjavík peninsula. Find the small warm pool. If you're lucky, you can even walk out to the lighthouse.

1hr walk from Grandi

Old Downtown & Laugavegur
Uncover the history of Reykjavík among the pubs and cafes; see the countless cats of Reykjavík and have a taste of Iceland.

1hr walk from Grótta

Öskjuhlíð
Woodlands close to the city centre. Explore the WWII bunkers, encounter curious rabbits and perhaps end by taking a swim in the sea in Nauthólsvík geothermal beach.

40mins from downtown

EXPLORE BY THE GLASS/SHUTTERSTOCK, OLANA22/SHUTTERSTOCK

Grandi
Discover the hidden diamonds in the old fishing district of Reykjavík. Grandi is home to many cultural and culinary gems.
🚶 *20min walk from downtown*

Viðey
Board the ferry to iconic Viðey and explore a diverse collection of outdoor art, witness the massive avian fauna of the island and enjoy the proximity to the sea.
⛴ *5mins from Skarfabakki*

Elliðaárdalur & Around
Take a long walk, cool your feet in the river or simply enjoy the outdoors while picnicking. Visit Árbæjarsafn open-air museum for a *kleinur* (twisted doughnut).
🚗 *15mins from downtown*

Heiðmörk
Visit Heiðmörk at the edge of the city, a seemingly endless source of outdooring that shows that Reykjavík is, in fact, next door to nature.
🚗 *35mins from downtown*

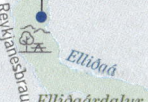

Hafnarfjörður
Walk through the old town and visit Hafnarborg museum.
🚗 *25mins from downtown*

THE RING ROAD
Trip Builder

TAKE YOUR PICK OF MUST-SEES AND HIDDEN GEMS

▬▬ Eyes on the road. The famous 'Ring Road' is a 1322km loop connecting most towns and villages via mountain passes, one-lane bridges and diverse scenery that changes every 10 minutes. Many of Iceland's most iconic sites are literally roadside.

📖 Trip Notes

Hub towns Selfoss, Höfn, Egilsstaðir, Akureyri, Borgarnes

How long Allow at least 7 days

Getting around For the ultimate road trip, hire a car. Otherwise, buses run year-round, but have a sporadic schedule outside of summer.

Tips Monitor weather forecasts and road conditions, particularly for the mountain passes on Holtavörðuheiði and Öxnadalsheiði. If you don't have driving experience in snow and ice, consider joining a tour. Summer traffic is heavy between Selfoss and Vík. And watch out for sheep!

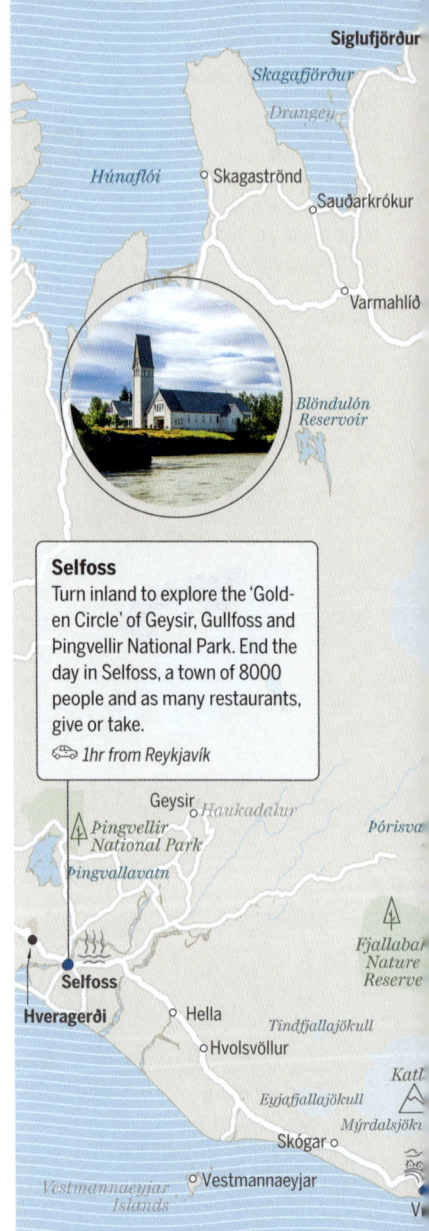

Selfoss
Turn inland to explore the 'Golden Circle' of Geysir, Gullfoss and Þingvellir National Park. End the day in Selfoss, a town of 8000 people and as many restaurants, give or take.
🚗 1hr from Reykjavík

WALKABOUT TRAVEL/SHUTTERSTOCK,
DANIEL DORSA/LONELY PLANET

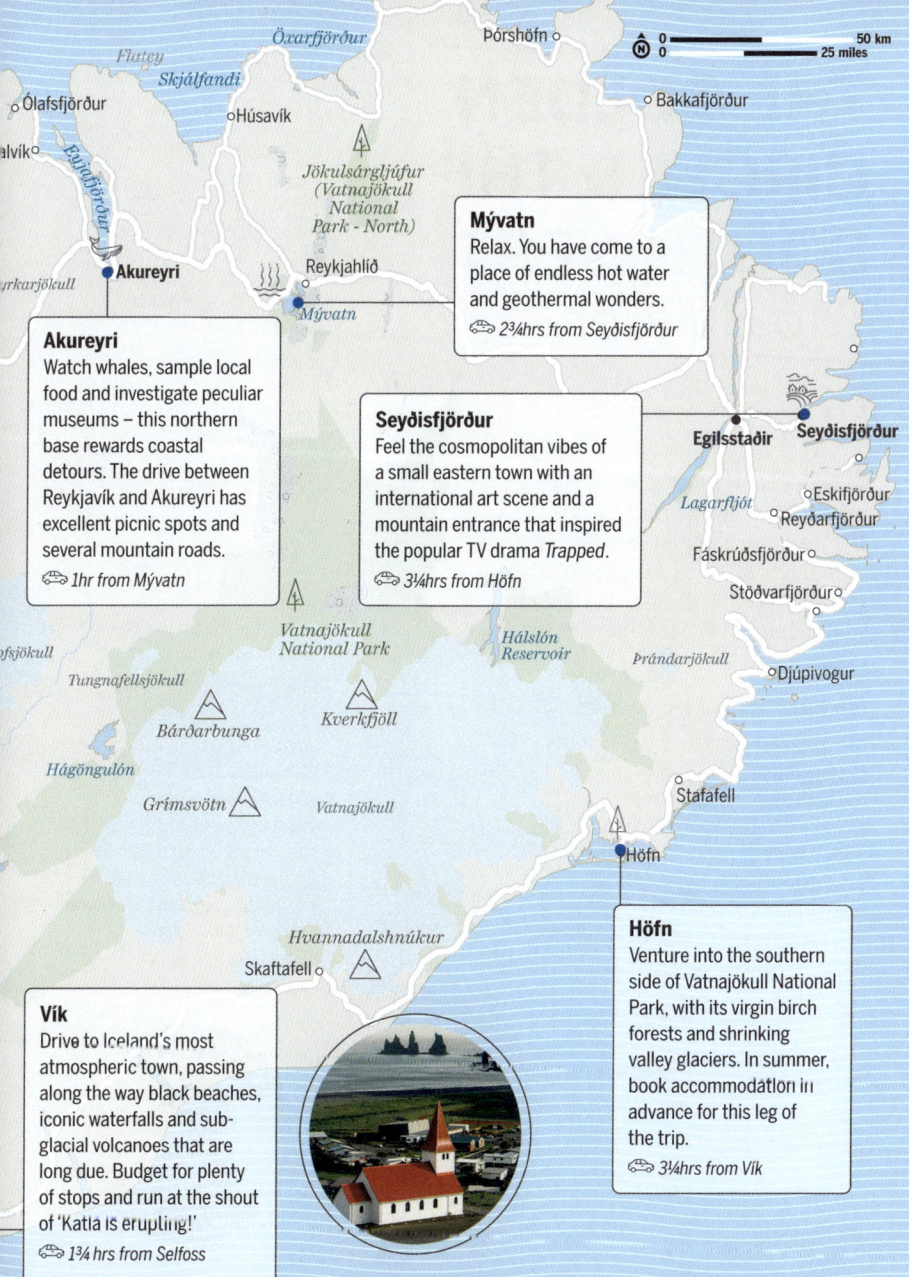

Akureyri
Watch whales, sample local food and investigate peculiar museums – this northern base rewards coastal detours. The drive between Reykjavík and Akureyri has excellent picnic spots and several mountain roads.

🚗 1hr from Mývatn

Mývatn
Relax. You have come to a place of endless hot water and geothermal wonders.

🚗 2¾hrs from Seyðisfjörður

Seyðisfjörður
Feel the cosmopolitan vibes of a small eastern town with an international art scene and a mountain entrance that inspired the popular TV drama *Trapped*.

🚗 3¼hrs from Höfn

Höfn
Venture into the southern side of Vatnajökull National Park, with its virgin birch forests and shrinking valley glaciers. In summer, book accommodation in advance for this leg of the trip.

🚗 3¼hrs from Vík

Vík
Drive to Iceland's most atmospheric town, passing along the way black beaches, iconic waterfalls and sub-glacial volcanoes that are long due. Budget for plenty of stops and run at the shout of 'Katla is erupting!'

🚗 1¾ hrs from Selfoss

THE GOLDEN CIRCLE & THE SOUTHWEST
Trip Builder

TAKE YOUR PICK OF MUST-SEES AND HIDDEN GEMS

For adventure seekers who want a big bang for their bucks. The Southwest region is close to the capital city of Reykjavík so you're not spending too much time driving, but still seeing some incredible sights.

Trip Notes

Hub towns Keflavík, Reykjavík, Selfoss, Vík

How long Allow 1 week

Getting around Rent a car to drive at your own pace and stop at hidden gems. Alternatively, join an organised tour group if you want to sit back and enjoy the view.

Tips June to August is peak tourist season. Be prepared for the crowds. Roads are paved and well-maintained, but can be difficult in winter conditions.

Reykjanes Peninsula
This usually overlooked area packs a big punch: the jagged basalt columns of Reykjanestá, the geothermal mudpots of Seltún, and the newest attraction: Fagradalsfjall volcano.

🚗 45mins from Reykjavík

LUIGI MORBIDELLI/SHUTTERSTOCK, VICTOR MASCHEK/SHUTTERSTOCK, BEKETOFF/SHUTTERSTOCK

The Golden Circle
Walk between continents at Þingvellir National Park, watch bubbling geysers spout into the air at Haukadalur valley and take in the thunderous roar of Gullfoss waterfall.

🚗 *45mins from Reykjavík*

Landmannalaugar
Multicoloured mountains, lava fields, geothermal hot springs and outstanding hiking. Note: only accessible via 4WD or bus from June to September.

🚗 *3¼hrs from Reykjavík*

Þórsmörk
A hikers' paradise of lush green mountains and glaciers in the rugged highlands. Between June and September, drive a 4WD or hop onto a bus to bring you, or take a guided super-Jeep tour year-round.

🚗 *1hr from Reykjavík*

South Coast
Known for massive waterfalls, breathtaking glaciers and black-sand beaches, the South Coast hosts some of the country's most iconic landmarks.

🚗 *1½hrs from Reykjavík*

Vík
A charming coastal village and a great place to stay the night after all your South Coast adventures.

🚗 *2½hrs from Reykjavík*

THE NORTH
Trip Builder

TAKE YOUR PICK OF MUST-SEES AND HIDDEN GEMS

Experience the North by boat or horse, discover varied waterfalls and geothermal gems, hike birding trails or snow-covered summits and ski to the shore. Also remember to take it easy, explore the cultural scene and go for a swim.

Trip Notes

Hub towns Hvammstangi, Blönduós, Akureyri, Húsavík

How long Allow 10 days

Getting around Best to hire a car. But you can also travel by bus, SBA highland bus or plane between the South and North.

Tips Highland roads are open in summer and require a highland-suited 4WD. ICE-SAR patrols the region and assists with rivers crossings (the driver is always responsible). See safetravel.is for more information.

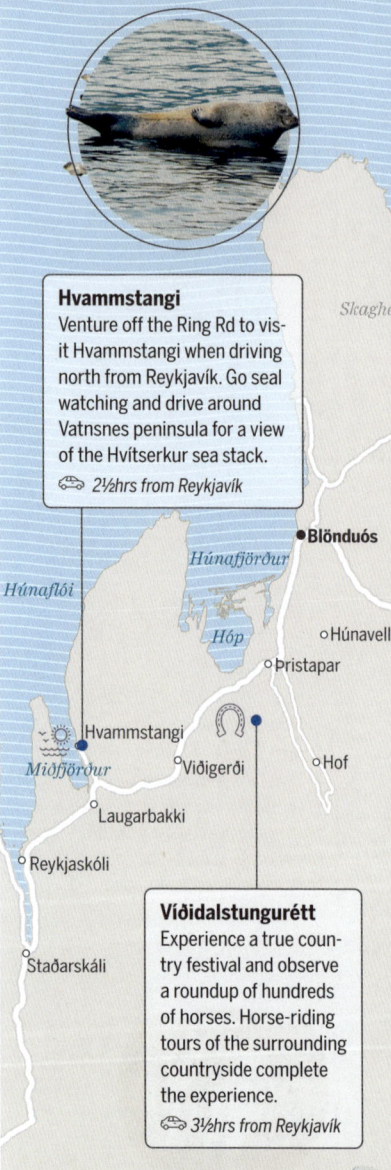

Hvammstangi
Venture off the Ring Rd to visit Hvammstangi when driving north from Reykjavík. Go seal watching and drive around Vatnsnes peninsula for a view of the Hvítserkur sea stack.
🚗 2½hrs from Reykjavík

Víðidalstungurétt
Experience a true country festival and observe a roundup of hundreds of horses. Horse-riding tours of the surrounding countryside complete the experience.
🚗 3½hrs from Reykjavík

DANIEL DORSA/LONELY PLANET,
JONAS TUFVESSON/SHUTTERSTOCK, GESTUR GISLASON/SHUTTERSTOCK

The Diamond Circle
This 250km tourist route in Northeast Iceland includes the region's best-known attractions: waterfalls, volcanoes, whale watching and geothermal baths.

🚗 6hrs from Reykjavík

Tröllaskagi
This peninsula between Skagafjörður and Eyjafjörður is characterised by tall, rugged mountains and small glaciers, great for hiking and skiing of all adventure levels.

🚗 4¾hrs from Reykjavík

Eyjafjarðarsveit
A centre for dairy production and other agriculture. Discover quirky museums, countryside churches and local food, and enjoy quiet contemplation in nature.

🚗 5½hrs from Reykjavík

Hveravellir
Road F35 lies across the ancient highland route of Kjölur between Langjökull and Hofsjökull glaciers. A 4WD is required. Stay to explore the highlands from Hveravellir.

🚗 4hrs from Reykjavík

THE WEST
Trip Builder

TAKE YOUR PICK OF MUST-SEES AND HIDDEN GEMS

Go west to discover the road less travelled and explore a bounty of fjords, hot springs, islands, glaciers, mountains, waterfalls and stunning coastlines. The region also boasts culinary and cultural highlights.

Trip Notes

Hub towns Borgarnes, Stykkishólmur, Patreksfjörður, Ísafjörður

How long Allow 2 weeks

Getting around Hire a car and travel at your own pace. Organised tours are also available. Buses run to some destinations, but are infrequent.

Tips Most roads are sealed, but allow extra time for slow and safe driving on gravel roads in the Westfjords and when roads are icy. Some services have limited opening hours or are closed October to April.

GIEDRIIUS/SHUTTERSTOCK,
MIKE TOWERS/SHUTTERSTOCK

Suðureyri
Sample local foods and learn about the fishing industry on a guided walking tour.
🚗 6hrs from Reykjavík

Patreksfjörður
Base yourself in this small fishing village for a trip to Látrabjarg Bird Cliffs and golden-red Rauðasandur beach.
🚗 5hrs from Reykjavík

Snæfellsnes Peninsula
Explore the region's national park and journey to the top of Snæfellsjökull glacier. Wander the jet-black sand of Djúpalónssandur beach and dine in colourful Stykkishólmur.
🚗 2hrs from Reykjavík

Ísafjörður

Join your adventure tours of choice, from kayaking, hiking, diving, cycling and wildlife watching to sailing and snow sports. Visit Hornstrandir Nature Reserve, the only place in Iceland where Arctic foxes are protected and tame

🚗 5½hrs from Reykjavík

Hólmavík

Inform yourself at the Sheep Farming Museum (12km from town) or the Museum of Icelandic Sorcery & Witchcraft. Soak up warm water and views at nearby Drangsnes Hot Pots.

🚗 3hrs from Reykjavík

Akranes

Make this harbour town the start or end of your journey. Hike nearby Akrafjall and take a dip in Guðlaug Baths on Langisandur beach, which is popular with sea swimmers.

🚗 50mins from Reykjavík

Borgarfjörður

Discover a fjord full of surprises. Learn about the sagas at the Settlement Centre in Borgarnes, take in Hraunfossar and Barnafoss waterfalls and explore Langjökull ice tunnel.

🚗 1hr from Reykjavík

7 Things to Know About ICELAND

INSIDER TIPS TO HIT THE GROUND RUNNING

1 Fragile Environment

Iceland is a nature lover's paradise, but its vegetation is delicate due to the harsh climate and short growing season. Moss can take years to recover after being damaged by footprints or tyre marks. Going off the beaten track and removing rocks to make cairns can also cause erosion. Remember that off-road driving can cause irreparable damage and is punishable by huge fines.

▶ Get more tips on how to leave a lighter footprint on p246

2 Geothermal Energy

Hot springs, volcanic fumaroles, mudpots and that sulphurous 'rotten egg' smell from hot-water taps are signs of the country's geothermal energy. Being located on a major fault line, Iceland has abundant volcanic activity and hot water. Hydropower is actually the main source of electricity, but geothermal makes up most of the rest. The hot water is also used to heat buildings, greenhouses, fish farms, swimming pools and to keep footpaths ice-free in winter.

▶ Learn more about volcanoes on p112

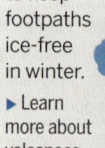

3 Ring Road

A road trip along Iceland's national highway gives you a taste of the best the country has to offer. Watch out for one-lane bridges and animals on the road, and don't try to see it all in a weekend.

▶ Discover the Ring Road on p18

4 Alphabet

The Icelandic alphabet has 32 letters. You might not be familiar with these ones:

Ð ð – as 'th' in 'rather'

Þ þ – as 'th' in 'thin'

Æ æ – as 'ai' in 'aisle'

Ö ö – as 'u' in 'nurse'

▶ Learn more about the Icelandic language on p250

5 Northern Lights

The aurora borealis is only visible when it's dark – so not in summer. The less cloud cover the better, so follow forecasts. It is often even visible in downtown Reykjavík, but less light pollution is best, so head away from built-up areas – or at least street lights – to really see the sky come alive.

▶ For the best spots to see the Northern Lights, see p176

6 Pools & Etiquette

All that geothermal energy means nearly every town has a swimming pool. Most poolgoers don't actually swim, but a soak in the hot tub is a daily ritual for many. There's usually a steam bath; some have a sauna and, more recently, a cold tub too. Entry is cheap.

To uphold hygiene and lower chlorine levels, visitors must thoroughly shower with soap without a swimsuit before entering. There are separate changing rooms for men and women – and gender-neutral areas at some. Some pools have a private shower, but mostly showers are communal. Having grown up with this, Icelanders don't bat an eyelid when they run into each other stark naked.

Trying to get out of the mandatory no-swimsuit shower will only draw attention. It's frowned upon so don't be surprised if the person standing next to you or the shower warden points out the rules. Just dive in.

▶ Prepare yourself with the dos and don'ts of pool etiquette on p106

7 Wild Weather

Icelandic weather is notoriously fickle. Don't be surprised if it's rainy and cold in summer – or if you get all four seasons in one. But you didn't come to Iceland for warm and sunny weather. Be prepared, wear layers and embrace it! The landscape is still stunning.

▶ Discover the best – and worst – of Iceland's seasons on p26

Read, Listen, Watch & Follow

 READ

Independent People (Halldór Laxness; 1934–35) Classic novel filled with satire and humour by the 1955 Nobel laureate.

The Sagas of the Icelanders (1997) Collection of medieval Icelandic literary treasures; stories of love, hate and adventure.

Burial Rites (Hannah Kent; 2013) Historical novel featuring the gruesome fate of a servant accused of murder in 1830.

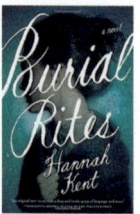

How Iceland Changed the World: The Big History of a Small Island (Egill Bjarnason; 2021) Iceland's role in historical events.

 LISTEN

Medúlla (Björk; 2004) Almost entirely an a cappella album. Recorded with choirs, a throat singer and a beatboxer.

My Head Is an Animal (Of Monsters and Men; 2011) The album, which contains hipster hit 'Little Talks', vaulted this Icelandic folk-rock band to global fame.

Sól rís 1980-2020 (Bubbi Morthens; 2020) Bubbi is a local legend whose career has spanned punk, rock, blues, reggae and folk.

Re:member (Ólafur Arnalds; 2018) This celebrated, irresistible multi-instrumentalist spans electronica and chill.

Haglél (Mugison; 2011; pictured) Blues-rock and first Icelandic-language album by this Westfjords local.

WATCH

Children of Nature (1991) Oscar-nominated love story about a couple escaping their retirement home for the Icelandic wilds.

Game of Thrones (2012; pictured top) Look for Þingvellir, Fjaðrárgljúfur, Grjótagjá, Kirkjufell and Reynisfjara.

I Remember You (2017) Mystery horror film about people who move to an abandoned town.

Noi the Albino (2003; pictured bottom) The trials and tribulations of a teenage outsider in Bolungarvík.

Trapped (2015–) Crime drama TV series by Baltasar Kormákur set in remote Iceland.

FOLLOW

All Things Iceland (@allthingsiceland) Expat view of life in Iceland.

The Reykjavík Grapevine (@rvkgrapevine) News, life, culture and travel magazine and website.

Benjamin Hardman (@benjaminhardman) Photographer and filmmaker covering Iceland, Greenland and Svalbard.

Gunnar Freyr Gunnarsson (@icelandic_explorer) Reykjavík-based photographer and storyteller.

Ása Steinarsdóttir (@asasteinars) Photographer and adventure-content creator.

▸ Get in the mood with the perfect playlist at lonelyplanet.com/articles/playlist-for-iceland-road-trip

REYKJAVÍK

FRIENDLY | CULTURAL | CALM

- ▶ **Trip Builder** (p50)
- ▶ **Practicalities** (p52)
- ▶ **Eat Reykjavík** (p54)
- ▶ **Icelandic Food** (p58)
- ▶ **A New Icelandic Cuisine** (p60)
- ▶ **Into the Night** (p62)
- ▶ **A Brief Take on Icelandic Craft Beer** (p66)
- ▶ **Culture Night** (p68)
- ▶ **A Capital of Culture** (p72)
- ▶ **A Path to Musical Excellence?** (p76)
- ▶ **Urban Hiking** (p78)
- ▶ **Listings** (p80)

REYKJAVÍK
Trip Builder

Stroll the beach and find the footbath near **Grótta Lighthouse** (p82)
🕒 ½ day

Discover cultural and culinary gems in **Grandi** fishing district (p57)
🕒 1 day

Stroll through the various **Reykjavík Art Museum** locations (p73)
🕒 1 day

Unearth how people lived at the **Aðalstræti Settlement Exhibiton** (p81)
🕒 ½ day

Explore Icelandic history at the **National Museum of Iceland** (p81)
🕒 ½ day

Care to take a bath by the seaside? Would you like to meet farm animals in the city? Or do you want to prowl for food and drinks in the darkest days of winter? Reykjavík offers plenty no matter the season.

PREVIOUS SPREAD: SURADECH SINGHANAT/SHUTTERSTOCK
ENDORPHINE/SHUTTERSTOCK,
GABRIELE66/SHUTTERSTOCK,
PALMI GUDMUNDSSON/SHUTTERSTOCK

Practicalities

ARRIVING

Keflavík International Airport About 40 minutes' drive from Reykjavík. As there are no trains in Iceland, there are two main transport options to and from the airport: the bus (Flybus, Airport Direct or Strætó public bus 55) and a taxi. The Flybus makes stops in a few places on its way to the BSÍ terminal, right next to downtown. From there, you can add a Flybus shuttle to town stops or take a taxi to reach your destination; walking is also viable.

HOW MUCH FOR A

Happy-hour beer 900kr

Icelandic hot dog 600kr

Bus fare 490kr

GETTING AROUND

Walking While the capital region is quite large, the centre is small and walkable. Within a 30-minute radius of downtown, you can find four different swimming pools, a public beach, several public parks and outdoor areas, museums, galleries, restaurants and more.

City bus and taxis For longer distances, the **Strætó** (bus.is) city bus is a rapid and convenient way to get around. Download its Klappið app. While not cheap, taxis are just a phone call away.

Rentals Rent bikes in the Old Harbour. E-scooters and are plentiful around town and can be rented via various apps such as Hopp and Zolo. They're a swift and delightful way to explore and get around Reykjavík.

WHEN TO GO

MAR–MAY
Expect wind and rain; great for a cultural visit in the city.

JUN–AUG
The ideal season for excursions and outdoor activities.

SEP–NOV
A relatively calm season; outdoors and cultural activities.

DEC–FEB
Perfect for winter sports and cultural activities.

EATING & DRINKING

Laugavegur The main shopping street in Iceland, Laugavegur and its surroundings hold a huge variety of restaurants and pubs.

Old Harbour & Grandi The Old Harbour (p57) is home to a diverse collection of cultural and culinary spots.

Must-try craft-beer pub Skúli Craft Bar (p80; pictured top) has a really good menu of Icelandic brews on tap at all times and knowledgeable staff.

Best food hall Pósthús Mathöll is an excellent food court in a former post office. Other interesting food halls, like Grandi Mathöll (p57; pictured bottom), dot the town.

CONNECT & FIND YOUR WAY

Wi-fi and mobile networks Available for use everywhere you go. Wi-fi access codes are displayed openly in most cafes, bars and restaurants. 5G SIM cards are also relatively affordable.

Navigation software This is pretty accurate in Iceland, but beware the loss of signal in the countryside – preload the maps in advance for viewing offline or ask locals for directions.

WHERE TO STAY

Accommodation is expensive in Iceland, but there are feasible midrange options, as well as a wide variety of rentals via Airbnb and similar services.

Neighbourhood	Pro/Con
Central Miðborg (Old Reykjavík)	The liveliest part of the capital area. Significantly higher prices, but closer to most things.
Kópavogur & Hafnarfjörður	These two capital-area towns offer cheaper accommodation, but at the cost of 30-minute bus rides to downtown.
Anywhere else in the capital area	Rental apartments available around town; different locations with their own pros and cons.

REYKJAVÍK CITY CARD

The Reykjavík City Card – available online in 24-, 48- and 72-hour variations – offers free access to the bus system, plus a trip to Viðoy, the swimming pools and various museums.

MONEY

Visa, MasterCard and contactless payments are accepted just about everywhere. Low-cost supermarkets (Bónus and Krónan) are great for stocking up on snacks and groceries.

01 Eat
REYKJAVÍK

RESTAURANTS | PUBS | FOOD

Looking for a place to eat? Strolling through downtown or nearby Grandi (the old fishing harbour) is a worthwhile and enjoyable way of discovering culinary gems. Offerings include 'honest' burgers, New Icelandic Cuisine and fish courses. Work up an appetite by sightseeing historical and cultural spots, and much more.

How To

Getting around Most buses go downtown near the pond Tjörnin, and from there it's an easy and enjoyable walk out to Grandi (10 minutes), while bus 14 goes straight to the harbour. Other options include grabbing a taxi or renting an electric scooters via app services.

Cost There are both cheap and expensive options. A sit-down dinner easily averages 2900kr to 5000kr per person, excluding drinks, and goes well above that for fine dining.

Out on the Town

Iceland's foodie scene has grown exponentially in the past 15 years. Today the culinary universe has grown so much that only the most dedicated foodies have an overview of the city's dining options. New locations of various styles and price ranges proliferate, as do progressive explorations and fusions of Icelandic cuisine. The number of luxurious or unique food experiences is also on the rise.

A significant portion of the restaurants can be found downtown: on Laugavegur, the main shopping street in Iceland; on Hverfisgata; and in and around Old Reykjavík. Strolling around downtown is both an architectural and gastronomical delight.

Café Loki serves simple, home-style Icelandic dishes. In good weather, sit outside the cafe to enjoy the views of Hallgrímskirkja

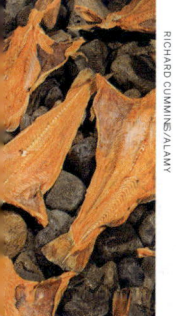

Reykjavík Maritime Museum

The main attraction at this Old Harbour **museum** is an exhibition called 'Fish and People – 150 Years of Maritime History'. It offers an interactive insight into the culinary past and present-day fishing industry, walking you through the phases of seafaring, fishing and production.

Top left Skólavörðustígur **Top right** Herring plate, Café Loki **Left** Dried cod

church and the constant flow of people. **Mat Bar** is an excellent choice for a more intimate dinner experience, sharing Nordic/Italian fusion dishes and tasting wine in the tight but lovely restaurant. **Skál!** serves beautifully presented fine-dining fare with verve, alongside wines and Icelandic craft beer. Italian-Japanese fusion may not seem like a natural pairing, but at **OTO** dishes sing with creativity and nuance. Delicious cocktails, too.

Hlemmur Mathöll fills a former bus station with varied vendors. Or seek out the city's famous hot dogs at the **Bæjarins Beztu** truck near the harbour (patronised by Bill Clinton, Anthony Bourdain, Kim Kardashian and late-night bar-hoppers). Its hot dogs are made of lamb, pork and beef. Use the vital phrase '*eina með öllu*' (one with everything) to get the quintessential favourite with sweet mustard, ketchup, remoulade and crunchy onions.

Reykjavík's Best Bites

Dill The first Michelin-starred restaurant in Iceland.

Óx Fantastic restaurant fronted by a speakeasy.

Mat Bar A stylish spot with a good vibe.

Skál! A top-tier restaurant with creative Icelandic cuisine.

Recommended by **Ólafur Örn Ólafsson**, *TV personality and owner of Vínstúkan Tíu Sopar.*

Left Dill
Below Marshall House, home to La Primavera

The Old Harbour

It feels natural to dine at the Old Harbour, but to this day there are boats still coming in. It's home to a range of restaurants, cafes and bars, mixed in with cultural attractions, ice-cream parlours and light industry.

Among the Old Harbour dining options is **Matur og Drykkur**, which reimagines classical Icelandic dishes, presenting them in a six-course menu. It also has a fantastic wine-pairing menu. **La Primavera** is located in Marshall House (which also houses **Nýló** aka Living Art Museum, **Kling & Bang**, **i8 Grandi** and **Þula** galleries, plus the workshop of artist Ólafur Elíasson). It's a perfect chaser after exploring the art. Located in a tiny house on the fringe of the Old Harbour, **Hamborgarabúlla Tómasar** is the burger joint of choice. It serves honest burgers and fries, no hassle and isn't trying to be anything more than just that.

Grandi Mathöll is located in a former fish factory turned food hall. In good weather you can drink and eat outside while overlooking the harbour and the downtown opposite. In the food court, **Kore** serves Korean fusion street food. Also in the food court, **Fjárhúsið** (Sheep House) specialises in Icelandic lamb. Then head over to **Omnom Chocolate**, offering premium Icelandic bean-to-bar chocolate and ice cream.

Icelandic **FOOD**

01 Blood sausage
Sheep's blood, mixed with lard and grains, is stuffed into animal intestines, sewn shut and boiled. To this day, it's widely available.

02 Lamb
By many considered the pinnacle of Icelandic raw ingredients, lamb is both a tasty and affordable meat. Available in most restaurants.

03 Foal meat
Icelanders love to ride their horses, but perhaps less known is that they love to eat them too.

04 Rice pudding
Contrary to everywhere else in the world, Icelanders consider rice pudding to be dinner, not breakfast or dessert.

05 Skyr
You've heard of *skyr*, right? The Icelandic yogurt is, in fact, not a yogurt but more akin to cheese.

06 Blueberries
One of only a handful of berries that grow wild in Iceland, blueberries are a delicacy that are commonly enjoyed soaked in cream.

07 Fermented shark
More commonly eaten as an appetiser or with a shot of Icelandic Brennivín, fermented shark is not as strong-smelling as skate.

08 Salted fish
Before coolers, fish was salted to keep it consumable. Salted fish with boiled potatoes is still a common dinner option in Icelandic homes.

09 Fermented skate
A traditional Christmas Eve dish. Also an item of controversy that traditionally causes feuds in apartment buildings because of the rancid smell from the preparation of it.

10 Brennivín
Until 1989 beer was banned in Iceland. Strong alcohol like Brennivín were the go-to drinks for many until then.

11 Coffee
While not necessarily sophisticated in terms of the art of coffee, Icelanders take coffee very seriously and consider it a staple of their identity.

12 Rye bread
Probably the most Icelandic bread you can get. It comes in solid, square pieces that are sometimes even baked in geothermal hot springs.

13 Fish jerky
The true sports snack of Iceland. Lightweight, high in protein and very chewy.

A New Icelandic Cuisine

TEACHING OLD FOOD NEW TRICKS

The first things that come to mind when most people think about Icelandic cuisine are probably lamb, fish and a variety of unusual courses that unaccustomed diners may find daunting. New Icelandic Cuisine puts a modern twist on traditional staples and repays intrepid eaters for their sense of culinary adventure.

Left Kombu tempura with Brennivín sauce **Middle** Matur og Drykkur **Right** Ling with root vegetable mousse, celery root and carrot salad

For many residents of Reykjavík, talking about Icelandic cuisine is a combination of talking about old Icelandic food-preservation methods and curiosity around the burgeoning restaurant choices in the capital area. Generally speaking, travellers are often unfamiliar with the look, smell and taste of true Icelandic cuisine. In fact, it's a great opportunity to press beyond your normal boundaries and have a culinary adventure.

Knowledge, preconceptions and stories colour people's reactions too, so when it comes to Icelandic ingredients, set aside your preconceptions and seize the opportunity to explore your senses.

Uncharted Territory

Ólafur Júlíusson is floor manager at **Matur og Drykkur**. To meet the challenges that recent years have thrown at the tourism and restaurant industries, Matur og Drykkur reduced its menu to a single culinary experience that would be rotated and rediscovered continuously. According to Ólafur, this metamorphosis has had a huge positive effect: 'We're never turning back.'

Having a single menu has its challenges and its benefits. He admits that sometimes locals wrinkle their noses at courses they generally don't associate with fine dining: blood pudding, cod heads, beans or cocoa soup. Ólafur concedes that Icelanders may suffer from an inferiority complex based on their gastronomical heritage, before adding: 'But it certainly doesn't have to be that way.'

The restaurant works almost exclusively with locally sourced ingredients and focuses on delivering Icelandic

cuisine in an unfamiliar shape and form. It uses a diverse set of local suppliers, obtaining, among other things, rhubarb and rhubarb juice for cocktails and goat cheese and meat from places like Háafell farm.

Some ingredients the chefs themselves go out and harvest in person, such as oarweed, chervil and wild celery. This approach enhances sustainability and results in a barely noticeable carbon footprint without compromising Matur og Drykkur's primary goal: to make great food and present diners with a unique take on Icelandic dishes.

> Travellers intrepid enough to eat cod's head or savour blood pudding in blueberry sauce will never look at Icelandic cuisine in the same way.

Stories Behind the Food

While storytelling isn't the main selling point of Matur og Drykkur, there's a story nonetheless behind each and every course on the menu. These stories include the methods to which early Icelanders resorted to survive winter, the ingredients they had to choose from, and how those dishes coloured their attitude towards food culture. Then there's the story behind each ingredient, from knowing that the goat cheese comes from a farm whose goats got their 15 minutes of fame in *Game of Thrones* to learning that the Atlantic halibut on the menu is yesterday's catch. And as you walk out after a night at Matur og Drykkur, you'll have stories of your own. Travellers intrepid enough to eat cod's head or savour blood pudding in blueberry sauce will never look at Icelandic cuisine in the same way.

Fermented Shark

In the case of fermented shark *(hákarl)*, Anthony Bourdain claimed that it was 'the single worst, most disgusting and terrible-tasting thing' that he had ever tasted. Gordon Ramsay famously spat it out, and Ainsley Harriott claimed it was 'like chewing a urine-infested mattress'. Archaeologist Neil Oliver, researching Viking diets, claimed it was like 'blue cheese but a hundred times stronger'. If you need to give this one a pass, that could be for the better: the Greenland shark that is used for this dish has a conservation status of 'vulnerable' globally.

Into the NIGHT

NIGHTLIFE | CLUBS | BARS

You're in a new town and you've been craving a night out for the longest while, but don't know where to start. This handy guide was based on the habits of a resident creature of the night, to help you to find your way around the Icelandic party scene. Now get out: party like an Icelander.

How to

Getting around The Reykjavík club scene is concentrated around downtown, on and around Laugavegur, and in the old downtown. Walking is the way to go.

When to go All year round as long as it's evening. Dress for the weather, though.

Prices A beer costs 1000kr to 2000kr, depending on location. Expect to pay upwards of 2200kr for a long drink or cocktail.

On a normal weekend night downtown is teeming with life, with partygoers flocking hither and thither as they migrate from one bar or club to the next. You'll find the different subclasses of partygoers, naturally, at different times throughout the evening and night. We'll give you some ideas that, depending on your clubbing and bar-hopping preferences and whether or not you're in for the full experience, you'll find useful on your prowl.

Lemmy & Bird

Lemmy is a pub and live-music venue and with a great beer garden. More recently, nearby **Bird** has become a haven to the LGBTIQ+/alternative/drag scene.

Food & Drink: 5pm to 11pm

Do you enjoy a happy-hour beer and a meaningful conversation, or perhaps a glass of wine in good company with lively discussion? There are plenty of comfortable sit-downs with good atmosphere around, and even some really nice spots for sitting outside if weather permits. If you'd like a little sustenance with your

Top left Prikið (p64)
Top right Lemmy
Left Twilight, Reykjavík

drinks, check out **Daisy**, **KEX Hostel**, **Skál!** and **Port 9**. Otherwise, **Jungle Cocktail Bar**, **GILLIGOGG**, **Veður**, **Vínstúkan Tíu Sopar** and **Bodega** are great places for drinks and company. In good weather Bodega is highly recommended, as it extends into the square where it's located.

11pm & Onwards

Many Icelanders don't venture out until closer to midnight and prefer partying into the night. **Prikið** is one of the oldest bar/cafes in Reykjavík and is a staple of the Icelandic bar and club scene, which during weekends is packed tight by guests. There's little space, but that doesn't stop the crowd from dancing to the beats laid down by that evening's DJ. Prikið is welcoming and cross-generational, but in the late evenings during the weekends it's mostly crammed by under-30s. **Röntgen** is a little more recent and has taken part of the overflow from Prikið, mainly those patrons who are over 30. It's also a late-night bar/club and has a similar vibe to Prikið, though it's a bit more refined.

The Day After

A curated hangover day by our resident creature of the night.

01 Carb up at **Grái Kötturinn** (Grey Cat); American pancakes and coffee until 2pm.

02 Walk to **Grandi**; let the sea breeze heal your wrecked nerves.

03 Take an afternoon nap in the park by the **Einar Jónsson Museum** if weather permits.

04 Down a Gleym-mér-ei burger and a peach schnapps at **Vitabar** for dinner.

05 Swim in the evening at **Sundhöllin** swimming pool. There's nothing like soaking in a hot-pot with the locals.

Recommendations by **Arnar Ingi**, *graphic designer, musician and resident creature of the night.*

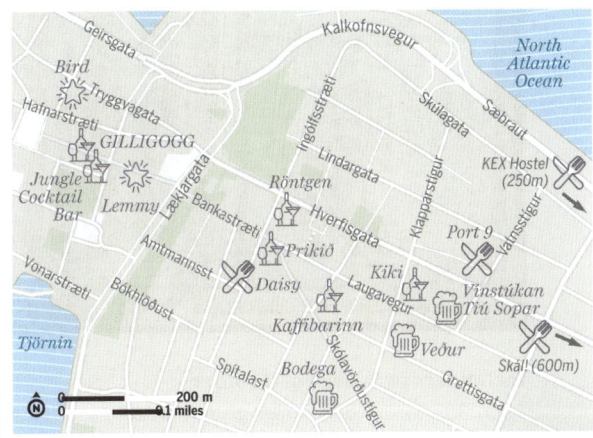

Left Grái Kötturinn (Grey Cat)
Below Kiki in Laugavegur

The DJs read the crowd well, playing anything from electro to funk.

A Deeper Dive

The clock is ticking ever closer to 2am. Heading home might be a good idea, but perhaps you're longing for a deeper dive. Both Prikið and Röntgen are perfectly good spots to keep going, but at this hour a few other spots are coming into their prime, including two major players that are worth a special mention.

Kaffibarinn This bar has been a prime location for the deep divers of the Reykjavík nightlife for over 25 years. It's remained rowdy, crowded and sweaty forever, and it feels like it's always open. It's the kind of place you might enter for a quiet coffee in the afternoon and find yourself stumbling home 14 hours later after drinking and partying. It has a long list of regulars from the neighbourhood, but welcomes non-regulars and tourists alike.

Kiki The heart of the local LGBTIQ+ scene in Reykjavík, but inclusive and approachable to everyone, Kiki is a bar that turns into a nightclub. It's tuned high in terms of party amplitude, plenty of dancing and cheerful intimacy under the beat of various great Icelandic DJs, playing all sorts of music: electro, Eurovision, you name it. This is absolutely the place to lose yourself in until morning.

A Brief Take on Icelandic Craft Beer

INFUSING CRAFT BREWS WITH LOCAL FLAVOURS

On 1 March 1989, after a prohibition that lasted 74 years, the purchase of beer became legal in Iceland. Until then neither bars, the alcohol monopoly nor anyone else could sell beer. Hence beer was a rarity and contraband. Today the 1st of March is celebrated in Iceland as 'Beer Day'.

Left Ægir Brewery
Middle Kaldi beer
Right Gæðingur Microbar

Icelanders in Search of Choices

After 1989, two major beverage giants produced and supplied Iceland with beer for over 17 years, until a couple in North Iceland, Agnes and Ólafur, started a brewery of their own, **Kaldi**, claiming the title of the first craft brewery in Iceland. A few years later, in 2010, a small group of dedicated beer enthusiasts formed a home-brewing club. Their aim was to learn how to brew beer and to create a supply chain to import the necessary ingredients into the country, and in so doing violate yet another prohibition remnant: the ban on home brewing.

In the same period, three craft breweries were formed: **Ölvisholt**, **Mjöður** and **Gæðingur**. Since then, the number of craft breweries has grown rapidly. At the time of writing, there are 27 established craft-beer breweries in Iceland. The majority of these were established in 2017 or later.

What Makes Beer Icelandic?

Iceland isn't a great agricultural source for beer-making. What little barley and wheat are grown here are in limited supply, very hardy and not a great source of starch. Furthermore, no malting takes place in Iceland, so in order to use those grains the brewers would need to mix in imported grains or use additional enzymes. For this reason most grains for beer-making, and hops of course, are imported. Then there's Iceland's water, which though crisp and clear lacks the minerals for optimal beer-making, and so the minerals you'd normally find in water abroad need to be added too. So what makes beer Icelandic?

Breweries have taken various approaches to Icelandifying beer. **Og Natura**, for example, uses Icelandic herbs and berries in its products, pairing them with hops in a most inventive manner. **Álfur** uses potato discards, from a local potato manufacturer, as a source of starch mixed in with the wheat and barley. **RVK Brewing Company** puts an entire Christmas tree into the boil for an added spirit of festivities. **Ölverk** uses geothermal heat to do their mash and boil, and many breweries employ the local *skyr* (yogurt-style delicacy) to start a lacto-fermentation in kettle-soured beers, adding a very recognisable flavour.

> So what makes beer Icelandic? Breweries have taken various approaches to Icelandifying beer...

So what are you waiting for? There are plenty of brewery taprooms all around Iceland and a variety of craft-beer pubs in downtown Reykjavík.

The Reykjavík Scene

Downtown and the Old Harbour are home to a number of craft bars and breweries with taprooms. Among them are **RVK Brewing Company** and **Bastard Brew & Food**, **BrewDog Reykjavik**, **Ægir Brewery**, **Skúli Craft Bar**, **Session**, **Microbar** and more. If you're willing to venture a little further, you may find yourself in **Gæðingur Microbar** or the **Malbygg Taproom** where the brewers themselves will gladly pour you a pint or five.

The Monopoly on Alcohol

The Icelandic government retains a monopoly on the retail sale of alcoholic beverages in Iceland through their countrywide stores called Vínbúðin ('known as Ríkið'). It is illegal for private companies to sell alcohol in any shape or form in Iceland. This has been a contentious issue in Iceland for years, and some companies have started selling alcohol via web stores anyway, challenging the government and claiming the laws are unjust since companies outside Icelandic jurisdiction are allowed to sell and distribute to Iceland. So far they remain in business, but only time will tell how this issue is resolved.

03 Culture NIGHT

FESTIVAL | DOWNTOWN | MUSIC

▬▬ Culture Night, first held in 1996 as a birthday celebration for the city of Reykjavík, is easily the biggest single event in Iceland, with over a third of the population of Iceland attending on a yearly basis.

📖 How to

What? Culture Night is a huge collection of simultaneous cultural events.

Where? Culture Night is held 'downtown' in the wide sense of the word, with the festival area extending west and east of downtown as well.

When? The event generally takes place on the first Saturday after 18 August.

Price? The festival is open to everyone, but particular events within the festival may charge for participation.

Culture Night During the Day

Particular locations and events have become staples of the festival, but by far the largest part of it is independently organised and executed by various individuals and groups, so each festival is mostly comprised of 'wildcard' events. Many of them go on the schedule, but others don't, so keep an eye out! Just walking around, not least in the residential areas of downtown, will surely bring you to flea markets, independent art exhibitions, home concerts and...waffles.

The city gives so called 'waffle grants' to residents who are willing to accept hundreds of guests into their homes or into their gardens and serve them waffles all day long. The mayor, at the time of writing, has personally baked waffles in the thousands for guests in his own home. Another staple

☆ Planning Your Day

The **Culture Night** *(menningarnott.is)* website has a glossary of events and activities. It's the best source of information to plan your day. Take into consideration that there will be over 100,000 people in town, so travel times will be longer than normal.

Top left A choir entertains the crowd
Top right Aerial silks performance
Left Drumming performance

event is the Reykjavík Marathon. It is the first event of the day and generally has around 10,000 participants from Iceland and all over the world. Runners can choose five different distances to run, ranging from 600m to the marathon.

What to Expect During the Day?
On a stroll through town you'll find a variety of events. Events vary from year to year, but past years included a bread-cake-decorating competition at the Reykjavík Art Museum, a street-food convention by the harbour, dance exhibitions, tightly packed events at the art galleries, backyard concerts, a silent disco at the library, a guided tour through the art collections of the downtown bank, poetry readings, an interactive VR theatre experience for one, and numerous street performances.

A Word from the Former Mayor

My best advice on Menningarnótt.

01. Start the day by participating in the Reykjavik Marathon. You can run the shorter distances, it does not matter, but it is a great way to experience the city from street level, go into neighbourhoods and run by the ocean. And you start the day with endorphins in your veins.

02. Go with the flow. Be welcomed into people's homes and houses or experience music in a backyard. There are interesting things going on everywhere. Go for the unplanned and unexpected.

03. Attend the numerous concerts during the evening, and end the night watching the dancing fireworks in the sky.

Dagur B Eggertsson, *former mayor of Reykjavík. @Dagurb*

Far left Fireworks light up the city
Left Arnarhóll hill concert
Below Street jazz performance

The Evening

Dinner may need a bit of planning if you're hoping to grab a table. Book tables in advance. However, many restaurants will host food-related events throughout the day and early evening as well, so you'll probably be able to refuel on the go. The final big event of the day is a concert by Arnarhóll hill where, each year, a diverse cast of performers entertain a crowd. It generally starts around 8pm. Slowly but surely the hill and surrounding areas fill with people. As the concert comes to a close at around 11pm, it culminates in a countdown in which everyone participates, chanting and anticipating one of the biggest fireworks displays of the year (perhaps beaten only by the chaotic battering of fireworks on New Year's Eve). Following the fireworks most people head home, and the Reykjavík nightlife takes over. What you decide to do next is a whole other chapter.

04 A Capital of **CULTURE**

ART | HISTORY | CULTURE

Reykjavík was designated one of the European capitals of culture in the year 2000. It was for good reason, too, as Reykjavík's heritage, cultural institutions and independently run spaces are both plentiful and diverse.

How to

Get around Most of the locations are in, or close to, downtown. For more distant places, a car or the city bus are the best modes of transport.

When to go Year-round, though for outdoor cultural spots it's ideal to aim for late spring, summer or early autumn. Or any time the weather decides to be less antagonistic.

Prices The Reykjavík City Card will save you money if you're planning a cultural day or three.

Downtown & Around

The city of Reykjavík plays host to many of the country's cultural institutions, and for the most part they're located downtown or within walking distance of it. It is easy to compose a full day or two of cultural exploration.

An integral part of the art scene in Reykjavík is the **Reykjavík Art Museum** with its collections of local artists. Emphasising 21st-century art, it is actually split into three separate locations: Hafnarhús, Kjarvalsstaðir and Ásmundarsafn. They can all be visited with the same ticket of admission. **Reykjavík Art Museum – Hafnarhús** is the largest and most central of the locations. For an ideal day trip, visit them in this order and end your day by bathing in **Laugardalslaug**, which incidentally is close by Ásmundarsafn.

Reykjavík City Card

The **Reykjavík City Card** (*visitreykjavik.is/reykjavik-city-card*) grants you admission to all of the museums and exhibitions run by the city and more. It also grants access to the swimming pools and the city bus too! It can be purchased in one- to three-day variants.

Top left Reykjavík Art Museum, Kjarvalsstaðir **Top right** Hafnarfjörður (p75) **Left** Medieval wood church door, National Museum of Iceland (p74)

There are plenty of cultural locations in the downtown vicinity. The **National Gallery of Iceland** by the pond is responsible for the art that's nationally owned and houses a variety of events and exhibitions of art from the 20th and 21st centuries. The **Einar Jónsson Museum** and sculpture garden is located next to the landmark Hallgrímskirkja and is dedicated to the art of Einar Jónsson, considered to be Iceland's first sculptor. Even when the museum is closed, the garden is a worthwhile excursion: it's great for picnics! The **National Museum of Iceland** is also only a short walk from downtown and offers a fantastic glimpse into how Iceland got to where it is today. It houses both permanent and temporary exhibitions with audio tours available in many languages.

Off the Beaten Path

Reykjavík is obviously bigger than just downtown and its surrounds. Some days you simply might want to explore a little more.

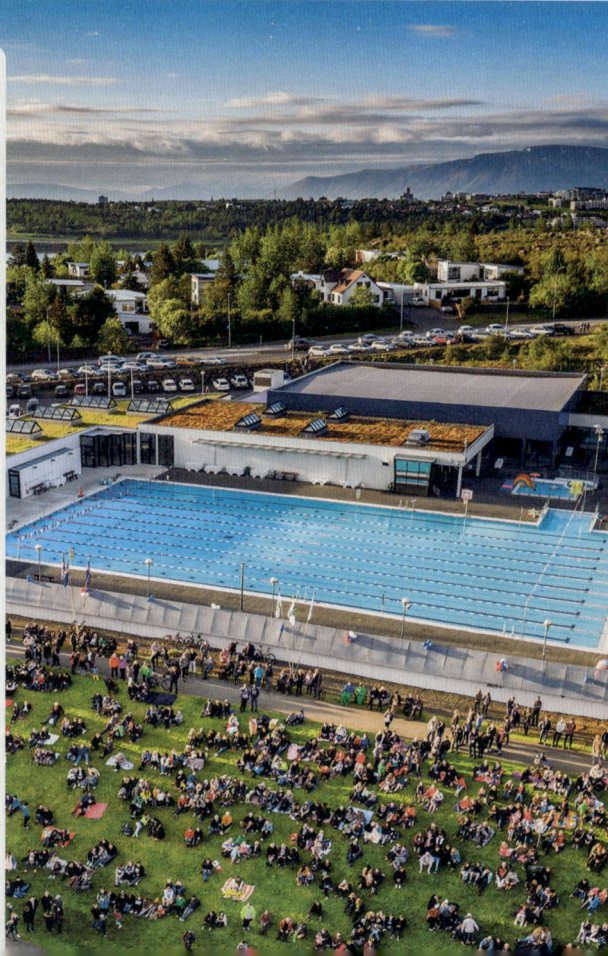

Art in Public Spaces

A selection of outdoor art by a local expert.

Þúfa (Tussock), by Ólöf Nordal A significant landmark in the cityscape. The *Tussock* is a taunt as it's not local to cities, it's a pest in farming, and constructing one is essentially an oxymoron.

Áfangar, by Richard Serra An unusual work by the artist, as *Áfangar* is made of basalt. Located on Viðey island, it deals with height contours in the Icelandic landscape.

The Tree of Signs, by Gabríela Friðriksdóttir Located far from the beaten path for a traveller, it's visible from the local IKEA and Costco but is simultaneously in seemingly untouched nature.

Harpa Þórsdóttir, *director of the National Gallery of Iceland.*

Left Kópavogslaug
Below Reykjavík Art Museum – Hafnarhús (p73)

In the town of **Hafnarfjörður**, south of Reykjavík, you can visit **Hafnarborg**, which houses the town's art collection. There are rotating exhibitions of both modern and contemporary works by various artists from the museum archives or as guest exhibitors. It's absolutely worth a visit in combination with a nice exploration of the old town of Hafnarfjörður, which is built on the edge of an old lava field and the sea.

Kópavogur, another Reykjavík neighbour, has its own cultural institution called **Gerðarsafn Art Museum**. It's as much a beautiful building to visit as an interesting museum for discovering Icelandic modern and contemporary art. On top of that it's located right next to the main transport hub of Kópavogur, and has a very good outdoor area for picnics and children. Close by the museum is **Kópavogslaug**, easily one of the best swimming pools for children.

The **Museum of Design & Applied Art** is located on Garðatorg square, in adjacent municipality Garðabær, and has exhibitions in various different design categories. It's a hidden gem if you're willing to make the trip.

REYKJAVÍK ESSAY

♪ A Path to Musical Excellence?

LOCAL SOUNDS, GLOBAL AUDIENCES

Iceland has produced many globally known musicians. Whether that number is the highest per capita, as many Icelanders proudly proclaim, is debatable. Regardless, given Iceland's size, the extent of the musical footprint it has left on global consciousness is extraordinary.

Starting Early

It's common in Iceland for parents to send their children to choirs from an early age. Once children start school, other options open up, such as learning classical instruments at music schools or getting lessons in primary school. Lessons prepare kids to participate in school bands, and these bands expose them to a variety of instruments. Alongside this, the children take obligatory music lessons in school where they learn the basics of music and creation and cooperation, and get exposed to the musical heritage of Iceland and other cultures.

Creating Platforms

Part of running a successful nationwide music programme is creating the platforms from which bands and musicians can launch.

Tónlistarþróunarmiðstöðin The Centre for Music Development, run by an old Icelandic punk legend, is a place where bands can get rooms to keep their equipment and practise their craft. Furthermore, it organises events at which the bands can perform.

Músíktilraunir At this event, bands from across Iceland compete annually in front of a live audience. Among the bands to have featured in the competition are Sigur Rós, Mammút, Of Monsters and Men, RetRoBoT (Daði Freyr's band before he went solo), Vök, Samaris and Agent Fresco.

Iceland Airwaves The biggest music festival in Iceland hosts performances from local and overseas talent. Alongside the festival is a brilliant off-venue programme crowded with upcoming names on the Icelandic music scene.

Left Trombone player **Middle** Musical performance at school **Right** Of Monsters and Men on stage.

The Present

Sigtryggur Baldursson, iconic musician and advisor to Iceland Music, is optimistic about the future of Icelandic music. His dream scenario is a music scene where musicians can make a living without being household names. To this end, he's been involved in a project that creates guides for young musicians on managing their career and their rights, among other things.

> While there may be enough work available in Iceland for bands to survive, to grow they may need to operate from abroad.

Although Icelandic music has come to be identified with the ethereal sound of internationally recognised performers such as Sigur Rós, Hjaltalín and Björk, they're not the totality of Icelandic music. You might be familiar with bands and musical projects without realising they're Icelandic. Did you know, for instance, that Of Monsters and Men, Kaleo and Gus Gus are Icelandic bands?

Baldursson says that bands that become popular locally face a tough choice: while there may be enough work available in Iceland for bands to survive, to grow they may need to operate from abroad.

So what's the best way to get acquainted with Icelandic music? Baldursson recommends the Spotify playlists at icelandmusic.is. Furthermore, if you're looking for events, the gig list in the **Reykjavík Grapevine** (grapevine.is) is the go-to list for concerts.

♫ Girls Rock!

The Girls Rock camp is a project that originated in the USA with the goal of instigating social change by creating a platform for girls, women and trans/non-binary people to take space in popular music culture where they are severely underrepresented. This project also took flight in Iceland and is now actively recruiting girls and hatching new bands en masse. The programmes are mostly run for children and teenagers, but they also have occasional programmes for adults. What's remarkable is that no prior music experience is required; the goal is to create new opportunities, after all.

05 Urban HIKING

WALKS | NATURE | CATS

Put on your good shoes, pack your swimsuit, visit the nichest museum in Iceland, see the first settlements, smell the sea and bathe with locals. Oh, and don't forget to pet the cats of Reykjavík.

Trip Notes

How long? This walk, while only about 4km long, can easily take a whole day with the activities suggested.

Tips Bring a swimsuit and make sure you dress according to the weather. On the way there are plenty of good places to stop for lunch.

Costs The entry fee for the Phallological Museum is 3500kr, the Aðalstræti Settlement Exhibition is 3000kr and the pool is 1380kr.

Cats of Reykjavík

Perhaps the true locals of Reykjavík, cats are everywhere and it can be fun to keep that in mind when walking around. They are popular as pets in Iceland and generally get to roam freely – a bother to some and celebrated by others. Cat patrols can be spotted wherever you go.

05 You packed a swimsuit and fresh socks, right? That wasn't for the beach! Sit back, relax and converse with the locals about the news and the weather in **Vesturbæjarlaug** swimming pool.

02 Icelandic Phallological Museum displays penises from over 100 species of mammals, including a human and, supposedly, a specimen from hidden folk, more commonly known as elves.

03 During building work in 2001, a well-preserved settlement partly dating back to the year 871 was discovered. A **Settlement Exhibition** was ingeniously integrated into the building being worked on.

01 The Protestant church of **Hallgrímskirkja** was until recently the tallest building in Reykjavík. Its construction started in 1945, and it wasn't formally opened until 1986.

04 Visit the seafront, explore the sloppy kelp jungles of **Ægissíða** and have a stroll around the old fishing sheds of **Grímsstaðavör**. Ægissíða is a popular path and beach to walk along and enjoy.

Listings

BEST OF THE REST

 ### Craft Beer & Gin

Microbar
The location near the bus station in Kópavogur was the first true craft bar in Iceland. Cosy but off the beaten path. Or pop into their Laugavegur location.

Skúli Craft Bar
A charismatic little craft bar next to Ingólfstorg downtown. Great location and atmosphere, and a good bottle list.

Malbygg Taproom
Malbygg is the cool kid of the Icelandic brewery scene. Its taproom is stocked with its own beers and plenty of imports. The location in Skútuvogur is tough to reach.

RVK Brewing Company
Ten minutes' walk from Hlemmur food court. Its small taproom has a good view into the brewery.

BrewDog Reykjavík
BrewDog is located off Laugavegur. A franchise of a UK taproom, it has an ambitious selection of Icelandic craft beer. Its staff and attitude are top-notch.

Ægir 101 Taproom
Beer bar in the heart of the Laugavegur pedestrianised area for the Grandi-based brewery.

Þoran Distillery
It's worth booking ahead for a visit. Here, the friendly distiller, Biggi, will walk you through how Icelandic gin is made and you'll sample his award-winning Marberg gin. *(thoran.is)*

 ### Restaurants

Dill €€€
The first Michelin-starred restaurant in Iceland. It works hard to make your experience unique while maintaining a sustainable approach. Downtown location.

Skál €€
Experience luxury dining with a good variety of slow food, creative small dishes and Icelandic craft beer.

Óx €€€
A rarefied, tiny spot, hidden behind a speakeasy called Amma Don. It's more of a dining experience than a traditional restaurant. Few seats available, so book ahead.

Mat Bar €€€
A nicely located spot across the corner from Laugavegur serving an ever-changing Italian/Nordic fusion menu. A great variety of wines and knowledgeable staff.

Austur Indíafélagið €€€
Fancy Indian food? This is as authentic as you

Reykjavík City Library

can get it in Iceland. Prime downtown location and a simple and relaxing interior.

Sægreifinn €€
Sidle into harbour shack 'Sea Baron' for the capital's most famous lobster soup plus fish skewers grilled on the spot.

 Quick Bites

Brauð & Co €
Watch hipsters make some of the city's best home-baked breads and pastries.

Baka Baka €
Baked goods and small plates play second fiddle at night when wood-fired pizza dominates.

Le Kock €€
Some of Reykjavík's best burgers paired with drinks at Tail, and bagels and doughnuts at its bakery Deig.

Mama Reykjavík €€
Globally inspired vegan stews, juices, salads and sandwiches in a space for wellness, art and spirituality.

Hamborgarabúlla Tómasar €
Tómas' burger joints are local, simple and in a league of their own. His original joint is located five minutes' walk from downtown.

Vitabar €
You've had a long Saturday night and you're craving a sloppy burger. Vitabar on Vitastígur, downtown, has you covered.

Art & Culture

Icelandic Punk Museum
Right downtown there's a stairway down from the pavement where Frikki Punk runs an exhibition dedicated to Iceland's punk scene.

Árbær Open Air Museum

i8
A gallery located downtown and in Grandi, i8 has exhibitions by current art powerhouses, both Icelandic and from abroad. A must visit for the visual-arts-oriented travellers.

Reykjavík City Library
The library's main building sits downtown. In addition to its customary function, it's home to concerts, culture walks, poetry readings and the Icelandic Photography Museum.

History

Árbær Open Air Museum
The open-air museum is a collection of old buildings and a vision of life in the olden days. Visit one of the turf houses and have a taste of homemade pastry.

Viðey
Originally an active volcano, then a significant location in Icelandic history and now a glorious place to enjoy geology, birds, history and art all in one place. Grab a ferry to Viðey!

Saga Museum
Iceland's Viking past is brought to life by eerie silicon models and a multi-language soundtrack featuring the thud of axes and hair-raising screams.

🌿 Public Parks & Outdoors

Klambratún
Klambratún park is a five-minute walk from Hlemmur food court. It's home to part of the Reykjavík Art Museum and a perfectly good frisbee golf course. Great for picnics.

Elliðaárdalur
Elliðaárdalur is the biggest green area in the capital region. It's home to birds and is one of the few areas where wild rabbits reside. Easily accessible by bus.

Höfðaskógur Forest & Hvaleyrarvatn
Take a short hike around this small lake and its pretty environment, including a large woodlands area (by Icelandic standards). Close by it's possible to go horse riding with Íshestar.

Grótta Lighthouse
Grótta is the tip of the Reykjavík peninsula Seltjarnarnes. It has a lighthouse and is thrillingly close to the sea. There's also a warm pool, Kvika Footbath, to dip your feet into.

Mt Esja
A bus ride away, Esja is a pretty tall mountain considering it's next door to Reykjavík. It has great views, facilities and walking paths. See Reykjavík from across the bay.

Reykjavík Zoo & Family Park
Do you like sheep? In Laugardalur you can find the only zoo in Iceland where you can meet those exotic animals and many more in person! Actually way more fun than it sounds.

Öskjuhlíð
Woodlands close to the city centre. Explore the WWII bunkers, encounter curious rabbits and perhaps end by taking a swim in the sea in Nauthólsvík geothermal beach.

Heiðmörk Nature Reserve
Visit Heiðmörk at the edge of the city, a seemingly endless source of outdooring that shows that Reykjavík is, in fact, next door to nature.

〰️ Swimming Pools

Sundhöllin
The city's oldest swimming pool is located downtown. It has been upgraded to modern standards, and has an outdoor swimming pool and hot tubs.

Vesturbæjarlaug
A 25m outdoor swimming pool, a children's pool and hot tubs. Close by is an ice-cream parlour, a cafe and a fast-food diner.

Laugardalslaug
One of the largest pools in Iceland, with the best facilities: an Olympic-sized indoor pool and several outdoor pools, a string of hot-pots, a saltwater tub, a steam bath and a curling 86m water slide.

Kópavogslaug
A 50m outdoor swimming pool, nice hot tubs, slides and an indoor swimming pool. This pool is in the next town over from Reykjavík, but is easily accessed by bus.

A trail on Mt Esja

Lágafellslaug

It sports a 25m swimming pool, hot tubs and three slides outside, and an indoor swimming pool for the kids. Located in Mosfellsbær, on the way in or out of the city.

Nauthólsvík Geothermal Beach

Nauthólsvík geothermal beach is a half-hour walk from downtown or five minutes by bus. How about lying in the tub or bathing in the North Atlantic?

 Music Venues

Harpa

Harpa Concert Centre is located harbourside in downtown. Its architecture is the pride of Reykjavík, and it's home to various events and to the symphony orchestra.

Mengi

Mengi is a venue operated by artists; it hosts diverse music and art events. It's located in a prime location downtown and its schedule is progressive. *(mengi.is)*

Gamla Bíó

Premier 1926 Art Deco cinema Gamla Bíó is now an excellent small concert venue. *(gamlabio.is)*

 Other Attractions

Tjarnarbíó

Tjarnarbíó theatre, the cinema by the pond, has a variety of shows on its calendar, plus plays (some performed in English), contemporary dance, concerts and more. *(tjarnarbio.is)*

Perlan, Wonders of Iceland

Kolaportið

Kolaportið (the coal storage) is the only flea market in Iceland. It's only open on weekends and is definitely worth a visit.

FlyOver Iceland

In Grandi you can experience flying over Iceland in a state-of-the-art cinema. It offers motion, curved cinema, wind, smell and more – immersive cinema like you've never seen before.

Whales of Iceland

Right next to FlyOver Iceland you can visit the whales. Walk among life-sized models of 23 types of whales.

Wonders of Iceland

In Perlan, a landmark building in Reykjavík, you can experience the sounds of earthquakes, visit Látrabjarg cliff in augmented reality, walk through an actual ice cave and see the aurora in Iceland's only planetarium.

THE GOLDEN CIRCLE

NATIONAL PARKS | WATERFALLS | GEOTHERMAL SPRINGS

- ▶ **Trip Builder** (p86)
- ▶ **Practicalities** (p87)
- ▶ **Þingvellir National Park** (p88)
- ▶ **The History of Iceland** (p90)
- ▶ **Waterworks** (p94)
- ▶ **Get Outside** (p96)
- ▶ **Listings** (p98)

THE GOLDEN CIRCLE
Trip Builder

The Golden Circle tourist route can be completed in a day. Its main sights include Þingvellir, Geysir and Gullfoss, but the region is also packed with hidden-gem waterfalls, important historical sites and unique geological landscapes.

Marvel at **Gullfoss**, a cascading two-tiered waterfall that drops into a ravine (p95)
🚗 10mins from Geysir

Watch the geyser spout water up to 40m into the air at **Geysir** (p95)
🚗 40mins from Þingvellir National Park

Soak in the **Secret Lagoon**, an outdoor natural hot spring pool (p99)
🚗 30mins from Gullfoss

Walk between the North American and Eurasian tectonic plates at **Þingvellir** National Park (p88)
🚗 40mins from Reykjavík

Walk the rim of **Kerið**, a colourful volcanic crater filled with bright-blue water (p97)
🚗 15mins from Selfoss

PREVIOUS SPREAD: DANIEL DORSA/LONELY PLANET
DANIEL DORSA/LONELY PLANET

0 — 10 km
0 — 5 miles

Practicalities

ARRIVING
Keflavík International Airport Around 90km from Þingvellir, all international flights come and go through here. The drive from Reykjavík is short and the roads are good. Tours depart regularly from Reykjavík.

FIND YOUR WAY
A tourist-information centre can be found at Þingvellir National Park.

MONEY
Expect to pay for parking at Þingvellir, Geysir and Kerið and for toilets at Þingvellir and Gullfoss. Credit and debit cards are widely accepted.

WHERE TO STAY

Town	Pro/Con
Laugarvatn	Has quaint guesthouses for those who don't want to complete the entire Circle in one day.
Flúðir	Detour to overnight at a B&B and soak in nearby hot springs.
Selfoss	Abundant hotels and guesthouses, and a good location to continue to the South Coast.

EATING & DRINKING
Geothermal bakery Eat rye bread that was baked using geothermal energy at Laugarvatn (p98).

Best tomato-themed menu Friðheimar (p98; pictured top)

Must-try ice cream Efstidalur II (p98; pictured bottom)

GETTING AROUND

Car Driving is the best way to explore places off the beaten path.

Tour bus For those who want to sit back and take it all in.

Private tour Often you can add adventure activities.

APR–MAY
Cooler temperatures, Northern Lights equinox peak

JUN–AUG
Everything is green, fair temperatures, midnight sun

SEP–OCT
Rain and wind are common, Northern Lights are back

NOV–MAR
Snowy with limited daylight hours

06 Þingvellir National PARK

HISTORY | TECTONIC PLATES | OUTDOORS

Þingvellir National Park is a UNESCO World Heritage Site for its history and geological elements. Here you will find multiple fissures caused by the rifting of the North American and Eurasian tectonic plates. It's also the site of the Alþingi, Iceland's democratic parliament established in 930 CE.

How To

Getting here Rent a car or join a guided tour.

When to go To avoid crowds, skip the park between 10am and 1pm when tour buses come. Early and late are best, especially with the midnight sun.

Parking There are multiple car parks around Þingvellir (from 1000kr depending on vehicle size).

Amenities Hakið Visitor Centre has an interactive history and nature exhibit, plus a snack bar and shop. Leirar Service Centre has a cafe/mini-mart.

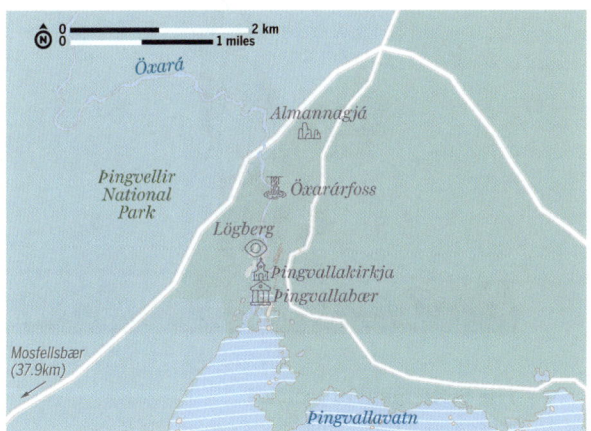

Iceland sits directly on the boundary between the North American and Eurasian tectonic plates, and the boundary runs through Þingvellir. The plates are spreading apart at a rate of 2.5cm per year, which create cracks and canyons in the landscape.

Viewing platform Near the main car park sits a large platform that overlooks the entire park, including Þingvallavatn, the largest natural lake in Iceland.

Almannagjá The official rift where you can walk between continents. The walls of the ridge are made up of the North American and Eurasian tectonic plates to the west and east, respectively. *Game of Thrones* fans will recognise one of the canyons as the filming location of the 'Bloody Gate'.

Þingvallabær Translating to 'Þingvellir town', it's made up of five houses that are now used as the park warden's office and the prime minister's summer house.

Þingvallakirkja Just past the houses is the church of Þingvellir. It's usually closed, but opens twice a day for free guided park-ranger tours from June to August.

Lögberg The approximate location of where parliament gathered. It translates to 'Law Rock', which is where the speaker would stand to make announcements during gatherings.

Öxarárfoss At the end of the Almannagjá rift, a beautiful waterfall cascades over the cliff of the North American plate into a river gorge.

Top Almannagjá
Bottom Þingvallakirkja

 Around Þingvellir

Enhance your time at Þingvellir by adding an activity or tour around the area. Hikers can stop in the visitor centre for a map of multiple trails of varying distances around the park, while local tour operators conduct tours of the area on horseback. There are also water-based activities: you can angle for trout and char in the clear cold waters of lake Þingvallavatn, or the cold-resistant can snorkel or dive between continents in crystal-clear glacier water (p97). And the area around lake Þingvallavatn is also a great place for bird-watching or spotting mink or the Arctic fox (Iceland's only native mammal).

■ **With thanks to Dale Kedwards**, who researches medieval Icelandic culture at the Árni Magnússon Institute for Icelandic Studies.

The History of Iceland

ICELAND'S POLITICAL HISTORY LOCATED BETWEEN TECTONIC PLATES

To Icelanders Þingvellir is more than simply the place where tectonic plates split apart. Literally meaning 'assembly plains', Þingvellir was once a gathering place for major historical events and is now a national shrine and UNESCO World Heritage Site.

Left Monument to Ingólfur Arnarson
Middle and right Þingvellir

The Settlement of Iceland

Iceland is unusual in that it was settled late. Around the year 870 there were no permanent inhabitants of Iceland. As kingdoms developed in the Middle Ages, the Norwegian king was known for being overbearing, so a lot of powerful landowners wanted to move and make new settlements. Norwegian seafarers headed west and found a new land to settle. Ingólfur Arnarson is known to be the first settler on the island. When Iceland became known, Scandinavians started migrating via boat. There was never a king or executive authority, but rather a decentralised and widespread distribution of power. For that to work, the people came together once a year to form a national assembly, or Alþing, held at Þingvellir.

Founding the Parliament

In the Middle Ages, Iceland didn't have towns or cities. Landowners were powerful as they owned land and slaves. Once the land was fully settled, locals needed to establish a way of governing themselves to counterbalance the growing power of a small number of landowners. District assemblies were formed in the beginning, but as the population grew it became apparent that a general assembly was needed. So in 930 Þingvellir was established, and parliament remained there for hundreds of years.

Annual Assemblies

Due to accessibility as well as an abundance of fresh water and forests, Þingvellir was chosen as the meeting

location. People from all regions of Iceland would travel for days to arrive at the annual assembly. The powerful regional leaders known as *goði* came together to make decisions. Once there, everyone would build booths out of stone, turf and cloth. It was the biggest event of the year and reminiscent of a festival, with attendees entertaining one another.

At the centre of the assembly plains was a structure known as Lögberg (Law Rock). Here anyone could stand and give a speech on matters they found important. News was reported, information was exchanged, conflicts were resolved, and marriages were arranged.

> People from all regions of Iceland would travel for days to arrive at the annual assembly.

The Law Speaker

But it was the law speaker, elected by the *goði* chieftains, who held the power at these meetings. Around the year 1000, the country was divided between pagans and the new religion of Christianity. The law speaker at that time had to decide what to do about the new religion. He hid under a cloak for a day to meditate on the decision. When he emerged, he stated 'We are one land and one people so we should have one law' and peacefully decided on Christianity with three caveats: people could still worship the pagan gods in private, still eat horse meat, and still expose unwanted babies to the elements. Today, an Icelandic flag stands in the spot where the Lögberg (Law Rock) was thought to be.

Icelandic Sagas

The sagas are an important part of Icelandic heritage. Written in the 13th century about events occurring between the 9th and 13th centuries, these books recount struggles and conflicts during the Settlement Era. Many of the sagas have moments at Þingvellir. Topics include the settlement, geological events, famine, witchcraft, and bloody feuds and battles. For those interested in reading the sagas, see the **Icelandic Saga Database** (sagadb.org).

Since the sagas were written some 200 years after the actual events took place, it is accepted that exaggerations are found in the writings. Icelanders embrace this, as it makes the stories that much more entertaining. Nevertheless, the sagas are important documents of courage, perseverance and what life was like at the time.

The Present Day

The national assembly continued meeting at Þingvellir until 1798, when it was moved to Reykjavík. In 1930 Þingvellir became Iceland's first national park, and in 2004 it was listed as a UNESCO World Heritage Site. Today Þingvellir looks the same as it always has: aside from the pathways to accommodate tourism, you're standing on a field that has always been a field, and is one of the biggest parts of the nation's history.

> In 1930 Þingvellir became Iceland's first national park, and in 2004 it was listed as a Unesco World Heritage Site.

Heart of Iceland

Inside the Hakið Visitor Centre, you'll find the Heart of Iceland, an interactive exhibit that beautifully portrays the history and nature of Þingvellir and why it means so much to Icelanders. Using state-of-the-art technology, it allows you to reveal artefacts from the area, trace the routes locals travelled to get to the annual assembly, and visualise the law counsel and what went on at the meetings. You will also learn how water travels from the glacier through filtered lava rock and into nearby lake Þingvallavatn, and what the future of Þingvellir holds. Admission is adult/child 1200kr/free.

Left Þingvellir **Above left** Manuscript exhibit, Saga Museum (p81), Reykjavík **Above right** Icelandic flag, Lögberg (Law Rock)

07 Water **WORKS**

WATERFALLS | GEYSERS | HIDDEN GEMS

Water is a common theme in Iceland, whether it's melting from a glacier, cascading over a cliff, or heated with geothermal energy from the ground. Along the Golden Circle you will find all of these elements in a relatively small geographical area.

How To

Getting here Rent a car and drive yourself to reach places off the beaten path.

When to go Geysir, Gullfoss, Brúarfoss and Faxi can be accessed year-round.

What to wear Warm layers and waterproof clothing from head to toe are essential no matter what time of year you're visiting.

Top Brúarfoss
Bottom Strokkur

The horse's mane Faxi is a small but mighty waterfall just south of Gullfoss. A 1000kr parking fee gets you access to this serene oasis. A small cafe and picnic area on-site are good spots to enjoy a midday bite. The surrounding nature is a great spot for bird-watching, and you might even see salmon jumping up the river in the summer.

Geothermal valley Geysir is a geothermal area in the Haukadalur valley that is home to geysers, fumaroles and mud-pits. The main attraction is **Strokkur**, which erupts up to 40m (131ft) every 10 to 15 minutes.

Crown jewel of the Circle Gullfoss translates to 'Golden Falls' and is a double-cascade waterfall dropping 32m into a massive gorge. The water comes from the nearby Langjökull, Iceland's second-largest glacier.

Vivid blue falls Bright-blue water cascading over black lava rock makes **Brúarfoss** waterfall unique. The car park (750kr) allows you to drive to about 500m from the falls. Or take a 7km (three-hour) return hike from the southern Brúará Trail car park to the waterfall, passing **Hlauptungufoss** and **Miðfoss** along the way. Stick to the trails. People have died after being swept away.

ⓘ Dress for Adventure

'There's no such thing as bad weather, only bad clothing.' This Icelandic saying might leave some people scratching their head. What's good versus bad clothing is not obvious to everyone, especially if you're not used to rain, high winds and low temperatures. The weather is notoriously unpredictable in Iceland, so proper attire is important, especially when travelling the Golden Circle. Its location away from the coast means it tends to be colder and windier. Wear layers that you can remove or add as conditions change. Sturdy footwear and waterproof outerwear (head to toe) are also critical.

08 Get OUTSIDE

ADVENTURE | TOURS | EXCURSIONS

Whether you prefer water or land activities, there is plenty of outdoor fun to add to your Golden Circle adventure. Hold on tight as you plunge through glacier rivers, snorkel in icy waters between continents, or ride over lava fields on an Icelandic horse.

How To

Getting here Drive a rental car, or join an organised tour. Most tour companies are Reykjavík-based and can provide hotel pick-up.

When to go These experiences can be accessed year-round but are subject to availability. Book in advance.

How much 18,000kr to 40,000kr.

What to wear Tour companies will outfit you with the necessary equipment and safety gear. Bring warm layers, sturdy hiking boots and a change of clothes.

Snorkel between continents **Silfra** is one of the prominent fissures in Þingvellir National Park, only this one is filled with freezing-cold water. Here you can snorkel (or dive if you're certified) between continents. The water is extremely clear, as it comes from the Langjökull glacier and is filtered through lava rocks. In Silfra, there are no fish or coral, just some bright-green algae and visibility can be up to 100m!

Snowmobile on a glacier Take sightseeing to a whole new level by snowmobiling on top of a glacier. **Langjökull** glacier is Iceland's second-largest ice cap and is just 30km from Gullfoss waterfall. This tour is offered year-round and creates memories to last a lifetime.

Paddle through canyons Just below **Gullfoss** is the canyon that forms the Hvítá river. Get your adrenaline pumping while white-water rafting between volcanic walls. Great for a novice or experienced rafter. It's possible to meet on location or get picked up from Reykjavík. Book with **Arctic Adventures** (adventures.is) or **Arctic Rafting** (arcticrafting.com).

Ride over lava fields Take in the landscape on horseback with an adorable Icelandic horse. Known for their short stature and even temperament, Icelandic horses are an important and beloved part of the culture. They have five gaits, two of which are rare: the *tölt* and the flying pace (p196). But don't worry, a riding tour would be a basic slow walk, perfect for adults and children alike.

Top Diving, Silfra
Bottom Icelandic horses

Walk a Volcanic Crater

A lesser-known sight along the Golden Circle route is **Kerið**, a volcanic crater lake. Thought to be 6500 years old, the crater is 55m deep and 170m wide. Its vibrant red walls dotted with green moss and filled with turquoise water make it one of the most picturesque places in the country. Walking the crater rim takes about 30 minutes to an hour. On one end of the crater is a pathway to walk down to the water to get a perspective of the crater's size. There's a fee of 600kr, which helps the landowner maintain the area.

Listings

BEST OF THE REST

Farm-to-Table Fare

Efstidalur II €

Enjoy delicious farm-fresh ice cream while hanging out with the cows at this family-run farm turned ice cream shop and restaurant. A short drive east of Laugarvatn.

Friðheimar €€

Located in the small town of Reykholt, this sustainable and eco-friendly greenhouse has a tomato-themed menu. The most popular dish is the all-you-can-eat tomato soup served with homemade bread. Reservations required.

Vínstofa Friðheima €€

Located within a greenhouse, the wine bar at Friðheimar boasts an extensive selection of vintages paired with light food. Perfect if you couldn't get a reservation at Friðheimar.

Flúðasveppir Farmers Bistro €€

Delish mushroom soup, burgers and more, with locally grown toppings at Iceland's only mushroom farm, in Fluðir.

Sólskinsbúðin €

Fluðir's adorable farmers market is the spot to stock up on local strawberries and capsicums.

Ylja €€

Laugarás Lagoon's excellent restaurant is run by Gísli Matt, a leading chef who creates inventive, hyper-local Icelandic cuisine. The menu uses locally sourced produce and evolves with the seasons. They harness the geothermal heat for some of the cooking techniques.

Græna Kannan Café €€

Try Sólheimar Eco-Village's own organic food in a buffet; daily soup comes with a cup of their roasted coffee.

Our Picks for Eating Around Þingvellir & Laugarvatn

Laugarvatn Fontana Geothermal Baking Tour €

Sample homemade rye bread baked using geothermal energy from the ground. Top it off with Icelandic butter and locally sourced smoked trout.

Lindin €€€

In a sweet little silver house facing Lake Laugarvatn, with high-concept Icelandic fare featuring local ingredients (including reindeer burgers).

Silfra Restaurant €€€

Beautifully presented, well-proportioned meals featuring locally sourced, seasonal ingredients at Ion Adventure Hotel south of Þingvellir.

Vinastræti Veitingahús €€

Cheerful bistro with Italian grilled sandwiches, pizzas and an airy rustic dining room in Laugarvatn.

Culture & History

Skálholt Cathedral

Historic location for culture, spirituality and music; the first school to educate clergy was founded here in 1056. Tour the church, crypt, tunnel and archaeological site.

Slakki Petting Zoo

Petting zoo with Arctic foxes, cows, puppies, pigs and more. The zoo also has a mini-golf putting course inside a greenhouse.

 ## Hot Water

Laugarvatn Fontana

Hot-spring spa with hot tubs of varying temperatures. Take a dip in the cold lake nearby for the ultimate therapeutic experience.

Laugarás Lagoon

Luxury spa with a beautiful riverside setting and top restaurant Ylja, run by leading chef Gísli Matt, centring sustainability and local sourcing.

Gamla Laugin (Secret Lagoon)

Oldest constructed pool in Iceland fed by a natural hot spring. The area around the pool consists of mossy lava, geothermal spots and a small bubbling geyser. Near Flúðir.

 ## Spectacular Stays

Skógarhólar Lodge €€

Horse-riding lodge in a five-bedroom house with a barbecue grill and a full kitchen near Þingvellir.

Lake Thingvellir Cottages €€

Four pine cottages with kitchenettes and views of the lake sit near the national-park entrance along Rte 36.

Ion Adventure Hotel €€€

Chic, with sustainable practices, a geothermal pool, a spa and a restaurant.

Buubble Hotel €€€

Sleep under the stars in a clear bubble tent in the countryside near Reykholt. Recline and watch the midnight sun or, in winter, look for the aurora borealis. A once-in-a-lifetime experience.

The Wine Bar at Friðheimar

Hótel Geysir €€

Right on the doorstep of the geothermal area of Geysir, this four-star hotel is minimalist cool, highlighting its stunning surroundings. For the ultimate indulgence, visit the spa.

Hótel Gullfoss €€€

Clean rooms and comfortable beds as close to the waterfall as you can get. Ask for a room facing the valley hot-pots and a restaurant.

Torfhús Retreat €€€

Luxury cabins made of reclaimed oak, complete with every creature comfort, north of Reykholt. Geothermic basalt pool.

Fellskot Guesthouse €€€

Sweet horse-farm house makes a cosy base, featuring comfortable rooms with country views and shared kitchen, north of Reykholt.

Camping at Þingvellir €

Sleep under the stars at the year-round campsite at Nyrðri-Leirar, adjacent to the park's service centre north of the lake, which has a small cafe. Restrooms and laundry are available year-round. Showers close December to March. Campsites at Syðri-Leirar and Vatnskot are open from June to August.

SOUTHWEST ICELAND & REYKJANES PENINSULA

LAVA FIELDS | SEA CLIFFS | GEOTHERMAL SPRINGS

- ▶ **Trip Builder** (p102)
- ▶ **Practicalities** (p103)
- ▶ **The Blue Lagoon** (p104)
- ▶ **Pool Etiquette** (p106)
- ▶ **Not the Blue Lagoon** (p108)
- ▶ **Eruptions & Lava** (p110)
- ▶ **Volcanoes** (p112)
- ▶ **Listings** (p114)

SOUTHWEST ICELAND

Trip Builder

Although most famous for the Blue Lagoon, this prominent geothermal area – named a UNESCO Global Geopark in 2015 – has countless other unique geological landscapes, too. A hub for spelunkers, geothermal hot springs and bird cliffs, it's now also home to brand new earth as live volcanoes have erupted.

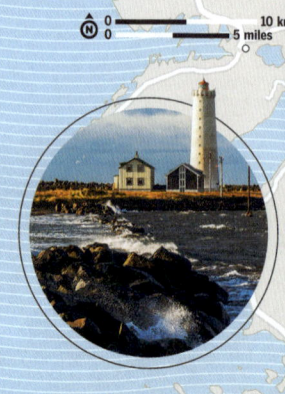

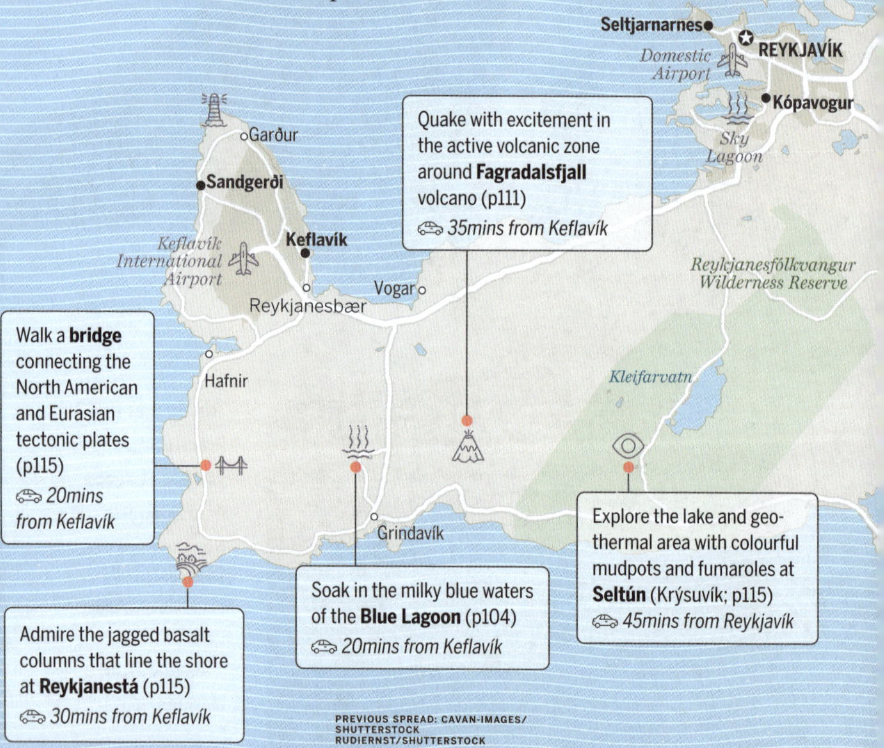
0 10 km
0 5 miles
Seltjarnarnes
REYKJAVÍK
Domestic Airport
Kópavogur
Sky Lagoon
Garður
Sandgerði
Keflavík
Keflavík International Airport
Reykjanesbær
Vogar
Hafnir
Grindavík
Reykjanesfólkvangur Wilderness Reserve
Kleifarvatn
Quake with excitement in the active volcanic zone around **Fagradalsfjall** volcano (p111)
35mins from Keflavík
Walk a **bridge** connecting the North American and Eurasian tectonic plates (p115)
20mins from Keflavík
Explore the lake and geothermal area with colourful mudpots and fumaroles at **Seltún** (Krýsuvík; p115)
45mins from Reykjavík
Soak in the milky blue waters of the **Blue Lagoon** (p104)
20mins from Keflavík
Admire the jagged basalt columns that line the shore at **Reykjanestá** (p115)
30mins from Keflavík

PREVIOUS SPREAD: CAVAN-IMAGES/SHUTTERSTOCK
RUDIERNST/SHUTTERSTOCK

Practicalities

ARRIVING

Keflavík International Airport On the Reykjanes peninsula, 50km from Reykjavík. The drive to and from Reykjavík is short and the roads are good. Flybus, Airport Direct and Strætó buses run regularly between Keflavík Airport and Reykjavík.

FIND YOUR WAY

A tourist information centre can be found at the Duus Museum in Reykjanesbær.

MONEY

Volcano visitors can park in a paid car park (1000kr). Credit and debit cards are widely accepted around the peninsula.

WHERE TO STAY

Town	Pro/Con
Reykjanesbær (Keflavík & Njarðvík)	Close to the airport, with cultural museums and restaurants.
Grindavík	Charming fishing village but impacted by recent eruptions.
Suðurnesjabær	Quiet coastal villages with few tourists; limited eating options.

EATING & DRINKING

Fish and chips An active fishing industry provides tasty freshly caught fish for places like Issi food truck in Njarðvík.

Beer Sample a local brew on tap at Litla Brugghúsið in Suðurnesjabær.

Must-try fish soup Cafe Bryggjan (p113)

Best spot for a drink Cafe Petite (p113)

GETTING AROUND

Car Driving is the best way to explore places off the beaten path.

Tour Bus tours for those who want to sit back and take it all in.

Bus Strætó (straeto.is) buses service Keflavík Airport and the Blue Lagoon.

APR–MAY
Cooler temperatures, , brown landscapes.

JUN–AUG
Everything is green, fair temperatures, midnight sun

SEP–OCT
Rain is common, but it's peak Northern Lights viewing when clear

NOV–MAR
Snowy with limited daylight hours

The Blue LAGOON

OTHERWORLDLY | RELAXING | REJUVENATING

When you think of Iceland, no doubt one of the first things that comes to mind is the Blue Lagoon. Walking out in a fluffy white bathrobe to milky-blue water surrounded by lava is the epitome of relaxation and luxury. Conveniently located 20 minutes from the airport, there's a reason it's the most visited tourist destination on the island.

How To

When to go Early in the morning or after 6pm to avoid tour-bus crowds. Reservation required for entry.

Getting here It's only 20 minutes from Keflavík International Airport and 40 minutes from Reykjavík. Destination Blue Lagoon and Reykjavík Excursions both offer bus services. Taxis are available from Keflavík or Reykjavík.

Luggage Storage is available on-site.

Changing facilities Private lockers are included with entrance as are shampoo and conditioner in the showers.

Admission to the Blue Lagoon includes the following perks.

Lagoon Relax and soak in the milky-blue waters, which are full of minerals, algae and silica. Kept at a comfortable 38°C, it doesn't matter if it's cold or snowy outside, the water will keep you warm. Most people spend about two hours here.

Mask bar Apply an algae or silica mud mask to your face and arms for a fresh glow. Algae contains collagen, so it helps reduce fine lines and wrinkles. Silica is cleansing and brightens the skin. The perfect jet-lag cure.

Steam room and sauna Take a break from the lagoon and hop into the dry or moist heat. Nourishing for the whole body.

Swim-up bar Refresh with a selection of juices, smoothies, beer and wine. Your electronic bracelet keeps your tab, so you can pay as you leave.

Viewing deck Grab your robe and head to the 2nd floor for a great view over the lagoon.

Tips for Your Visit

First, follow pool etiquette (p106). Second, load up on conditioner, as the minerals in the water are tough on hair. Third, leave all jewellery in the lockers to avoid damage. Fourth, bring your own swimsuit, robe or slippers, or rent them at the counter; also bring a waterproof case for your phone – it'll be handy if you want to take it with you into the lagoon. Finally, don't just hang out by the entrance and the mask bar. The lagoon is large and quiet corners can be found if you explore.

💎 Indulge Yourself

Upgrade your Blue Lagoon experience with a premium add-on.

Massage Treat your muscles to a massage while suspended in the water.

Retreat Spa The ultimate five-hour luxury spa experience, including body scrubs and private facilities.

Dining Experience fine dining at the **Moss** or **Lava** restaurants or grab a bite at the **Spa Restaurant** or cafe.

Accommodation Stay overnight at the luxurious **Silica** or **Retreat Hotel**.

Pool Etiquette

GUIDELINES TO ENJOY ICELAND'S MOST LOVED TRADITION

Icelanders love swimming pools. Almost every town has one. Baby swim classes are offered starting from four months' old. Families spend weekends soaking in hot water and splashing down slides. However, in order to enjoy the pools, there are rules you must follow.

Admission

Stop at the entry counter and pay the admission fee. Entrance is 1000kr to 1300kr for adults, 300kr to 700kr for kids, and free for babies and the elderly. If you don't have a swimsuit, you can often rent one.

Shoes Off

Before entering the changing room, take off your shoes. There is a rack outside where everyone leaves their shoes.

Changing Rooms

There are separate changing rooms for men and women, and, increasingly, small ones for people who do not identify as either. Young children can use any, under parental supervision.

Inside the changing rooms you will find lockers. They are free to use and have a key attached to safely store your belongings. Leave your phone and camera as they are forbidden inside the locker room and there's nowhere to put them once outside. Get undressed, grab your suit and towel, and head to the showers. There will be cubbies to store your towel until you are finished.

Wash First

The most important rule is to wash your hair and your entire body without a bathing suit on. Soap is provided, but you are welcome to bring your own. There is a poster in every shower detailing the areas that need to be washed with soap before entering the pool. The pools use minimal

Left Swimming during a festival, Reykjavík **Middle** Seljavallalaug (p131) **Right** Outdoor geothermally heated shower

chlorine, so this is important to keep everything sanitary. Some pools have a stall with a shower curtain if you want more privacy.

Entering the Pools

After showering, put your bathing suit on and head to the pool. Leave your towel in the cubbies so that it's ready when you come back inside. In the pool area you will find hot-pots of varying temperatures as well as a lap pool and possibly a slide or splash area for kids. Hop around to as many hot-pots as you like, and take a dip in the cold pool to cool off in between. Some pools are indoors, others are outdoors, and some have a combination of pools.

> Hop around to as many hot-pots as you like, and take a dip in the cold pool to cool off in between.

Post-Swim Treat

After your relaxing session at the pool, do as the Icelanders do and head to an ice-cream shop. For the local experience get the Bragðarefur, which is soft-serve ice cream blended together with your choice of fruits or candies. Go-to places include Ísbúð Huppu and Ísbúð Vesturbæjar, or if you prefer hand-scooped ice cream look for Skúbb or Valdís.

Time to Go

When you are finished enjoying your time, go back and do everything in reverse. Shower, dry yourself off completely (do not enter the changing area with wet feet!), find your locker and get dressed, and put your shoes on outside as you leave.

Congratulations! You have now experienced one of the essential parts of Icelandic culture, and you did so while following the best tourist etiquette. Go forth and have a great day now that you are in a state of bliss.

10 Not the Blue LAGOON

LOCAL | RELAXING | REFRESHING

In Iceland, going to the pools is a way of life. Every day locals gather in hot tubs heated with geothermal water. They're more than a place to swim; they're a place to discuss the news, gossip about neighbours and soak away stress. It's part of the daily routine, and no matter the weather – under the midnight sun or during a winter snowstorm – you will find the pools packed.

How To

Getting here Rent a car to choose your own hot-pot adventure.

When to go Year-round, rain or shine.

Expect to pay 15,990kr for Sky Lagoon; 1380kr for local pools.

What to bring Swimsuit, towel and toiletries.

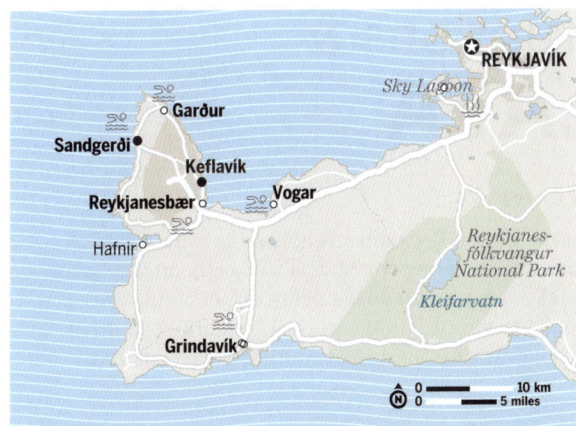

Top Sky Lagoon
Bottom Sauna, Sky Lagoon

Sky Lagoon

'Where the sea meets the sky' is the motto of this beloved spa experience that rivals the Blue Lagoon. The architecture is inspired by Icelandic design elements using turf, water and lava. The infinity pool overlooks the Atlantic with views all the way to the Snæfellsnes Peninsula. A swim-up bar serves a selection of non-alcoholic and alcoholic drinks. It's the ultimate place for relaxation and rejuvenation, just minutes from downtown Reykjavík. The complete Sky Lagoon experience is based on a series of thoughtful, curated steps designed to help you relax from head to toe.

Hot dip Wade in the hot waters of the lagoon, get a natural massage under the waterfall, or rest on the lava rocks.

Cold dip Plunge into the cold pool to get your blood pumping.

Sweat it out Step into the sauna for quiet serenity with an incredible view.

Refresh Walk through a cold mist to reinvigorate your senses.

Exfoliate Massage with their signature body scrub, a mix of sea salt and oils.

Steam Step into a hot steam room and allow the scrub to melt into and hydrate your skin.

Relax Shower and hop back in the lagoon.

If you worked up an appetite, the lounge inside serves a selection of quick bites and beverages. Reservations to the lagoon complex are recommended.

Sundlaug

If you're looking to experience Icelandic pool culture without the spa price tag, a town's local *sundlaug* is your best bet. There's no need to reserve ahead, but make sure you check opening times in advance. The following villages have pools worth exploring.

Reykjanesbær

Four hot tubs, steam bath, indoor and outdoor lap pool, and children's pool.

Vogar

Hot tub, lap pool, and solarium.

Garður

Two hot tubs, sauna, lap pool, children's pool, and waterslide.

Sandgerði

Two hot tubs, sauna, lap pool, children's pool, and two waterslides.

Grindavík

Two hot tubs, cold tub, sauna, lap pool, children's pool, and waterslide.

Eruptions & LAVA

VOLCANOES | LAVA FIELDS | CAVES

The geological landscape on the Reykjanes Peninsula is evidence of hundreds of years of volcanic activity. The peninsula sits directly on diverging fault lines on which earthquakes have created lava fields, craters and caves. But you don't have to be a geologist to appreciate the unique formations: a drive around the peninsula reveals captivating areas just waiting to be explored.

📍 How To

Getting here Rent a car or join a tour.

When to go Lava-tube tours take place year-round, but hikes shouldn't be attempted between November and March due to dangerous snow and wind conditions. Never drive off-road or hike off-trail.

Expect to pay 8400kr to 49,000kr for cave and crater tours.

What to wear Warm layers and waterproof clothing from head to toe no matter the time of year. Sturdy hiking boots are a must for the rugged volcanic terrain.

Top Fagradalsfjall eruption, 2021
Bottom Flowing lava, Fagradalsfjall

Hike the Cooling Craters of Fagradalsfjall

What better way to experience the power of an erupting volcano than by witnessing hot flowing lava in person? **Fagradalsfjall** (erupted in 2021), **Litli-Hrútur** (erupted in 2023) and **Sundhnúksgígar** crater-chain fissures (2023–present) allow just that. Trails have been carved out so that people can walk to Fagradalsfjall's craters and enjoy this once-in-a-lifetime experience from a safe distance.

Note: daylight hours vary according to the time of year. In June, when the sun essentially never sets, you could be at the eruption site at 2am and feel like it's the middle of the day. By contrast, the sun sets around 10pm in August, meaning it's possible to view the red-hot lava in complete darkness.

Paid **car parks** (1000kr), off Rte 427, are just east of the village of Grindavík. Expect the return hike to last three to four hours. Sturdy hiking boots are essential, as are warm layers and waterproof gear. Consider hiking poles and headlamps too, and bring a backpack with water and a snack.

Due to volcanic gases or active lava flowing from Sundhnúksgígar crater chain, hiking routes are closed at times. **Reykjanes Geopark** (reykjanesgeopark.is) maintains hiking maps, and the Wapp smartphone app has GPS waypoints. Check safetravel.is for the latest information on the hiking routes, GPS coordinates and weather conditions. It's possible to sidestep access problems by observing from the air. Try helicopter operators **Norðurflug** (helicopter.is) and **Glacierheli** (glacierheli.is).

Lava Tubes & Magma Chambers

Lava tubes are formed when lava hardens over a flowing magma channel. On the Reykjanes Peninsula there is a prominent tube and a magma chamber that you can explore with a guided tour.

Raufarhólshellir
Walk through the tube where lava flowed during the Leitahraun eruption about 5200 years ago. Natural holes in the ceiling reveal multicoloured rocks. (thelavatunnel.is)

Þríhnúkagígur
From May to October, descend via lift into a 200m dormant volcano that could house the Statue of Liberty! Expert guides ensure safety during the slow six-minute descent as you marvel at the walls where magma once flowed. You'll hike 3km across lava fields to reach the volcano. (insidethevolcano.com)

■ **With thanks to Sara Barsotti**
Sara works for Veður as a volcanic hazards coordinator.

Volcanoes

HOW THE ISLAND WAS FORMED

Iceland sits atop a hot spot on the divergent Mid-Atlantic Ridge. This results in frequent volcanic activity and landscapes filled with lava fields, black-sand beaches, peaks and craters. The island has about 30 active volcanic systems, one of which is currently erupting.

Earthquakes & Eruptions

Iceland formed 20 million years ago when the plate boundaries of the Mid-Atlantic Ridge spread apart, releasing magma from the centre of the earth, creating what we now call Iceland. Iceland is still a work in progress, with current eruptions and lava flow creating new earth.

Because of its plate-boundary location, earthquakes are common in Iceland. Around 500 are recorded in an average week. Most of these are mere tremors at less than magnitude 3 and not felt by humans. Occasionally a magnitude 4 or 5 will hit an active volcanic zone, which can be felt around the area. Because the plates are diverging, a magnitude 5.0 and above is significant. Bigger earthquakes are rare, and the largest ever recorded was a magnitude 7.1 in 1784.

Iceland is among the most active volcanic areas on Earth, with about 30 active systems. On average, eruptions occur every five to 10 years. Since Iceland's settlement, 13 systems have erupted. Most were from fissures or shield volcanoes that produce basaltic lava. The dangers of volcanic eruptions include hot lava flow, poisonous gases, ash fall, lightning and glacial flooding. Depending on the location and type of volcano, any combination of these hazards is possible. Eruptions can happen at any time, but are usually preceded by an earthquake.

On 19 March 2021, after three weeks of seismic activity, a fissure opened on the Reykjanes Peninsula. Over several weeks, a number of vents opened and increasing lava flow filled Geldingadalur valley, spilling over into neighbouring valleys. Less than two months after the onset, one

Left Bárðarbunga eruption, 2015
Middle Grímsvötn ash plume
Right Magma flows from Fagradalsfjall

massive crater took over, spraying magma up to 300m into the air. The fissure, aka **Fagradalsfjall** volcano, is a subset of the Krýsuvík volcanic system, one of four systems on the Reykjanes Peninsula. The last eruption happened over 800 years ago, but in 2021, after weeks of seismic activity, a dyke intrusion finally found a weakness in the crust at Fagradalsfjall, erupting. This effusive eruption halted, but then the nearby Litli-Hrútur volcano erupted in 2023. That same year, the **Sundhnúksgígar** crater-chain fissures began erupting around Grindavík, flowing, halting and requiring berms to be built to protect the Blue Lagoon and Grindavík where fissures opened in the middle of the road and subsumed buildings. Current dangers to the public are gas emissions and the spread of hot lava – always check safetravel.is before going.

> The country is a major advocate of renewable energy, producing 30% of its electricity from geothermal stations.

A Way of Life
Despite their dangers, Icelanders have come to rely on volcanic systems. Geothermal energy brings hot water directly to homes and allows greenhouses to grow fresh fruits and vegetables year-round. The country is a major advocate of renewable energy, producing 30% of its electricity from geothermal stations. Swimming pools, part of Iceland's social fabric, are naturally heated with this hot water, and the tourism industry utilises volcanoes for tours and excursions.

Other Recent Eruptions

Eldfell Heimaey, the inhabited island of the Vestmannaeyjar archipelago, erupted without warning in January 1973. Residents had to evacuate on fishing boats and the lava flow caused massive destruction to the town.

Eyjafjallajökull Located under the glacier in South Iceland, ash from its April 2010 eruption disrupted airspace for days, affecting millions of travellers.

Grímsvötn Iceland's most active volcano, situated under the Vatnajokull glacier in the central highlands, erupted in May 2011, sending a massive ash cloud into the sky.

Bárðarbunga The largest eruption in over 200 years lasted from August 2014 to February 2015. Locals were concerned with gas pollution and glacial flooding.

Listings

BEST OF THE REST

Lighthouses & Views

Garður
At the northernmost tip of the peninsula is a small village with two lighthouses. It's a beautiful area to explore the coastline and spot birds or seals if you're lucky. Stop by the nearby heritage museum, which has a collection of old machine engines, or visit the exhibitions inside the larger of the two lighthouses.

Reykjanesviti
Located on the southwestern part of the peninsula near Reykjanestá and Gunnuhver hot springs. It was originally built in 1878, but an earthquake destroyed it a few years later. It was rebuilt in 1929 made of white concrete in a new location. Walk up to the lighthouse for a great view over the area.

Stafnesviti
A picturesque orange lighthouse sits between Hafnir and Sandgerði. Large waves can usually be seen crashing around the shore of the surrounding dramatic landscape. The farm nearby was the site of the most prominent fishing area on the peninsula in the 17th and 18th centuries.

Hópsnesviti
Just south of the village of Grindavík sits a small orange lighthouse. Accessible by car or foot, the route to the lighthouse runs through a lava field dotted with remnants of old rusted shipwrecks.

History & Culture

Viking World
In Njarðvík, this museum showcases the settlement of Iceland and the Nordic role in discovering North America. The main hall features the *Íslendingur,* an exact replica of a 9th-century Viking ship that sailed from Iceland to New York to commemorate Leifur Eriksson's journey to the New World.

Stekkjarkot
Next to Viking World is a turf-house replica of how Icelandic families once lived. Occasionally open with free admission.

Duushús
Houses multiple art and cultural exhibits in the charming old harbour of Keflavík. Also a tourist centre for information about the surrounding area.

Giantess in a Cave
A nod to the troll and elves folklore that exists in Iceland. Visit a 5m-tall giant sitting in a cave on the Keflavík old harbour.

Sudurnes Science & Learning Center
In Sandgerði, a fascinating exhibit about Polar explorer Jean-Baptiste Charcot, whose ship *Pourquois Pas?* wrecked near here in 1936 (all but one sailor perished).

Gunnuhver

👁 Interesting Geological Features

Reykjanestá & Gunnuhver
Jagged basalt columns, a lighthouse, and a geothermal area with colourful mudpots and fumaroles.

Bridge Between Two Continents
A built bridge connecting the North American and Eurasian tectonic plates.

Brimketill
A seaside pool naturally carved by the ocean. Legend has it that trolls used to bathe in it.

Seltún (Krýsuvík)
Lake Kleifarvatn and Seltún make up this geothermal area with fumeroles and coloured mudpots.

Grænavatn
A 6000-year-old crater lake with green water. Located north of Seltún and easy to walk around.

Stampar
This series of calderas is around 2000 years old. It's a short walk from the marked car park just off Rte 425.

Eldborg
The biggest of five calderas and 7000 years old. From Rte 427 it's possible to walk up to the crater or simply view it from afar.

Háleyjarbunga
A 9000-year-old 25m-deep caldera near Reykjanestá. It can be reached from a hiking path that starts from Gunnuhver.

Brimketill

☕ Coffee & Cake

Cafe Petite
Comfortable living-room furniture awaits you to sit down with your beverage of choice at this Keflavík cafe. Pour your own beer on tap right at your table, or order your favourite coffee drink.

Bryggjan
A spacious fishing-themed restaurant on the top floor of a former warehouse in the Grindavík harbour. Locals and tourists alike gather for a cup of coffee or a selection of homemade cakes and Icelandic waffles. If you're in the mood for something savoury, try the mouth-watering seafood soup with fresh baked bread.

Kaffi Gola
Go for cakes, waffles, sandwiches and coffee at this beloved small cafe alongside Hvalsneskirkja, with views of meadows and ocean.

12 Vestmannaeyjar SIDE TRIP

PUFFINS | BELUGA WHALES | VOLCANO HISTORY

An archipelago of 15 dome-shaped islands, collectively known as Vestmannaeyjar, sits atop a volcanic hot spot just 16km off Iceland's southern coast. The largest island, Heimaey, is inhabited by a community referred to as the Eyjamenn – the island people – by 'continental' Icelanders, as well as puffins and two beluga whales.

How to

Getting here The **ferry** *(herjolfur.is)* to Heimaey generally departs from Landeyjahöfn (35 minutes) in summer and Þorlákshöfn (three hours) in winter, meaning winter visitors should consider overnighting on the island. Reykjavik Domestic Airport has several flights a week.

Festival At the end of July, 10,000 to 15,000 Icelanders flock to Vestmannaeyjar for the four-day **Þjóðhátíð** pop-music festival.

Dining Some visitors travel to the island just to dine at the internationally praised **Slippurinn** restaurant.

The Backyard Volcano

In casual geological terms, the town of Vestmannaeyjar is the 'Pompeii of the North': in 1973, the town had to be rebuilt after a volcanic eruption forced the population to flee in the middle of a cold January night.

The eruption lasted six months and the **Eldfell** crater looming over the town is easily recognisable by its cone-shape and lack of vegetation. By foot it takes an hour from town, but if your legs are tired, quad company **Volcano ATV** *(volcanoatv.is; tour adult/child from 13,900/6900kr)* makes sure you have no excuse not to go.

Preserving the history of this major event in Iceland's history is the **Eldheimar Museum** *(eldheimar.is; adult/child 3400/1800kr)*, with an immersive exhibition set up in 2014 and an excellent sideshow on the 1963 Surtsey eruption.

Biggest Love Island

The Vestmannaeyjar archipelago is home to the world's largest Atlantic puffin colony. Every summer, starting in May or June, these 'penguins of the North' arrive at their seaside burrows at cape Stórhöfði, Heimaklettur and elsewhere to do a little dance, and make a little love. From mid-May to mid-September, **Eyjatours** (eyjatours.com; adult/child 10,500/7500kr) offers two-hour bus tours to the main sites on Heimaey, while the **Ribsafari** (ribsafari.is, one-hour tour adult/child 17,600/900kr, two-hour tour 26,300/13,900kr) speeds between sights in a rubber boat.

Little Gray & Little White

In 2019 a pair of beluga whales that previously lived at an aquarium in China came, via plane, to Vestmannaeyjar for a show-biz retirement at the **Beluga Whale Sanctuary** (belugasanctuary.sealifetrust.org/en; adult/child 3560/2610kr) Their new home is a 32,000-sq-metre sea pen at a pristine creek called Klettsvik – accessible by excursion boat – where one of the caretakers explains the mission of this sanctuary for cetaceans. The Sea Life Trust hosting the belugas also has a **visitor centre** explaining the island's marine life and the 6000-mile journey made by the two seasoned performers, Little Gray and Little White.

Above Puffino, Heimaey

SOUTH COAST & SOUTHERN HIGHLANDS

WATERFALLS | GLACIERS | BLACK-SAND BEACHES

- ▶ **Trip Builder** (p120)
- ▶ **Practicalities** (p121)
- ▶ **Chasing Waterfalls** (p122)
- ▶ **Coast Road Trip to Vík** (p124)
- ▶ **Trekking in Þórsmörk** (p126)
- ▶ **Landmannalaugar Hiking** (p128)
- ▶ **Listings** (p130)

SOUTH COAST
Trip Builder

Some travellers view this as a precursor to the wonders of the Southeast, but don't hurry past – famous waterfalls, Þjórsárdalur valley and the highland areas of Þórsmörk and Landmannalaugar will get you away from the crowds and into some incredible nature.

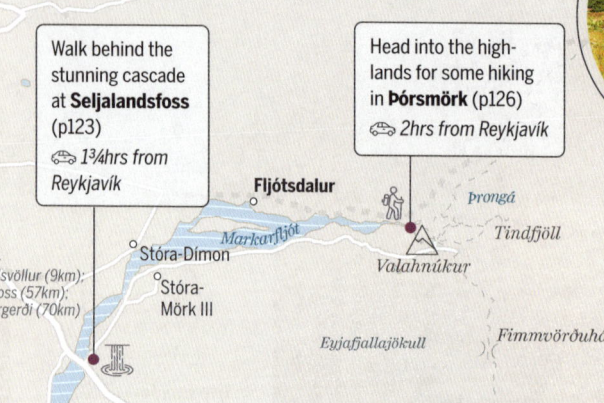

Hike the painted mountains of **Landmannalaugar** (p128)
🚗 3hrs from Reykjavík

Brennisteinsalda
Bláhnúkur
Fjallabak Nature Reserve

Walk behind the stunning cascade at **Seljalandsfoss** (p123)
🚗 1¾hrs from Reykjavík

Head into the highlands for some hiking in **Þórsmörk** (p126)
🚗 2hrs from Reykjavík

Fljótsdalur

Markarfljót *Prongá*
Stóra-Dímon *Tindfjöll*
Stóra-Mörk III *Valahnúkur*

Hvolsvöllur (9km); Selfoss (57km); Hvergerði (70km)

Eyjafjallajökull *Fimmvörðuháls* *Mýrdalsjökull*

Ásólfsskáli *Skógaheiði* *Sólheimajökull*

Skógar

Gape from the ground or above at **Skógafoss** (p123)
🚗 2hrs from Reykjavík

North Atlantic Ocean

Admire the weirdly wonderful rock formations at **Dyrhólaey** (p125)
🚗 2½hrs from Reykjavík

Walk on the black-sand beach and witness the basalt stacks at **Reynisfjara** (p125)
🚗 2½hrs from Reykjavík

Brekkur
Vík

0 — 20 km
0 — 10 miles

Practicalities

ARRIVING

Keflavík International Airport This is 165km from Seljalandsfoss. The roads from Reykjavík are good and buses run frequently.

FIND YOUR WAY
Tourist information centres can be found at Hveragerði, Selfoss and Vík. Each has free wi-fi.

MONEY
Expect to pay for parking at Seljalandsfoss and for public toilets at Dyrhólaey. Credit and debit cards are widely accepted.

WHERE TO STAY

Town	Pro/Con
Selfoss	Major hub with restaurants and accommodation; good location from which to tackle South Coast sights.
Hvolsvöllur	Small village with few amenities situated close to major landmarks.
Vík	Biggest town in the South but also the busiest and most expensive.

EATING & DRINKING

Dine in a barn Gamla Fjósið (p130) has the full farm-to-table thing sorted.

Fresh fish and chips Try the fresh local cod at Mia's Country Van (p130).

Local beer Craft brewery Smiðjan Brugghús (p130) in Vík offers brews on tap.

Best for viking-themed dining Ingólfsskáli Viking Restaurant (p130; pictured top)

Must-try cheese pizza Suður-Vík (p130)

GETTING AROUND

Car Driving is the best way to explore places off the beaten path.

Tour A bus tour is is ideal for those who want to sit back and take it all in.

Bus Strætó (straeto.is) buses stop at the villages along the coast.

APR–MAY	**JUN–AUG**	**SEP–OCT**	**NOV–MAR**
Cooler temperatures, brown landscapes, attractions reopen	Everything is green, fair temperatures, midnight sun	Rain and wind is very common, September can be excellent	Snowy with limited daylight hours, Northern Lights possible

13 Chasing WATERFALLS

NATURE | POWERFUL | ADVENTURE

Iceland has thousands of waterfalls, but some of the most popular, accessible and impressive are along the South Coast. Thanks to run-off from the glaciers, you can find yourself at the base of massive waterfalls within two hours of leaving Reykjavík. Each of the falls is unique in its size, shape, volume and surrounding nature, and all of them are worth a visit.

How To

Getting here Rent a car to visit hidden gems and to stay as long as you like. South Coast guided tours stop at the main waterfalls.

When to go These major attractions are always busy, but tour buses arrive between 10am and 4pm.

Paid parking It's 1000kr to park at Seljalandsfoss.

What to wear Waterproof gear from head to toe. Microspikes are needed to avoid slips on icy paths between November and March.

Seljalandsfoss You'll see this waterfall from afar as you're driving east on the Ring Rd. It's a 60m drop-off from a sheer cliff, but what makes it special is that you can walk behind the falls. Make sure you have waterproof outerwear because you *will* get wet, and sturdy boots are essential as the waterfall mist makes for slippery pathways. From November to March a thick layer of ice forms on the path making it impassable without microspikes.

Skógafoss In the village of Skógar, a handful of lucky locals have a massive waterfall in their backyard. A wide curtain of water falls 60m surrounded by lush vegetation. It's possible to approach the falls to feel the power up close, but be prepared to get wet. Don't forget to take the nearly 500 stairs to the top platform for sweeping views over the valley. This is also the start of the Fimmvörðuháls hike, a 25km trail that ends in Þórsmörk.

Gljúfrabúi Just 500m from Seljalanddsfoss and tucked behind a rock wall, this gem falls 40m down into a cave. To get inside, you walk through a river with slippery rocks by holding onto the cave wall. Once inside you're rewarded with thunderous falls.

Kvernufoss Behind the Skogar folk museum and tucked into a ravine is a surprising gem. A 30m drop from a cliff surrounded by black rock makes this remote location a must-see. To get here, head behind the museum and follow the river for about 20 minutes.

Top Seljalandsfoss
Bottom Gljúfrabúi

 Waterfalls

Glaciers cover 11% of the land in Iceland. Waterfalls on the south are fed from Eyjafjallajökull and Mýrdalsjökull glaciers. Melting of these ice caps means water finds its way to the sea through cracks and over cliffs. The result is stunning waterfalls in various locations and landscapes. The tallest waterfall in Iceland is easily Morsárfoss (240m) in the Vatnajökull National Park, in a remote area north of Kristínartindar peak in the region of Skaftafell. But as always in Iceland, it's not always the highest that is the most impressive.

Coast Road Trip
TO VÍK

ROAD TRIP | SIGHTSEEING | SELF-DRIVE

Massive waterfalls, sweeping black-sand beaches and glaciers that cascade down the mountainside are just a few of the things you will see between Reykjavík and Vík. Packed with breathtaking sights, this South Coast drive is a must-do during your time in Iceland.

Trip Notes

Getting here Rent a car or join a guided tour.

When to go Peak season is June to September. Difficult driving conditions could slow you down between November and March.

Top tip Rte 1 is a two-lane road with no shoulder, so stopping on the side of the road is dangerous. Find a rest area if you want to pull over for a photo op.

Worthwhile Detours

Detour off the main road to these incredibly scenic places.

Þórsmörk Part of the highlands with hiking galore. Reached via 4WD or guided tour due to difficult roads and river crossings.

Vestmannaeyjar Take the ferry to an archipelago of volcanic islands (p116). A village occupies Heimaey island, home to great puffin watching from May to August.

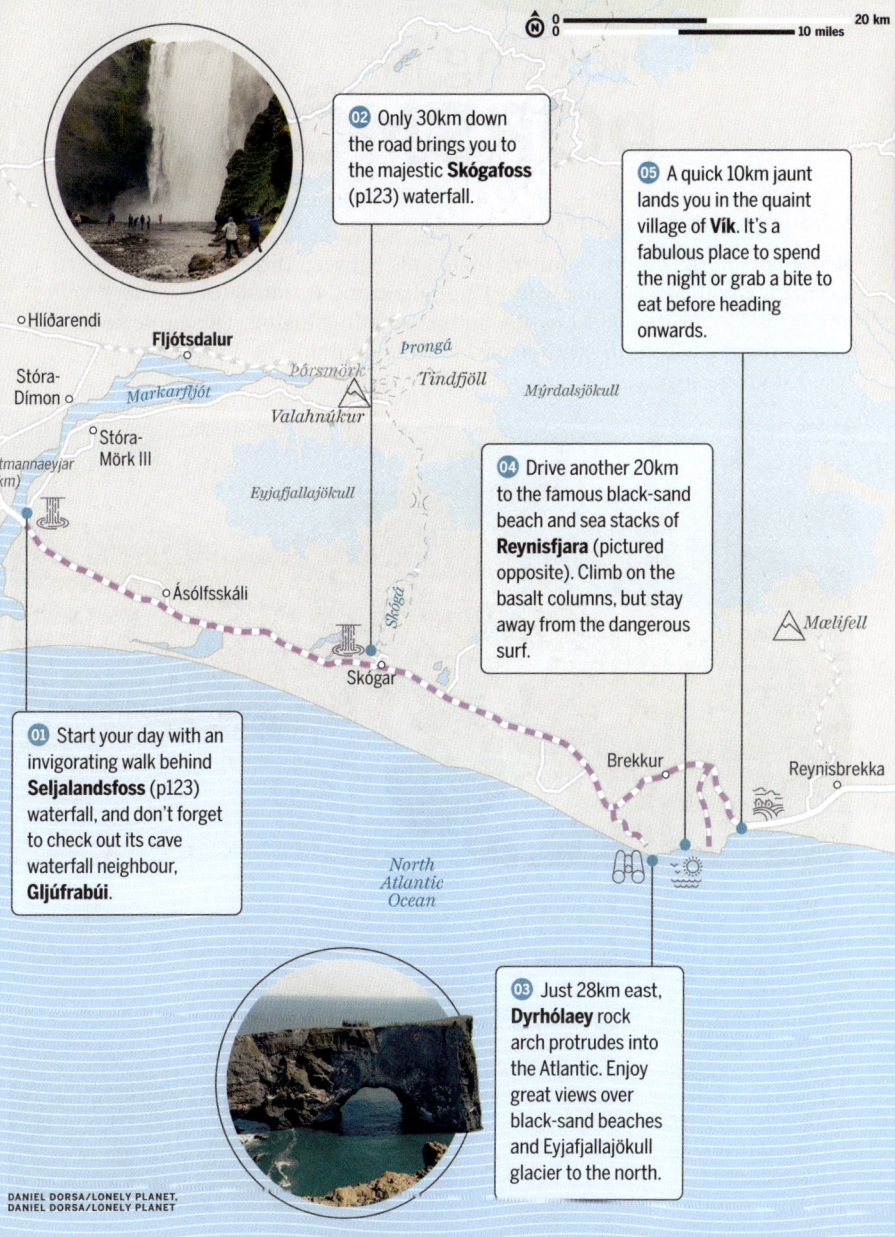

02 Only 30km down the road brings you to the majestic **Skógafoss** (p123) waterfall.

05 A quick 10km jaunt lands you in the quaint village of **Vík**. It's a fabulous place to spend the night or grab a bite to eat before heading onwards.

04 Drive another 20km to the famous black-sand beach and sea stacks of **Reynisfjara** (pictured opposite). Climb on the basalt columns, but stay away from the dangerous surf.

01 Start your day with an invigorating walk behind **Seljalandsfoss** (p123) waterfall, and don't forget to check out its cave waterfall neighbour, **Gljúfrabúi**.

03 Just 28km east, **Dyrhólaey** rock arch protrudes into the Atlantic. Enjoy great views over black-sand beaches and Eyjafjallajökull glacier to the north.

DANIEL DORSA/LONELY PLANET,
DANIEL DORSA/LONELY PLANET

15 Trekking in ÞÓRSMÖRK

OUTDOORS | HIKING | NATURE

Þórsmörk is in the southern highlands between three glaciers: Eyjafjallajökull, Mýrdalsjökull and Tindfjallajökull. It translates to 'Thor's Valley' and is known for its rugged nature and outstanding hiking. This protected nature reserve is teeming with jagged green mountains, deep ravines and braided glacier rivers.

How To

Getting here River crossings mean a 4WD will only get you so far; hop on one of the modified buses to complete the journey. In summer Trex, Sterna and Reykjavík Excursions run from Reykjavík. Hire a super-Jeep tour with Midgard Adventure.

When to go Year-round with a tour. June to September if driving yourself.

Top tip Bring food, as base camps have cooking facilities, or visit **LavaGrill** restaurant at Volcano Huts.

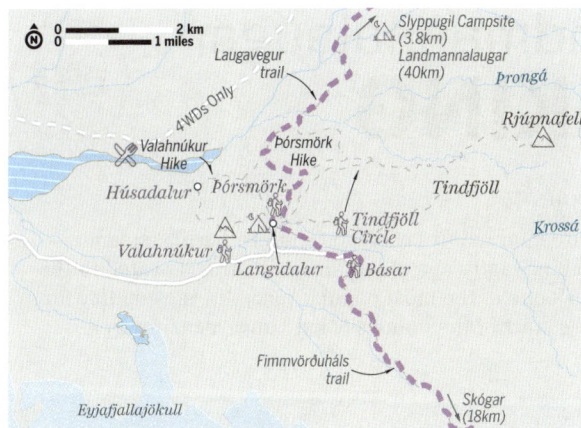

Top Skógafoss
Bottom Fimmvörðuháls

Hikes around Þórsmörk range from two hours to multiple days. Trail maps can be found at the base camps. Trails are generally marked with coloured stakes.

Valahnúkur This moderately difficult 2.4km hike starts at Volcano Huts in Husadalur and gives panoramic views over the entire valley. From the summit you can see two glaciers, glacial rivers and moss-covered mountains.

Tindfjöll Circle Trail markers begin at Langidalur, but it can also be reached from Volcano Huts. Parts of the trail are narrow with steep drop-offs. Sweeping valley views reward you along the way. Expect the 8km hike to take between five and six hours.

Multiday Hikes Both the Laugavegur and Fimmvörðuháls trails start and/or end in Þórsmörk. **Basar** marks the beginning of Fimmvörðuháls, and Laugavegur ends at **Langidalur**.

Fimmvörðuháls

This 25km trail runs between Skógafoss and Þórsmörk. The hike is broken up into three sections. Part 1 is Waterfall Way, a series of 26 waterfalls from the Skogá river. Part 2 passes between the two glaciers: Eyjafjallajökull and Mýrdalsjökull. Part 3 is in the lush green mountains of Þórsmörk. This hike requires appropriate gear, planning and preparation. Weather conditions are unpredictable, so warm layers, waterproof outerwear and sturdy hiking boots are essential. Bring plenty of food and water. Most hikers complete the trail within eight to 10 hours, but it's possible to overnight at a mountain hut halfway.

Stay Overnight

The following base camps are generally open June to September. You need to book for hut accommodation but not for camping. Remember Þórsmörk is a nature reserve, so camping outside designated areas is forbidden.

Basar Huts for 83 people, kitchen and outdoor sitting area, showers for a fee, and a campsite. (utivist.is)

Húsadalur – Volcano Huts Private cottages, shared dormitories, glamping tents and a campsite. Kitchen, sitting area and showers. The restaurant serves three hot meals daily. (volcanotrails.com)

Langidalur Hut for 75 people, a fully equipped kitchen, showers for a fee and a campsite. (fi.is)

Slyppugil Campsite Camping area with toilets and showers for a fee, but no kitchen or electricity. (tjalda.is)

16 Landmannalaugar HIKING

HIGHLANDS | CAMPING | HIKING

Multicoloured rhyolite mountains, lava fields and geothermal steam vents make up the breathtaking landscape of Landmannalaugar. Located in the Fjallabak Nature Reserve, it's one of the most popular places in the country for hiking. The base camp is the start of the famous 55km Laugavegurinn trek.

How To

Getting here Drive a 4WD on one of three routes: F208 from the north, and F225 or F208 from the south. Trex and Reykjavík Excursions have daily bus departures from Reykjavík.

When to go June to September when the highland roads open, depending on weather.

Top tip Mountain Mall is an old-school bus from the '70s that sells snacks and basic supplies. Otherwise, bring your own food.

Sleeping Camping and hut accommodation are available with kitchen and showers at the base camp.

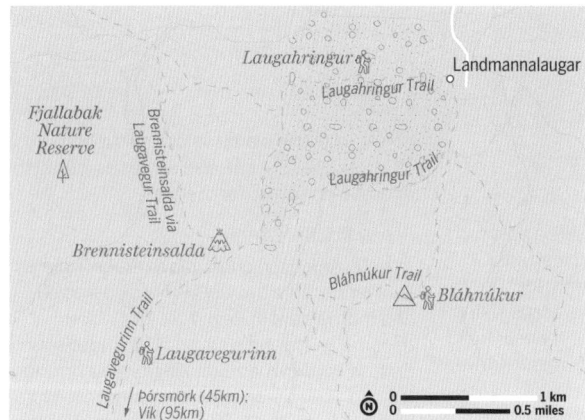

Top Landmannalaugar
Bottom Laugavegurinn

Popular Hikes

There are countless hikes of varying duration and difficulty around Landmannalaugar. Check at the base camp for maps of hiking trails around the area. The most popular routes are Laugahringur, Brennisteinsalda and Bláhnúkur.

Laugahringur A 5km loop through a lava field. Relatively easy walking, this path would be great for kids or families.

Brennisteinsalda An old volcano and an iconic mountain in Landmannalaugar known for its vibrant colours. The beginning of the hike is the same as Laugahringur before continuing upwards to the mountain peak. This 6km loop offers great highland views.

Bláhnúkur A more challenging route, but the one with the most rewarding views. A 6km loop with steep narrow paths has fantastic panoramic views at the summit. If you have time, it's possible to combine the Bláhnúkur and Brennisteinsalda hikes.

Laugavegurinn This 55km trek runs from Landmannalaugar to Þórsmörk, traversing some of Iceland's most incredible scenery. It's only accessible between July and September and is usually completed in three to five days with stops at mountain huts along the way. To reserve a bed or find camping info, check fi.is. Due to unpredictable highland weather, it's essential to have warm layers, waterproof outerwear and sturdy hiking boots. Hikers carry their own food with plenty of water reserves to fill up from the glacier streams en route.

Non-Hikers

Hiking isn't the only way to enjoy the beauty of Landmannalaugar.

Hot Spring
Landmannalaugar translates to 'the people's pool' for good reason: a big natural hot spring is located here. Relaxing with a dip in hot water is the perfect way to enjoy the surrounding nature.

Horse Riding
Let the Icelandic horse bring you to places that are difficult to reach on foot. Multiday guided tours can be arranged for more experienced riders.

Angling
Volcanic lakes around the area are full of brown trout and arctic char. With a licence, you can fish with your own pole, or join a tour where operators outfit you with everything you need.

Listings

BEST OF THE REST

Eat, Drink & Be Merry

Ingólfsskáli Viking Restaurant €€

A Viking-themed restaurant inside an old turf longhouse. Staff dress up in old Icelandic clothing and the food is made with local ingredients. If you want to feel like a true Viking, drink your beer out of a horn, or try your hand at axe throwing or archery. A 10-minute drive from Selfoss.

Gamla Fjósið €€

An old barn converted into a restaurant serving delicious food. A 40km drive southeast of Hvolsvöllur.

Mia's Country Van €

Just before you reach Skógafoss you'll find a colourful food truck selling fish and chips with fresh-caught fish from a nearby village.

Suður-Vík €€

This Vík restaurant is located inside an old aluminium home. Try the cheese pizza, which is made with four cheeses and served with jam – much better than it sounds!

Smiðjan Brugghús

Vík's hippest (and only) microbrewery, with craft beers on tap and windows onto the brew room. It also serves bar food.

Museums

Lava Centre

Hvolsvöllur is home to LAVA – an interactive exhibit about Iceland's volcanoes and earthquakes. Feel what it's like to experience an earthquake and watch volcanic eruptions in an HD movie. The site also serves as a tourist information centre for the area.

Bobby Fischer Center

In 1972, American chess player Robert James Fischer became the world chess champion at a tournament in Reykjavík. Years later he became an Icelandic citizen. This museum in Selfoss houses memorabilia from his time in Iceland. It also stands as a meeting place for chess players and hosts chess tournaments.

Skógar Museum

Open-air museum with turf houses as well as an indoor museum with artefacts from around the area. A short distance off the Ring Rd, 34km west of Vík.

Lava Show

Experience red-hot lava flowing up close and personal in Vík at this interactive demonstration of a volcanic eruption.

Skógar Museum

🥾 Hot Water & Hikes

Reykjadalur
Just outside the town of Hvergerði and tucked away in the mountains is a hot-spring river in which you can bathe. To get there, you must complete a moderately challenging 3km hike, but the views along the way are great, and relaxing in a hot spring at the end makes it worth it.

Seljavallalaug
One of the oldest pools in the country, this was built in 1923 by a local farmer who wanted to teach people how to swim. It sits at the base of Eyjafjallajökull glacier and is fed by natural hot water from the ground. To get there, take an easy 1.8km walk from the car park.

🥾 Tours

Glacier Hike
Solheimajökull is a glacier tongue off Myrdalsjökull and is a popular spot to walk on a glacier. Doing so should only be done with a professional guide, as the glaciers are unstable and dangerous. Multiple companies operate tours here.

Highlands
If you're not renting a 4WD, but want to get into Landmannalaugar or Þórsmörk, Midgard Adventure offers day and multiday super-Jeep tours to get you to locations off the beaten path.

Zipline Iceland
Zip between canyons as you experience the landscape from above.

Glacier hiking, Sólheimajökul

🚗 Other Sights Around Skógar

Sauðhúsvöllur Kofinn
Built by a farmer in the 1940s, this turf-covered shed was used to store milk cans.

Rutshellir Cave
Rutshellir is said to be the largest artificial cave in Iceland. Carved into the bottom of a big boulder, it's around five metres wide and 20 metres long inside, with a skylight and window. It's believed to have been an ancient dwelling before becoming a store place for hay and stockfish in more recent times.

Drangurinn í and Drangshlíð 2
These picturesque turf houses are set below a big rock face that forms part of the Eyjafjöll mountains, with a structure built below the rock itself. They were once used as cowsheds for hay – though local legend also claims that a man once married an elf-woman, and they lived inside Drangurinn rock.

THE EAST & SOUTHEAST

REMOTE FJORDS | GLACIERS & CAVES | SILENT PATHS

- ▶ **Trip Builder** (p134)
- ▶ **Practicalities** (p135)
- ▶ **Exploring Skaftafell** (p136)
- ▶ **Skaftafell on Foot** (p140)
- ▶ **Jökulsárlón Jaunt** (p142)
- ▶ **Glaciers** (p144)
- ▶ **Eastern Villages** (p146)
- ▶ **Eastern Escape** (p148)
- ▶ **Hallormsstaður Forest** (p152)
- ▶ **Borgarfjörður Eystri** (p154)
- ▶ **Listings** (p156)

THE EAST & SOUTHEAST
Trip Builder

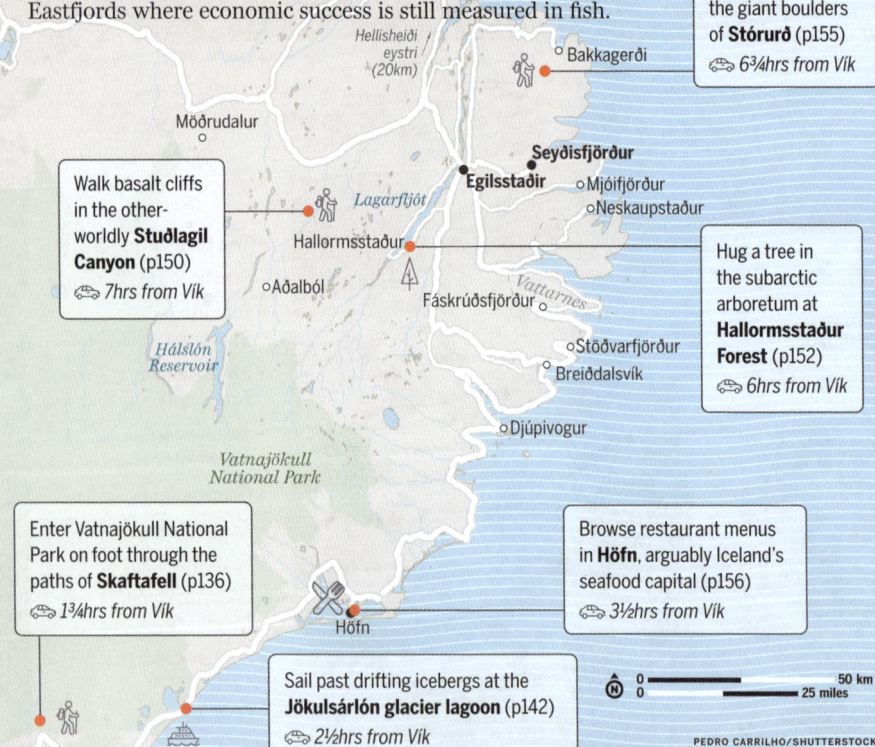

The itinerary for Iceland's eastern corner is written in the colours of the Icelandic flag – blue, red and white – representing water, fire and ice. The contrasts of the region will feed any traveller a balanced diet of excitement and calm energy: from the iconic scenes at Jökulsárlón to the less-explored Eastfjords where economic success is still measured in fish.

Find solitude among the giant boulders of **Stórurð** (p155)
🚗 6¾hrs from Vík

Walk basalt cliffs in the otherworldly **Stuðlagil Canyon** (p150)
🚗 7hrs from Vík

Hug a tree in the subarctic arboretum at **Hallormsstaður Forest** (p152)
🚗 6hrs from Vík

Enter Vatnajökull National Park on foot through the paths of **Skaftafell** (p136)
🚗 1¾hrs from Vík

Browse restaurant menus in **Höfn**, arguably Iceland's seafood capital (p156)
🚗 3½hrs from Vík

Sail past drifting icebergs at the **Jökulsárlón glacier lagoon** (p142)
🚗 2½hrs from Vík

PEDRO CARRILHO/SHUTTERSTOCK
PREVIOUS SPREAD: PANPILAS L/SHUTTERSTOCK

Practicalities

ARRIVING

Seyðisfjörður Ferry Terminal To bring their own car, many travellers take the *Norræna* ferry from Denmark.

Egilsstaðir & Höfn Airports Renting a car at the airports is the best option for onward travel.

FIND YOUR WAY

Vatnajökull National Park has excellent visitor centres in Skaftafell and Skriduklaustur. Information can be found online at vatnajokulsthjodgardur.is.

MONEY

Cards are accepted everywhere. Expect to pay 15,000kr for a three-hour glacial hike and 3000kr for fish and chips.

WHERE TO STAY

Town	Pro/Con
Höfn	Wooden guesthouses and renovated warehouses line this busy harbourside town.
Breiðdalsvík	One shop, one micro-brewery, one public pool.
Egilsstaðir	The regional capital has a peculiar history of French architecture and an elegant waterfront hotel. Year-round accommodation.

EATING & DRINKING

Seafood Never tried halibut? Mackerel (pictured)? Cusk? Browse the menus of this port region and learn new names of fish species. The langoustine (in a baguette or plated) in Höfn is worth crossing Iceland for.

Tea Vök Baths has a tea bar with colourful choices (p147).

Must-try restaurant Pakkhús (p157; pictured bottom), including its sheep-dung-smoked whisky.

Best Ring Rd snack Beitarhúsið Café (p156)

GETTING AROUND

Car Most practical way to travel. East of Höfn, the Ring Rd is less busy.

Bus Service is spotty. Try the carpooling website samferda.net.

Tunnels Several eastern villages are connected by mountain tunnels; the longest is 7km from Eskifjörður to Neskaupstaður.

NOV–MAR
Ice-cave season and snowstorm warnings.

APR–MAY
Iceland emerges from winter with roads and attractions reopening.

JUN–AUG
Average temperatures around 15°C; perfect hiking conditions.

SEP–OCT
Spectacular streaks of colour and smaller crowds in Vatnajökull NP.

Exploring
SKAFTAFELL

GLACIER | WATERFALL | ICE CAVES

Skaftafell is the gate to Vatnajökull National Park, a UNESCO World Heritage Site, where guests walk into virgin birch-tree forests and then reach for a jacket as temperatures drop, the closer they get to the massive Vatnajökull glacier. Take a boat, hike to a waterfall, walk atop the glacier and more.

🗺️ How to

Getting here Drive to most sights via the Ring Rd; additional walking is sometimes required. At Skaftafell visitors pay a parking fee (1000kr per car), then walk 2.5km to Svartifoss waterfall.

When to go Skaftafell is accessible year-round. Popular paths get overcrowded in summer. Glacier caves are only accessible October to March.

Planning ahead From July to August, book accommodation well in advance if you plan to overnight between Vík and Höfn.

Black Falls Most people have come across an image of the iconic **Svartifoss** waterfall before visiting Skaftafell – or even before visiting Iceland – so the actual site may be a little surprising: the waterfall is a stream, not a river, falling just 20m. But what it lacks in force is made up for by the spectacular basalt cliff, giving the waterfall an elegant picture frame. And as far as short hikes go, the 5km loop passing Svartifoss is one of the most pleasant walking experiences you could wish for.

The Hollywood glacier The name **Svínafellsjökull** may sound foreign, but for watchers of *Batman*, *Game of Thrones* and *James Bond*, the glacial site may be a familiar backdrop. The vista overlooking the glacier is halfway up a mountain and accessible via a short but bumpy gravel road about 2km east of the junction to Skaftafell. Rapid melting of

🌋 The Top of Iceland

At 2110m above sea level, the glacial **Hvannadalshnjúkur** is Iceland's highest point. On clear days, the frozen pyramidal summit is visible from Skaftafell, roughly a 12- to 18-hour hike away. **Icelandic Mountain Guides** (*mountainguides.is*) runs organised tours. Spring is by far the best time to go.

Above left Svínafellsjökull
Above right Skaftafell **Left** Svartifoss

the glacier has increased the risk of landslides and falling rocks, limiting access beyond the vista.

Puffins at Ingólfshöfði Decades ago, the farmer at Hofsnes pioneered organised tours in the area when he began driving his tractor with a passenger-adjusted hay cart to the nearby **Cape Ingólfshöfði**. The cape has a spectacular sand beach, a rich history chronicling the arrival of Iceland's first settlers, and from June to August puffins flock here to nest. There are better places to spot puffins, but the birdlife adds to a wonderful 2½-hour experience guided by a local from the tour company **Öræfaferðir** *(fromcoast tomountains.com)*.

On & Below the Glaciers

Get the crampons on 'Glacier walks' are a popular way to explore the basics of glaciology. Over summer most tours take place on **Falljökull** (near Skaftafell) and during

Vatnajökull National Park

Fire meets ice at the Vatnajökull National Park, with 10 active volcanoes – seven of them underneath the ice cap. The park is Europe's largest, covering 14% of Iceland altogether. The southern Ring Rd from Kirkjubæjarklaustur to Lónsöræfi has many wonderful detours into the park, accessible only in summer:

Lakagígar Moss-grown and serene today, the volcanic craters at Laki formed in a 1783 eruption that killed a quarter of the Icelandic population.

Morsárjökull This remote valley glacier, accessible only on foot from Skaftafell, gives visual evidence of the shrinking of Vatnajökull's surface.

Lónsöræfi This often-overlooked trek from Lónsöræfi to Snæfell is a multiday adventure.

Left Lakagígar
Below Ice cave, Vatnajökull

winter on **Breiðamerkurjökull** (near Jökulsárlón), lasting at least 2½ hours. Ice axe in hand, wearing massive crampons, guests are guided to see cracks, streams and ponds forming on the glacier. The pace is slow and the difficulty modest; getting on the glacier from the moraine can be steep. (You won't need the ice axe, but it looks great in photos!)

Ice-blue caves Every winter, local 'ice cavemen' go in their super-Jeeps to the foot of the Vatnajökull glacier searching for a natural entrance: the landscape changes every summer and is unsafe to visit outside the frozen months from October to March. The **Crystal Cave**, still used in some advertising, has reopened after a period of closure, and the **'Sapphire Cave'** is another common destination but each tour depends on weather conditions, cave structure and the number of sunlight hours. Tour operators include **Arctic Adventures** (adventures.is) and **Local Guide of Vatnajökull** (localguide.is). Expect to pay at least 30,000kr per person, since the massive trucks have limited seating.

Skaftafell on Foot

LOST IN A BIRCH FOREST? JUST STAND UP.

Skaftafell, a birch tree forest at the base of the Vatnajökull glacier, is a rare peek into what Iceland may have been like during the medieval warm period that preceded settlement. It's one of few forests in Iceland and a stunning spot close to glaciers and waterfalls.

Left Hikers brave the weather, Skaftafell **Middle** Footpath through summer foliage **Right** Iceland's iconic woolly willow

Historians debate *how* green Iceland was before settlement when a bunch of Norsemen arrived and practised an unsustainable slash-and-burn agriculture on a landscape where soil forms slowly but erodes quickly. According to *The Book of Settlements*, the 13th-century chronicle penned by Iceland's earliest nerd, a man called Ari the Learned, the island was covered in trees 'from the coast to the mountains' – some contemporary studies claim as much as 30% of the island.

A Local Perspective

'I love the calm', says local tour guide Sigurgeir Thoroddsen on a pleasant day in June, standing in front of the Skaftafell Visitor Centre with a busy car park and bathroom facilities for a thousand-plus visitors a day. The visitor centre doesn't look calm at all, but Thoroddsen insists: 'All you have to do is follow the trails not going to Svartifoss.' The landmark Svartifoss waterfall is small but picturesque, with black basalt walls filling the frame, and no less impressive during the frozen winter. The 5km path from the car park is great and is suitable for all ages. On warm summer days, expect company.

Local Landmarks

Hikers seeking a day of solitude should head into the valley of Morsár glacier or the Bæjarstaðaskógur forest; both paths are flat but long. Amateur mountaineers up for a challenge can spend the day hiking up the Kristínartindar peaks. The stunning view at 1126m gives scale to the massive Vatnajökull glacier covering 8% of Iceland; the valley glaciers visible down on the ground are in fact just

tiny outlets. The Kristínartindar also offers an exclusive look at Iceland's highest waterfall, which streams down the Morsár glacier; the water flow has been powered by increased melting of the glacier, and in 2011 it was acknowledged as a single drop falling 228m – a waterfall, indeed. (Morsár waterfall takes the crown as Iceland's highest from the 198m Glymur in West Iceland.) To manage expectations, the view is from a 6km distance.

Future Forests

Looking towards the south, you will note the flip side of climate change: young birch trees expanding over the once-grey glacial outwash. The self-seeded birch, native to Iceland unlike pine, usually takes decades to grow but the warming of Iceland has prompted an unprecedented growth spurt. At the current rate, the area currently named after sand – Skeiðarársandur – will become the country's largest forest. That, says plant ecologist Kristín Svavarsdóttir, is among 'the most amazing developments currently taking place in Icelandic nature'. In 2019, Skaftafell, along with most of Vatnajökull National Park, became a UNESCO World Heritage Site precisely for its ephemeral landscape; a sort of lab, UNESCO notes, to 'explore the impacts of climate change on world glaciers and the landforms left behind when they retreat'. The paths of Skaftafell will walk you through it.

> At the current rate, the area currently named after sand – Skeiðarársandur – will become the country's largest forest.

🥾 Top Trails

Svartifoss–Sjónarsker–Sel Passing several waterfalls and an old farmhouse, this 5km loop is, for a good reason, the most popular route. Allow 2½ hours.

Skaftafellsjökull Glacier The easiest trail available: some 2km on flat ground to a glacial moraine. Back the same way. Allow one to 1½ hours.

Bæjarstaðarskógur Forest Protected since 1935, this birch-tree forest is a wonderful 16km venture. Two beautiful ravines and long footbridges. Allow five hours.

Kristínartindar Mountain peaks with magnificent views. Bring an extra sweater and snacks – the hike is an 18km return trip and takes six to eight hours depending on your fitness and the time of year. Consult with staff at the visitor centre before attempting this outside summer.

For maps and more, visit vatnajokulsthjodgardur.is.

18 Jökulsárlón JAUNT

BOATING | KAYAKING | PHOTOGRAPHY

At Jökulsárlón glacier lagoon, Iceland lives up to its name: icebergs, calving from Europe's largest ice cap, drift towards the sea and, almost there, strand themselves on the sandbanks of the massive lagoon that was once entirely glacier.

How To

Getting here Rte 1, the Ring Rd, crosses the southern tip of the lagoon where the largest icebergs are usually visible from the road. Park and walk.

When to go The soft evening sun, as well as early mornings, is a particularly lovely time to visit. Winter travellers may spot the Northern Lights.

Top tip The lagoon is home to ringed seals, which are sometimes seen resting on the ice.

DANIEL DORSA/LONELY PLANET

Points of entry Icebergs, big and small, line the southern end of the lagoon, furthest away from the Breiðamerkur glacier itself. Most visitors stop by the bridge, where the icebergs are closest to shore. But a little further west (called 'the alternative car park' on Google Maps) are elevated paths with panoramic views.

Diamond Beach There was a time, in the not so distant past, when the small delta where the Jökulsárlón runs to the sea was known universally as Fellsfjara. Now, inspired by some humble photo captions, the site goes by the name 'Diamond Beach'. This is a reference to the small (and not-so-small) pieces of ice that have floated up onto the beach, where they shine against charcoal-coloured sand.

Boating The trailer yachts driving up and down the shores of Jökulsárlón (since there is no harbour) are among the oldest businesses in Icelandic tourism. At the peak of summer, some 40 tours depart every day, cruising around the icebergs for 40 minutes. A Zodiac driver will take you much closer to the glacier on a one-hour tour.

Kayaking The third option to explore the waters is by kayak, also departing from the main car park. Reasonable fitness is required, as this activity lasts for roughly an hour. Unlike other transport, kayaking is completely silent. Drip, drip, drip: listen hard and you will hear the water leave its frozen form.

Clockwise from bottom left Kayaking, Jökulsárlón; Jökulsárlón glacier lagoon; Diamond Beach

The Other Glacier Lagoon

Loners are generally out of luck when it comes to iceberg watching, such is its popularity. But the massive Fjallsárlón lagoon is less crowded than its famous neighbour. The area is private property, belonging to a nearby farm, which minimises the commercial chaos. It has only one cafe and one boating operator, **Fjallsárlón** (fjallsarlon is), which offers 45-minute dinghy excursions. Due to the lagoon's depth, the icebergs are more spread out than in Jökulsárlón, with fewer opportunities for a close-range sighting from land.

Glaciers

THE (EVER-RETREATING) FRONTLINE OF CLIMATE CHANGE

Iceland is roughly 10% ice – unless this guidebook is being read long after publication: every year glacial land twice the size of Keflavík International Airport disappears. Few frozen regions on the planet are as accessible to travellers, but keeping the glaciers alive goes beyond preserving a natural attraction.

Left Entrance to ice cave, Vatnajökull
Middle Hydroelectric plant
Right Skaftafellsjökull

Back in 1995, when Gudfinna Adalgeirsdóttir finished her PhD in glaciology, climate change in popular discourse was a punchline at best. 'Our summers are balmy, but we have high hopes for that global warming', whimsical Icelanders would tell visitors. Even the weatherman on TV would describe hot days as 'soon running Iceland out of business'. These jokes are no longer in good taste. Almost half of the total glacial melt Iceland has witnessed since the Little Ice Age has occurred within the last 30 years, roughly the span of Adalgeirsdóttir's career.

'I knew. Scientists knew', she says in her matter-of-fact manner. 'But I can lay out the facts more firmly today.' For one, the satellite images of today are impossible to argue: a time-lapse of Ok glacier shows a white circle in the western Highlands fade, decade by decade, year by year, into a tiny dot. Dead. In 2019, a funeral was held for Ok, the first glacier to lose its status.

The other 15 ice caps could go the same way, and the smaller ones most definitely will. Under the Paris Climate Agreement, a policy framework meant to keep temperatures from rising 2°C above pre-industrial levels, the mighty Vatnajökull glacier, up to 1km in thickness, will still shrink to 30% to 60% of its current size.

An Existential Threat

For the people of Iceland, a world without ice brings more than just an identity crisis. Waning glaciers lead to a phenomenon named 'crustal uplift' similar to when a heavy object is removed from a mattress; the nearby surface springs up. In the town of Höfn, where Vatnajökull

is close and visible, land rises by about 2cm each year, twisting the town's sewer pipes. The town's iconic harbour has already grown too shallow for large ships to use during low tide.

Roughly 70% of electricity in Iceland is produced by hydroelectric power plants in rivers streaming from the glaciers. As the glacial melt increases, the rivers grow more powerful, producing ever more electricity. But only for the time being. The state-run energy company Landsvirkjun is installing more wind turbines to prepare for a looming energy shift.

Where Tourists Walk

Tourism is booming in the Arctic, a trend attributed to the desire to see our frozen planet before it changes. Iceland, a relatively easy place to get to, has most of its major glacial sites concentrated south of Vatnajökull; the popular Jökulsárlón lagoon is within the range of an electric car from Reykjavík – and has a charging station on the parking site. The Breiðamerkur glacier, calving into the lagoon, covered the car park one hundred years ago. Jökulsárlón is altogether about 20 sq km, half the size of Iceland's annual loss of glacial land over the past decade.

The icebergs drift across the lagoon and run aground on the southern side, conveniently next to the Ring Rd. All lined up for a photograph, they melt, break and roll around. It's as if they are calling our attention to something...

> Almost half of the total glacial melt Iceland has witnessed since the Little Ice Age has occurred within the last 30 years.

The Melting Glacier Walk

Every afternoon, June to August, the Vatnajökull National Park offers a guided tour to the Skaftafellsjökull glacier. Free of charge, the hour-long walk starts at the Skaftafell Visitor Centre, approximately where the glacier was at the dawn of the 20th century. Tour leader Ari Másson says guests walk through the glacier's past; the trail enters moraines where the oldest hills date from the 1930s. 'Put into perspective, the landscape is shocking to most people', he says. A small lagoon now separates the walking path from the glacier's edge; the tour turns around on the highest sandhill, after some 2km of walking. Ask at the visitor centre.

19 Eastern VILLAGES

FRESH FISH | QUIRKY MUSEUMS | LOCAL ART

Home to fishermen and farmers, hotels and smelters, an artist commune and a finishing school, the villages of the East embody the contrasts of Icelandic life. The local *austfirðingar* are chatty at the local baths and eager for guests to try their speciality reindeer burgers with a milkshake or a Breiðdalsvík brew.

How To

Getting around Mountain tunnels make driving distances relatively short between the larger towns known collectively as Fjarðabyggð. The road to Mjóifjörður (population 11) is often closed over winter and the pass to Seyðisfjörður can be a hazardous drive.

When to go Most places stay open year-round, although with limited opening hours over winter.

Top tip Seyðisfjörður Church hosts concerts every Wednesday night from July to August with a fabulous lineup of prominent musicians.

Top Neskaupstaður
Bottom Seyðisfjörður

The artist colony Seyðisfjörður is a port town turned artist colony. With old timber houses painted in the colours of the rainbow, this charming town is best explored on a stroll. Starting from the blue church, several arts-and-crafts boutiques line the road to **Skaftfell Culture Centre** (skaftfell.is), a stronghold for visual artists. At the edge of Seyðisfjörður is the walk-in sound sculpture *Tvísöngur*, which is well worth the 15-minute walk uphill from the Brimberg Fish Factory. In 2020, a massive landslide destroyed part of the town, explaining the multiple construction projects.

Fish, straight from the pan The furthest town from Reykjavík, **Neskaupstaður** can sustain almost every desire of a modern cosmopolitan life despite its remoteness – or perhaps because of it. There is even a fabulous record shop. One of the country's largest fishing companies is based here; to taste the catch of the day head to Beitiskúrinn (Bait Shack), which offers an outside setting on a wharf and fried fish served directly in a black skillet.

Cold lake, hot bath Since opening in 2019, the top-of-the-line **Vök Baths** (vokbaths.is) has been a default destination for those seeking to soak in hot water at the edge of a cold lake. It's an architectural delight with a swim-up bar serving a selection of colourful teas. Located 5km from the regional capital of Egilsstaðir.

New Village, New Museum

Each eastern village prides itself on a landmark museum with a theme that draws out the character of its community. **Fáskrúðsfjörður** has the French Museum honouring the 19th-century legacy of French sailors; **Eskifjörður** the Maritime Museum in a wooden house from 1816; and **Reyðarfjörður** the neatly located Wartime Museum covering the occupation of Allied forces in WWII. But the most intriguing of all is at a private home in Stöðvarfjörður, where **Petra's Mineral Collection** (steinapetra.is) displays hundreds of colourful rocks. Stone collector Petra Sveinsdottir (1922–2012) began welcoming guests around 1975, soon after her husband passed away, and today the collection is maintained by her four children.

20 Eastern ESCAPE

HIKES | KAYAKING | ROAD TRIP

Ever since the days of early typography, the Eastfjords (which, roughly speaking, extend from Djúpivogur in the south to Vopnafjörður in the north) have been marked with vague lines of guesswork. To this day, the region remains Iceland's least explored. And that's precisely its charm.

🗺 How To

Getting around The stunning Rte 939, known as Öxi, is a shortcut to Egilsstaðir over summer. Winter snow shuts gravel roads.

When to go Planning to jump into the river Eyvindará, like the locals on sunny days? Then summer is probably best. Otherwise, take your pick.

Before you leave To realise your potential as a Nordic strongman, try to lift the 186kg boulder outside the swimming pool in Egilsstaðir.

The dancefloor cave Whether the **Easter Cave** (Páskahellir), located on a rocky beach in the Neskaupstaður Nature Reserve, is a cove or a small cave is debatable. Either way, this quiet spot is a favourite among locals. It's a 20-minute walk each way, from where the road ends a few kilometres east of Neskaupstaður. From the cave, 'one can watch the sun dance on Easter morning', a signpost claims, without elaborating on what that means exactly.

This way, Indiana Jones About a 10-minute drive from the town of Eskifjörður is a hole in the ground that once changed the world. It's the entry to the 70m-long mine **Helgustaðanáma**, where the largest and purest crystals to project light were once found. These led to the invention of telescopes and magnifiers. Known as Iceland Spar, the

🐾 Reindeerland

In the early 18th century, the Icelandic government imported reindeer and set them free for the benefit of sustainable game hunting. The same thing was tried with musk ox, native to Greenland. What remains of these experiments is the 3000 reindeer living solely in the East and often visible from the road – if not crossing the lanes!

Clockwise from left Reindeer; Stuðlagil canyon (p150); Easter Cave (Páskahellir)

biggest chunk ever extracted is on display at the British Natural History Museum. Today, only small pieces remain left at the site. Bring a torch and note the old train tracks.

To the kayaks! Paddlers are in paradise in the calm eastern fjords. In Neskaupstaður, the local kayaking club **Kaj** *(facebook.com/kajakklubburinnkaj)* rents out equipment and 'sometimes' offers guided trips. It's best to have some level of experience.

Old rocks, new view Although inland, and strictly speaking not part of the Eastfjords, nearby **Stuðlagil canyon** is a must-see destination. Its magnificent basalt formations existed, unseen, for hundreds of centuries. The explanation: the gigantic Kárahnjúkar Hydropower Plant dammed the glacier river streaming through the canyon. As the water level shrunk, basalt banks of unusual height and with streaks of earthy colours were revealed.

⚠ The Five-Summit Challenge

In 2020, local mountaineers placed stamps on top of the region's five iconic mountains: Kistufell, Hólmatindur, Svartafjall, Goðaborg and Hádegisfjall. Collect all five stamps in a special pamphlet widely sold for 500kr, and you have earned the title 'Fjallagarpur Fjarðamanna' – the Mountaineer of the Fjords. Respect!

How long will it take? Well, altogether the five summits are 5186m; roughly the equivalent of Mont Blanc.

So you may not have time, and that's fine! But this is all to say that the East is made for hiking. For ideas, check out the widely available booklet *The Pearls of Egilsstaðir Area*, published by the local touring club. It has 30 excellent hiking suggestions, long and short.

Left Hólmatindur, one of the region's five iconic mountains
Below Fardagafoss

It is possible to access the canyon from both sides of the river Jökulsá á Dal. The view is arguably better from the eastern side starting by the Klaustursel farm. Before crossing the bridge, guests are asked to park their car in the car park. From there, walk on the gravel road past a small waterfall and sheep barn, and then on to a path. Altogether it's 5km one way.

Alternatively, the vista on the western side requires almost no walking. To get there, continue past Klaustursel on the road Jökuldalsvegur and look for the Stuðlagil sign. Cars are parked pretty much on the cliff's edge.

Get behind this On the road to Seyðisfjörður, the **Fardagafoss** may seem like yet another waterfall. But look closer and you'll see there is a cave. The narrow entry is a wet adventure, but what else would you expect when going behind a waterfall? The sound of water falling some 20m blasts the cave, and if outlaws still existed, there would certainly be one hiding in there.

21 Hallormsstaður FOREST

FOREST TRAILS | WATERFALL | LOCAL HARVEST

Welcome to the best place in Iceland to be a tree. The arboretum in Hallormsstaður Forest is Iceland's largest, with hiking trails showcasing the surprising number of tree species able to thrive at latitude 65° north. Sometimes called 'the least Icelandic landscape', this is where local travellers far outnumber foreign tourists.

How To

Getting around The forest has 11 paths, covering 740 hectares. Maps are available at car parks and at Hotel Hallormsstaður.

When to go June to August. Summer solstice, on 21 June, is celebrated with a bonfire and the oddly exciting Lumberjack National Championship.

Top tip The Orkan petrol station is a de facto ice-cream shop.

Stroll the arboretum On a hot summer day, the pristine Atlavík Creek is hot property for tents and camper vans. This is where Icelanders go on holiday. (And just watch how quickly guests leave at the sign of clouds, off to a sunnier corner of the country.) From the car park, take a pleasant 2km path to the **arboretum** containing 80 tree species, following the cliffs of Lagarfljót river. There's plenty of excellent picnic spots.

Sheep sorrel pesto at Vallanes To get a delicious taste of this fertile region, and a sense for the practical use of forestry, visit **Asparhúsið, Móðir jörð** farm, which offers pancakes made from locally grown barley, homemade veggie burgers and pesto made of wild sheep sorrel. The **restaurant** *(modirjord.is)* is built entirely of local wood. Apple trees grow outside as part of a bold subarctic experiment, and purple grapes hang inside a colourful greenhouse.

Third-tallest waterfall The 128m **Hengifoss** was once Iceland's second-tallest waterfall, but lost its place when the melting Mosár glacier snapped the first seat. But silver or bronze, it's still much loved! Located at the top of a canyon, getting here is part of the fun. The pleasant path is about a 5km return trip and only moderately steep. Allow 1½ to two hours and keep an eye out for the magnificent basalt rocks by the smaller Litlanes waterfall midway.

Top Hallormsstaður Forest
Bottom Lagarfljót

The Lagarfljót Wyrm

Tempted to go for a swim in the calm river Lagarfljót with its inviting stony creeks? Think again. This wide river is fed by a murky glacial stream, making it cold and deep. And somewhere near the bottom, at 110m, swims the Lagarfljot Wyrm. This folkloric figure is arguably Iceland's most famous monster, first chronicled in a 1350 script and regularly spotted since. In the winter of 2012, a retired farmer on his afternoon walk caught the creature on camera. The internet has the proof.

22 Borgarfjörður EYSTRI

BIRDWATCHING | HIKING | SOLITUDE

The puffins are stoic, the stones home to elves, and the village from a bygone age. Borgarfjörður Eystri is a hiking destination in a remote fjord an hour's drive from the Ring Rd. Walking distances range from 15 minutes (the harbour bird cliff) to five days (the Víknaslóð trail).

How To

Getting here Rd 94 has been paved all the way to the village of **Bakkagerði** (population 77) and its two hotels, opening the area up to winter visitors, but check **road conditions** *(umferdin.is/en)* for the Vatnsskarð mountain pass during the months of snow.

When to go June to early August for the birdlife.

Top tip The **Musterið Spa**, located in the old fish factory, has three multi-temperature hot tubs with stunning views.

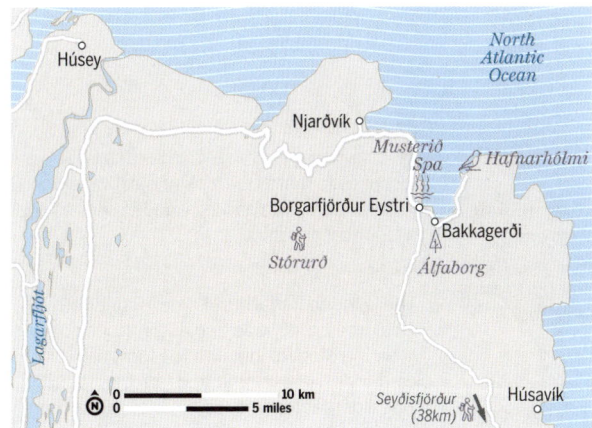

Top Breiðavík valley
Bottom Stórurð

Puffinland Some 7km from Bakkagerði village is a harbour where, during the summer when small boats fish freely, you'll find hard-at-work fishermen. The grassy rock of **Hafnarhólmi**, which shelters the harbour, is one of the best places on Iceland's mainland to see puffins up close. Along with fulmars and kittiwakes, the puffins nest in the Hafnarhólmi colony from June to August when the baby pufflings can survive on their own.

Hidden boulders A middle-of-nowhere lagoon of giant boulders, **Stórurð** is the highlight of the alpine Dyrfjöll mountain ridge. This pristine place owes its atmospheric beauty to how hard it is to get here: allow four to six hours for a return trip depending on your level of fitness. That said, the walk is relatively easy and flat, as the trail starts several hundred metres up on the Vatnsskarð pass on Rd 94.

Meet the elves The rocky hill above the local campsite is called **Álfaborg** – the City of Elves – and according to folklore a visit brings good luck, particularly to young people. At the very least, the hill has an excellent vista. The local church down the hill is usually open, and it's worth checking out the peculiar **altarpiece**; it depicts Jesus giving his 'Sermon on the Mount' on top of the Álfaborg hill.

Víknaslóðir Trail

The marked 55km trail from Borgarfjörður Eystri to Seyðisfjörður, known as Víknaslóðir, has over recent years become an increasingly popular alternative to the well-established highland routes like Landmannalaugar and Lónsöræfi. Here hikers travel in solitude. The route covers three landmark creeks – Brúnavík, Breiðavík and Húsavík – and can be done in three to five days depending on the destination. Most hikers end in the deserted Loðmundar Fjord and get a Jeep ride back to Bakkagerði; others add an extra day and end in the town of Seyðisfjörður.

Listings

BEST OF THE REST

Hot Baths

Selárdalslaug
Built on the banks of a salmon river in 1949, Selárdalslaug is a sudden surprise on the empty road north of Vopnafjörður. This part of Iceland has little geothermal heating, making it all the more special and appreciated.

Sundlaug Hafnar
Blue, red and yellow: the three waterslides at this swimming pool in Höfn offer serious rides. Hot tubs are nice, too.

Sundlaug Eskifjarðar
Three multi-temperature tubs (for the lazy) and two waterslides (for the crazy). And a 25m pool for swimming. Perfecto.

Djúpavogskörin
South of the village of Djúpivogur, on a random geothermal field, are two hot tubs, built by locals seeking to unwind and socialise. Everyone can visit; just treat this communal property with respect. No locker facilities.

Fresh Coffee, Traditional Atmosphere

Hjáleigan Kaffihús
Located outside a turf house hosting the Bustarfell Museum near Vopnafjörður, this summer-only cafe serves impressive homemade cakes from traditional recipes. Try the rhubarb pie called *hjónabandssæla* (happy marriage cake), with cream of course!

Nesbær
The bakery in Neskaupstaður is also a place for a good yarn. Friendly staff, good vibes and a cinnamon bun to go with it – you will leave knowing a little more about local life.

Kaupfjelagið Verzlun
art cafe, part grocery store in Breiðdalsvík. It's made to match the look of the town's old general store, with packed wooden shelves and a fancy cashier table.

Beitarhúsið Café
The wooden Beitarhúsið cafe – built from local trees, driftwood and a telephone pole – is on the Ring Rd junction to Möðrudalur, the country's highest inhabited farm. Its founder was a carpenter who returned to the farm to take over from his retiring parents. Don't miss the homemade *kleinur* (twisted doughnuts).

Seafood

Randulffssjóhús €€
In a wooden house, showcasing artefacts from the time Eskifjörður was a herring base, this seafood restaurant is a top place to taste East Iceland. Outside seating is on the water, and if you fancy catching the fish yourself the restaurant has a boat.

Café Sumarlina €€
In a landmark wooden house, this restaurant in Fáskrúðsfjörður has a family-friendly menu of fish and chips, pizzas and burgers.

Mjóifjörður

Hafnarbúðin €
Höfn's old harbour diner, serving burgers, milkshakes and most famously a langoustine baguette – with lots of mayo.

Pakkhús €€€
Fine dining in Höfn. The restaurant specialises in 'Icelandic lobster' – technically langoustine – caught by the fishermen working at the nearby harbour.

Outdoor Art

Eggin í Gleðivík
A 1km stroll from the village of Djúpivogur, artist Sigurður Guðmundsson has placed 34 egg-shaped rocks to represent local bird species. As with any good art, reviews are mixed.

The Red Chair
By the Ring Rd, next to the Þorgeirsstaðir farm between Höfn and Djúpivogur, is a red chair of gigantic size. Keep it warm for the troll and enjoy this picturesquely situated furniture.

The Phone Booth
At the edge of Seyðisfjörður is a mysterious phone booth titled *How Are Things...?* with Iceland's old coat of arms. Made in 2006 by artist Guðjón Ketilsson, the booth marked the hundred-year anniversary of a submarine telegraph cable from Scotland being brought ashore at Seyðisfjörður.

Festival Fun

LungA
LungA Art Festival is an art and music festival that has drawn big names and an engaged crowd to Seyðisfjörður every July since 2000. A wonderfully diverse celebration of all things art. *(lunga.is)*

Eistnaflug Metal Festival
The Eistnaflug Metal Festival is an indoor metal music festival held in Neskaupstaður during the second weekend of July, attract-

Rte 955 along the Vattarnes peninsula

ing international bands and metalheads. Wondering if this is for you? Try the Icelandic band Skálmöld.

Fjarðabyggð on Foot
The late-June hiking festival known as Á fætur í Fjarðabyggð is a week-long schedule of guided walks in the Eastfjords.

Summer Detours

Hellisheiði eystri
How steep is a 12% slope? Hellisheiði eystri, on Rte 917 between Egilsstaðir and Vopnafjörður, is the highest mountain pass still in wide use.

Vattarnes
Instead of taking the tunnel between Fáskrúðsfjörður and Reyðarfjörður, Rte 955 along the Vattarnes peninsula is a gravel road with wonderful views and sheep casually crossing the road. The Vattarnes sea cliffs, on the tip, make for a good stop.

Mjóifjörður
An hour-long zigzag on a gravel road into a fjord that is home to a community of 11 people. Over winter, the road usually closes and residents travel by ferry to Neskaupstaður. Check out the Klifbrekku waterfall and stop for coffee at Brekka. The road ends by the Dalatangi lighthouse, a landmark for fishermen since the 19th century.

AKUREYRI
SKIING | SOAKING | SAVOURING

- ▶ **Trip Builder** (p160)
- ▶ **Practicalities** (p161)
- ▶ **Adventure in Eyjafjörður** (p162)
- ▶ **Playing in the Snow** (p164)
- ▶ **Cultural Curiosities** (p166)
- ▶ **Listings** (p168)

AKUREYRI
Trip Builder

■ This little big town is a centre for outdoor activities in all seasons, with nature exploration, hiking, water sports, sledding and skiing. It also has a vibrant cultural scene, cosy cafes and plenty of opportunities for après-ski.

Go **dog-sledding** in the wintry landscapes around Akureyri (p165)
🚗 15mins from Akureyri

Immerse yourself in Akureyri history and culture at the **Akureyri Museum** (p166)
🚶 20mins from Akureyri

Listen to live Icelandic music at **Græni hatturinn** (p167)
🚶 5mins from Akureyri

Ski the varied slopes at **Hlíðarfjall** resort (p165)
🚗 15mins from Akureyri

Explore Eyjafjarðarsveit and enjoy a relaxing soak in the woodland **Forest Lagoon** (p163)
🚗 10mins from Akureyri

PREVIOUS SPREAD:
GHING/SHUTTERSTOCK

JIRI STOKLASKA/SHUTTERSTOCK,
TODAMO/SHUTTERSTOCK

0 — 10 km
0 — 5 miles

Practicalities

ARRIVING

Akureyri Airport Rent a car, take a taxi or walk along the fjord-side footpath (30 minutes).

Hof Buses from Reykjavík go to the Hof long-distance bus stop. The taxi station (BSO) and Miðbær town bus station are within a five-minute walk.

FIND YOUR WAY

There's a seasonal tourist office at **Hof Cultural Centre** (visitakureyri.is). Free wi-fi is widely available.

MONEY

Cards are widely accepted; there are ATMs downtown. Buy food at supermarkets and pack lunches to save money.

WHERE TO STAY

Town	Pro/Con
Camping, glamping	Two campgrounds – one in town, one on the outskirts. In Eyjafjarðarsveit you can sleep in a yurt.
Hostels, hotels, guesthouses	Many to choose from; varying price ranges and amenities.
Cottages, apartments	With cooking facilities; located in and outside town.
Farmstay	Outside town; country atmosphere.

EATING & DRINKING

Local institution Bautinn Restaurant (pictured top) has operated since 1971. Seek out lamb or fish on the varied menu.

Cocktails Sip cocktails on the porch overlooking downtown at Múlaberg Bistro & Bar.

Coffee and cakes Sample good coffee and tempting cakes at Kaffi Ilmur (pictured bottom).

Must-try bakery Lyst (p168)

Best rooftop view Strikið (p168)

GETTING AROUND

Walking Most of downtown is easily walkable, although some streets are steep.

Car Free parking is widely available. For pay parking, try **Parka** (parka.is).

Bus City buses (straeto.is) are free. All routes begin and end at the Miðbær town bus station in the central area. Taxis operate from the nearby BSO.

JAN–MAR
Resort ski season. Short days, dark nights. Northern Lights.

APR–JUN
Off-piste ski season. Long days, bright nights. Midnight sun in mid-June.

JUL–SEP
Best for hiking, wildlife watching, outdoors.

OCT–DEC
Storms, winter road conditions. Short days, Northern Lights.

23 Adventure in EYJAFJÖRÐUR

FOOD | FARMS | NATURE

Beginning just south of Akureyri, framed by tall mountains and accessed by Rtes 821 and 829, lies the rural paradise of Eyjafjarðarsveit. The area is often overlooked by visitors, but locals love it for weekend drives and cycling trips, its farmhouse cafes, quirky shops and museums, and the many opportunities it offers to rejuvenate in nature.

How To

Getting around Bring your own bike or hire a car at Akureyri Airport. Or, contact **Akureyri E-Bike** *(akureyri-ebike-tours.com)* for organised tours. There are no public buses.

When to go Year-round, but summer is especially lovely and is when most services are open. With its après-ski scene, winter is also appealing.

Where to stay You can overnight at a farm, in your own tent, in a yurt, or in classic guesthouses and hotels. Book at esveit.is/ferdathjonusta/gisting.

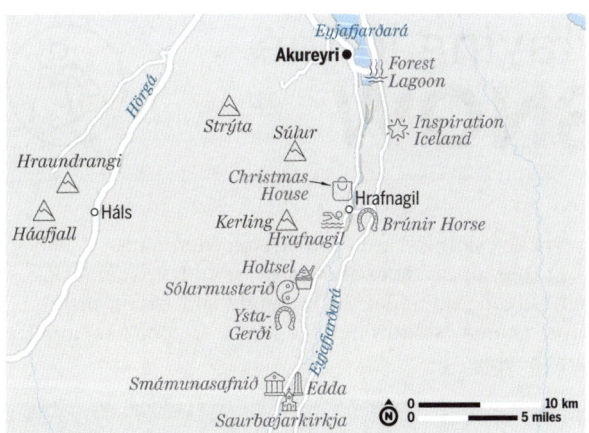

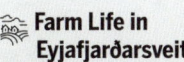

Top Eyjafjarðará river
Bottom Icelandic horses

Hiking For a challenging hike and splendid views, summit **Mt Súlur** (1213m). The trail starts on Súluvegur, on the edge of town just before the Glerá bridge (11km, five to six hours return).

Angling Eyjafjarðará river is known for big Arctic char. Fishing permits are **online** (sala.eyjafjardara.is/permits/eyjafjardara).

Riding Go horse riding at **Ysta-Gerði** (ysta-gerdi.com).

Yoga Join peace walks, storytelling and yogic events at **Sólarmusterið** (solarmusterid.is). **Inspiration Iceland** (inspiration-iceland.com) offers yoga classes, treatments, tours and hikes.

Swimming The **Hrafnagil swimming pool** has a fun waterslide and is great for families. Opposite Akureyri with views of the town and fjord is **Forest Lagoon** – a wonderful woodland spa.

The curious and the quirky Kristnes is where the region's first settler built his home. Later it became a tuberculosis healing centre. Walk around the Kristnes forest and visit the **Hælið Museum** (haelid.is). The **Christmas House** attracts visitors in all seasons, but especially around the holidays. The gingerbread house carries kitsch, sweets and collectables. If you dare, peek at ogress Grýla in her cave! **Smámunasafnið** showcases a local eccentric's amazing collection of tools, pencils, rusty nails and anything you can think of. The cafe serves old-fashioned countryside treats. Iceland's answer to Europe's Gothic cathedrals are tiny **countryside churches**. Eyjafjarðarsveit has six. Start at **Saurbæjarkirkja** turf church.

Farm Life in Eyjafjarðarsveit

With its fertile soil and amenable climate, Eyjafjarðarsveit has long been one of North Iceland's agricultural hubs. It is known as a centre for dairy production, but the region's farmers also produce beef, lamb, pork, horse meat, eggs and honey, and grow potatoes and greenhouse vegetables. Taste farm-made ice cream at **Holtsel**, attend a horse show at **Brúnir Horse** followed by a stop at their cafe for homemade bread and cakes, and say hello to **Edda**, a giant metal cow sculpture about 27km south of Akureyri near the Saurbæjarkirkja turf church.

24 Playing in the SNOW

SKIING | ADVENTURE | FAMILY

In and around Akureyri, the skiing season can stretch from mid-November well into June. Hit the slopes (there are tracks for all levels) and ski under the stars and Northern Lights, ski under the midnight sun, ski off-piste from summit, to sea and cross-country ski through the forest. Or, don't ski at all and opt for sledding or snowshoeing.

How To

Getting here It's easiest to hire a car. Bus 78 runs between Akureyri and nearby skiing towns north along Eyjafjörður.

When to go December to March for alpine and cross-country skiing. March to May for the main off-piste ski season.

How much A day pass at Akureyri's Hlíðarfjall costs about 7200/1950kr per adult/child.

Afterwards? Browse the selection of locally made Icelandic wool sweaters at **Lopi Og List** on Akureyri's Hafnarstræti.

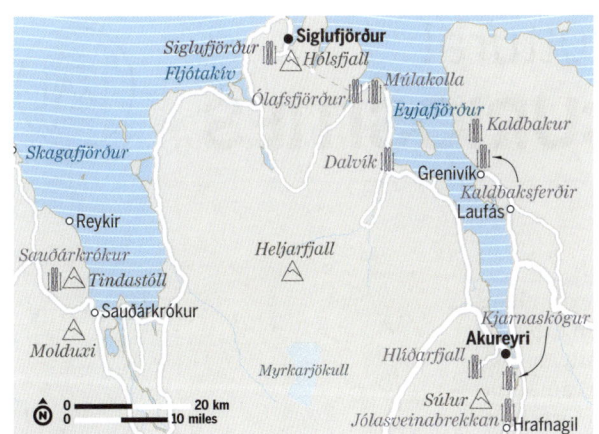

Top Skiing, Eyjafjörður
Bottom Sledding

Alpine skiing North Iceland's largest ski resort is Akureyri's **Hlíðarfjall** ski centre, with various lifts, slopes and ski lessons for children and adults, plus ski and snowboard rentals. There is also skiing at **Dalvík**, half an hour to the north; around **Ólafsfjörður** and **Siglufjörður** (30 minutes beyond Dalvík); and, at **Sauðárkrókur**, one hour on. Resorts vary in size and levels of service, but all have groomed pistes for alpine skiing and snowboarding. (northiceland.is/en/experiences/ski)

Cross-country Find tracks in and around **Kjarnaskógur** forest on Akureyri's outskirts and at all the resorts. Courses are offered in Ólafsfjörður and Siglufjörður (inquire at skidafelagolf@gmail.com).

Mountain skiing There are off-piste opportunities, including at **Mt Kaldbakur**, about 40 minutes from Akureyri across the fjord, and **Múlakolla**, near Ólafsfjörður. **Kaldbaksferðir** (kaldbaksferdir.com) offers snowcat tours. For ski touring and heli-skiing, contact bergmenn.com, vikingheliskiing.com and arcticheliskiing.com.

Snowshoeing For a slower-paced winter adventure, **Wide Open** (wideopen.is) offers half-day snowshoe tours in the frozen landscapes around Akureyri.

Sledding Locals go to **Jólasveinabrekkan** in Lundahverfi for sledding (no charge; parking in Brálundur). Or, skim over the snow on a dog sled with **Go Husky** (gohusky.is), just north of Akureyri, or **Snow Dogs** (snowdogs.is), near lake Mývatn.

Winter Festivals

Mývatn Winter Festival
Relish winter North Iceland style at this annual festival (vetrarhatid.com), held outside Akureyri around Mývatn in March. It is packed with special events like horse riding on ice, and also features dog-sledding, snowmobiling, cross-country skiing and ice fishing.

Yule Lads Bath
The trolls Grýla and Leppalúði have a wicked cat and 13 sons who live around Dimmuborgir near lake Mývatn. There is fun for all in early December when the sons – the Yule lads – take their annual bath in Mývatn Nature Baths, about an hour east of Akureyri. See jolasveinarnirdimmuborgum.com.

25 Cultural CURIOSITIES

ART | MUSIC | HISTORY

Akureyri is small but concentrated, and packed with things to do. As Iceland's northern capital, the town is known especially for its art and culture and for its cafe scene. Take things slowly and explore, visiting the art, history and heritage museums, learning about local authors and poets, listening to live music, warming up in a cafe or enjoying a night out.

How To

Getting around Most places are within walking distance. Town buses are free, or take a taxi.

When to go June to August is when the main cultural festivals take place. The A! performance festival is held in October. Many concerts are scheduled around Christmas and Easter.

Top Tip At Akureyri Museum in Innbærinn, the oldest part of town, you can buy a pass for seven museums and learn about the town's history.

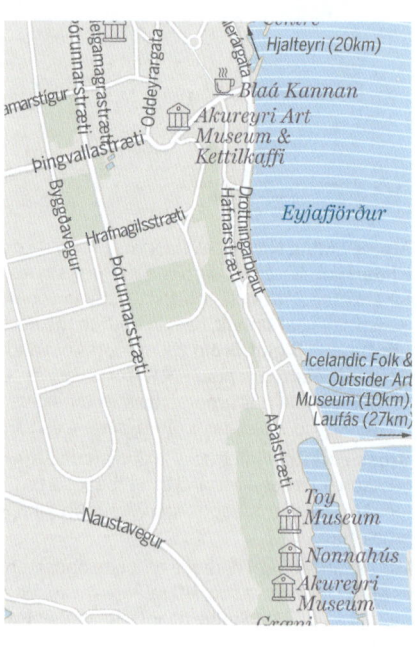

Art

Akureyri Art Museum, in 'Arts Alley' (Kaupvangsstræti), showcases the works of locally and nationally known artists. Finish with coffee, cake or wine at the museum's **Ketilkaffi**. A 20-minute drive to the north lies the hamlet of **Hjalteyri**, where the seasonal **Centre for Contemporary Art** operates inside an old herring factory. On the other side of Eyjafjörður is the **Icelandic Folk and Outsider Art Museum**, with its colourful and curious exhibits.

History

Akureyri Museum (minjasafnid.is) is actually a complex of museums. The main building at Aðalstræti 58 hosts the Schulte Collection – with ancient Icelandic maps, some with sea monsters – and rotating exhibitions on local history and life. Stroll in the museum park and visit the old timber church. **Nonnahús**, where children's book author Jón Sveinsson (Nonni) used to live, has been preserved

like a time capsule. Also visit the **Toy Museum**, **Davíðshús** (the house of poet Davíð Stefánsson) and turf farm **Laufás** on the other side of the fjord, portraying traditional country life.

Music

The landmark **Hof Cultural Centre** by the Davíðshús harbour hosts shows, concerts and conferences. Classical concerts are often held at Easter. Unassuming **Græni hatturinn**, in the basement of cosy **Bláa Kannan** cafe in the town centre (famous for its freshly baked cakes), is a popular concert venue and a good introduction to Iceland's music scene.

Akureyri Art Summer

The long-standing festival **Listasumar** *(Akureyri Art Summer; listasumar.is)* is held from late June until late July to celebrate Akureyri's long summer days and local talent, with a rotating programme of events held at various places around town. These include concerts and exhibits for all ages and tastes. Watch for pop or rock performances at Græni Hatturinn, classical concerts at the Hof Cultural Centre, visual art exhibitions at the Akureyri Art Museum, outdoor art exhibits, and art and craft workshops for children and adults. Check the festival website for a full listing.

Above Akureyri Museum

Listings

BEST OF THE REST

 ### Parks & Forests

Lystigarður
The Botanical Garden is at its loveliest from June to September. Stroll among trees and plants from around Iceland and beyond, and have a meal or slice of cake at Lyst.

Kjarnaskógur
Kjarnaskógur forest, about 5km south of town, has shady walking paths and bridges across a bubbling stream, playgrounds, communal barbecues and a beach volleyball court.

Vaglaskógur
About 30-minutes' drive through the Vaðlaheiði tunnel lies birch-filled Vaglaskógur, one of Iceland's largest forests. Nearby is the Daladýrð Petting Zoo, where kids can jump in the hay and meet the farm animals.

Art & Design

Vorhús
Established by designer Sveinbjörg Hallgrímsdóttir, Vorhús is popular in Iceland for its cups, bedsheets, ornaments and other objects with raven patterns and designs inspired by Icelandic flora and landscapes. *(vorhus.com)*

Islensk.is
In a historical house by the harbour, designer Hugrún Ívarsdóttir runs a shop carrying various products, including tablecloths, kitchen towels and platters with *laufabrauð* patterns inspired by the unique North Icelandic Christmas bread.

 ### Wining & Fine Dining

Eyja €€
This wine bar and bistro downtown is in an inviting yellow historical building with three-course options and a fish-of-the-day main.

North Restaurant €€€
Chef Gunnar Gíslason elevates Nordic cuisine to new levels here, with fresh, locally sourced Icelandic ingredients and creative menus. At Hotel Akureyri.

Strikið €€€
Large windows with fjord views lend glitz to this 5th-floor restaurant known for its Icelandic brunches and local focus (super-fresh sushi, lamb shoulder, shellfish soup).

 ### Beer, Draught & Craft

R5
At this micro bar you'll find the largest variety of beer in North Iceland, local and otherwise. Groups can book beer and food pairings.

Akureyri Backpackers
This hostel-cum-restaurant offers a selection of Icelandic beer, mass-produced and micro-brewed, along with no-fuss food and travel advice.

Ölstofa Akureyrar
In 'Arts Alley' you'll find the local Einstök Brewery's tasting lounge with eight types of

Lyst at Lystigarður

beer on draught and many more in bottles from around the world, plus sports TV.

Oceanic Adventures

Hjalteyri Kayak Rental
This company arranges family-friendly sea-kayaking tours on Eyjafjörður, both guided and non-guided, with options for fishing (and even whale watching) and a hot tub afterwards.

Fairytale at Sea
Based in Ólafsfjörður, about an hour's drive north of Akureyri, this company offers jet-ski tours to places usually hidden from view, in the shadow of mighty mountains surrounded by seabirds and breaching whales.

Strýtan Divecentre
A Hjalteyri-based dive centre that takes experienced divers to unique geothermal chimneys in Eyjafjörður. It also runs dives at Nesgjá fissure, about an hour's drive northeast of Akureyri.

Arctic Trip
This small, Grímsey-based operator offers diving and snorkelling with puffins and other seabirds around Grímsey, boat or land-based tours, and homey accommodation at its base, Sveinsstaðir.

Whale Watching Hauganes
From Hauganes village, 35km north of Akureyri, join a whale-watching tour of Eyjafjörður with optional sea angling. The local restaurant, Baccalá Bar, serves tasty fish dishes and there are hot tubs at the nearby beach.

Hiking & Nature Walks

Glerárdalur
Follow river Glerá, which runs through Akureyri, into Glerárdalur. A 10km walking path leads from the parking space on Súluvegur to the valley's end. Around the valley are many mountains worth hiking.

Humpback whale near Hauganes

Eyjafjarðará Estuary
The Eyjafjarðará estuary is known for its rich birdlife. Find walking paths south of Akureyri Airport and a bird-watching house. Bring a stick as protection from Arctic tern attacks.

Krossanesborgir
This nature reserve on Akureyri's northern outskirts has walking paths between boulders, a pond, diverse plant and birdlife, and a narrow sand beach.

Kerling
At 1538m, this is North Iceland's tallest mountain. A steep, unmarked path leads up from Finnastaðir (Rte 824) then down to Glerárdalur with views to Vatnajökull glacier. It's only for hikers in good shape and in good weather.

Hraunsvatn
This hidden lake lies at the foot of the Hraundrangi mountain range in Öxnadalur. Park at Háls farm, find the marked trail, and venture on a short and adventurous hike.

Golf

Akureyri Golf Club
Play golf at Jaðarsvöllur, Iceland's northernmost 18-hole golf course. The Arctic Open is held annually in late June when golfers compete under the midnight sun. (gagolf.is)

- **Trip Builder** (p172)
- **Practicalities** (p174)
- **Heavenly Showstopper** (p176)
- **Astronomical Iceland** (p178)
- **Looking Skyward** (p180)
- **Arctic Coast Way** (p182)
- **Flippers & Feathers** (p184)
- **Wild Things** (p186)
- **Journey Through Stories** (p188)
- **Modern Legends** (p190)
- **Island Explorations** (p192)
- **Icelandic Horse Culture** (p194)
- **Tölting Through Time** (p196)
- **Listings** (p198)

NORTH ICELAND
Trip Builder

North Iceland is a world apart, with its long winters, dramatic history and diverse landscapes. Waterfalls, mountains, volcanoes and geothermal areas yield to green pastures, free-roaming horses and birds galore. Many visitors don't make it this way, leaving plenty of space for exploration and solitude.

Head to **Grímsey** island, Iceland's northernmost corner (p193)
⛴ 3hrs from Dalvík

Join local food workshops at Brimslóð Atelier in **Blönduós** (p182)
🚗 40mins from Varmahlíð

Learn the herring history of beautiful **Siglufjörður** (p182)
🚌 1¼hrs from Akureyri

Go on epic horse treks and experience round-ups in **Skagafjörður** (p195)
🚗 30–60mins from Blönduós

PREVIOUS SPREAD: MUMEMORIES/SHUTTERSTOCK
DANIEL DORSA/LONELY PLANET, CREATIVE STOCK PHOTO/SHUTTERSTOCK, INBOUND HORIZONS/SHUTTERSTOCK

Practicalities

ARRIVING

Akureyri Airport Icelandair flies from Reykjavík to Akureyri. **Norlandair** *(norlandair.is)* links Akureyri with Grímsey, Þórshöfn and Vopnafjörður. For onward transport, hire a car or book taxis or shuttles.

Strætó *(straeto.is)* Line 57 buses go daily between Reykjavík and Akureyri via Blönduós, Varmahlíð and Sauðárkrókur. Line 79 links Akureyri with Húsavík, Line 78 goes from Akureyri to Siglufjörður via Árskógssandur, Dalvík and Ólafsfjörður, and Line 56 goes from Akureyri to Egilsstaðir via Skútustaðir (for Mývatn).

HOW MUCH FOR

Whale watching 13,000kr

Fish of the day 3500kr

Pint of beer 1500kr

GETTING AROUND

Car Hiring a car is the best way to get between places and to more remote areas. A 2WD is fine for most destinations in summer, including most of the Arctic Coast Way. However, in highland areas you will need to have a 4WD or arrange an organised tour.

Bus & taxi Straeto has almost-daily bus connections between major towns. Akureyri has taxis and free public buses. In most other towns you can easily walk, or watch for the occasional taxi.

Ferry Scheduled ferry trips link Árskógssandur with Hrísey daily, and Dalvík with Grímsey several times weekly.

WHEN TO GO

JAN–MAR
Short days. Northern Lights. Possible snow, ice. Ski season.

APR–JUN
Midnight sun (late June). Migrating birds. Possible snow. Off-piste ski season.

JUL–SEP
Tourist and festival season. Highland roads open. Best for outdoor activities.

OCT–DEC
Colder, shorter days. Northern Lights. Autumn colours.

EATING & DRINKING

Icelandic Most restaurants in coastal towns serve local seafood. Try the catch of the day. Lamb is a must; they graze in mountain pastures in the summer and have a slightly gamey flavour.

International Pizzas and hamburgers are everywhere. Larger towns have Italian, Asian, Middle Eastern and even African restaurants.

Skyr (pictured top) Buy this yoghurt-like dessert in supermarkets in classic or creative combinations.

Cafes and bakeries Open early in the mornings and popular among locals. Try the *kleinur* (twisted doughnut; pictured bottom).

Best small-town dining Hótel Norðurljós (p199)

Must-try dinner Brimslóð Atelier (p182)

CONNECT & FIND YOUR WAY

Wi-fi Free and available in most hotels, bars, restaurants and public buildings. There is good network coverage everywhere except the most remote areas.

Navigation Ask for guidance at tourist information centres and hotels. Google Maps is helpful, but check online for **road conditions and closures** (road.is) and also for general **travel updates** (northiceland.is, safetravel.is).

WHERE TO STAY

There are varied sleeping options throughout the region. It's best to book in advance.

Town	Pro/Con
Hvammstangi, Blönduós and Skagaströnd	Seal watching and horse riding
Skagafjörður (Sauðárkrókur, Varmahlíð, Hofsós)	Horse riding, river rafting, history
Siglufjörður and Ólafsfjörður	Water sports, skiing, museum
Eyjafjörður (Akureyri, Dalvík, Hrísey and Grímsey)	Hiking, skiing, boat tours, water sports, art and culture
Grenivík, Húsavík, Mývatn	Volcanoes and geothermal areas, whale- and bird-watching, highland tours
Ásbyrgi, Melrakkaslétta, Langanes	Nature exploration, bird watching, slow travel and solitude

DISCOUNT CARD

The Camping Card Provides access to campsites around Iceland (max 28 nights per family) for €179. Order online at campingcard.is (or buy it in Iceland).

MONEY

Cards (Visa and MasterCard) are accepted almost everywhere and are often preferred, although cash is also fine. There are ATMs dispensing Icelandic krónur in most towns.

26 HEAVENLY
Showstopper

STARGAZING | NORTHERN LIGHTS | MIDNIGHT SUN

The sky above North Iceland puts on a show in all seasons. Here, on the edge of the Arctic Circle, the sun never sets in summer and hardly rises in winter. Dark, clear skies are sprinkled with millions of stars and, sometimes, the Northern Lights come out to dance.

Trip Notes

Getting around Car is the best way to travel through North Iceland. Rte 870 and the other roads up around the peninsulas offer rugged but fine cycling.

When to go Late August to early May for stargazing and Northern Lights. Mid-June to mid-July for midnight sun. Meteor showers in August and November.

Top tip Search online for information on Northern Lights and the midnight sun: **forecasts** (auroraforecast.is), best **locations** (arcticcoastway.is) and **tours** (northiceland.is).

Monument to the Dwarves

Raufarhöfn's **Arctic Henge** has four 6m-tall gates around a 10m-tall arch and 360-degree views. The gates – called Austri, Norðri, Suðri and Vestri after the dwarves that hold up the sky in Norse mythology – function as sundials and are at their best at sunrise, sunset and around the summer solstice.

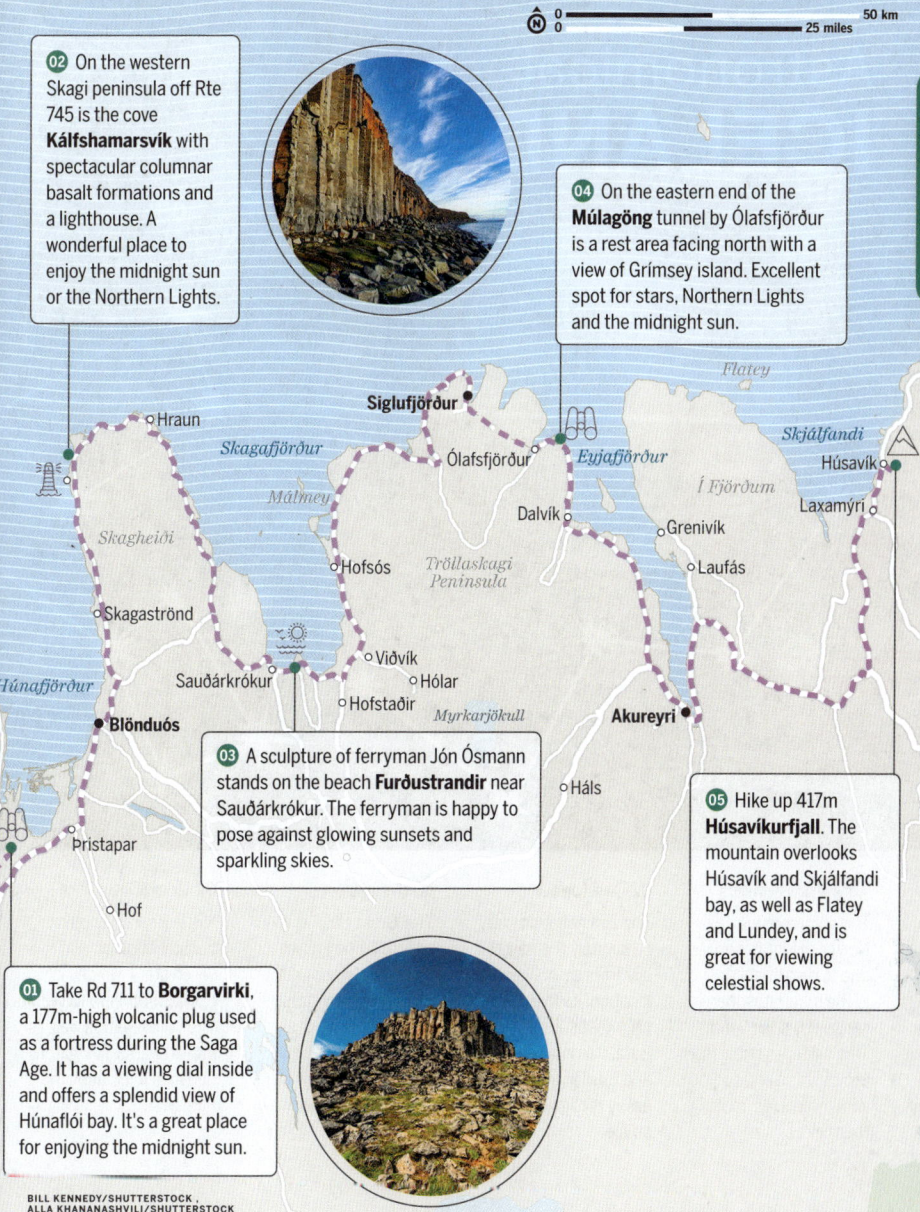

02 On the western Skagi peninsula off Rte 745 is the cove **Kálfshamarsvík** with spectacular columnar basalt formations and a lighthouse. A wonderful place to enjoy the midnight sun or the Northern Lights.

04 On the eastern end of the **Múlagöng** tunnel by Ólafsfjörður is a rest area facing north with a view of Grímsey island. Excellent spot for stars, Northern Lights and the midnight sun.

03 A sculpture of ferryman Jón Ósmann stands on the beach **Furðustrandir** near Sauðárkrókur. The ferryman is happy to pose against glowing sunsets and sparkling skies.

05 Hike up 417m **Húsavíkurfjall**. The mountain overlooks Húsavík and Skjálfandi bay, as well as Flatey and Lundey, and is great for viewing celestial shows.

01 Take Rd 711 to **Borgarvirki**, a 177m-high volcanic plug used as a fortress during the Saga Age. It has a viewing dial inside and offers a splendid view of Húnaflói bay. It's a great place for enjoying the midnight sun.

BILL KENNEDY/SHUTTERSTOCK ,
ALLA KHANANASHVILI/SHUTTERSTOCK

Astronomical ICELAND

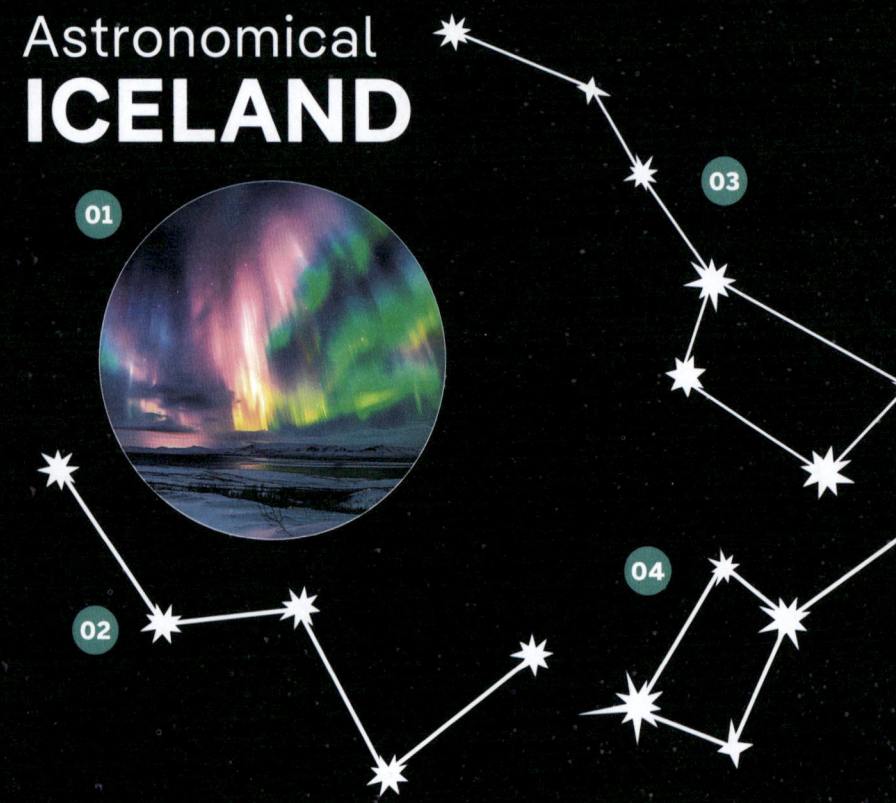

01 Aurora borealis

The mesmerising Northern Lights appear due to disturbances in the magnetosphere caused by solar wind. Tiny particles enter the atmosphere and collide with molecules, making them glow.

02 Cassiopeia

The constellation can be seen by the naked eye from a northern location. Its five brightest stars – Alpha, Beta, Gamma, Delta and Epsilon – create the easily recognisable 'W' shape.

03 Ursa Major

The 'Great Bear' is a constellation known from the asterism of its main seven stars. It's visible from the northern hemisphere and goes by many other names (Karlsvagninn in Icelandic).

04 Ursa Minor

'Little Bear' is another constellation of seven stars, which also resembles a ladle. The constellation was important for navigators because it includes the Pole Star.

Arctic Circle (66.5° N)
24 hours of daylight

05 Pole Star

Also known as Polaris or North Star, the Pole Star is a very bright triple star system. It lies nearly in a direct line with the Earth's rotational axis 'above' the North Pole and appears to stand still.

06 Milky Way

The galaxy that contains our solar system appears as a hazy band of light stretching across the winter sky from the east to the west. It's known as Vetrarbrautin (Winter Path) in Icelandic.

07 Meteor showers

These are celestial events in which a myriad of radiating meteors appear to fly at high speed from one point in the sky. The Perseids arrive in August and the Leonids in November.

08 The midnight sun

At summer solstice (around 21 June) – when the Earth has its maximum axial tilt towards the sun – there is no sunrise or sunset at Iceland's most northerly point, Grímsey island.

Looking Skyward

CELESTIAL PHENOMENA ABOVE ICELAND

The Northern Lights are a highlight for visitors to Iceland during the dark season. However, if the aurora borealis won't put on a show during your stay, direct your attention towards the twinkling stars and the moon. And sometimes, with luck, you may even be able to catch an eclipse.

Left Milky Way above Goðafoss **Middle** Northern Lights **Right** Star trails moving around the Pole Star

Auroras, Eclipses & Stars

The Northern Lights tend to be more frequent just after 'solar maximum' – the peak period of activity in the 11-year solar cycle. As the most recent maximum was in late 2024, from now to 2028 could be ideal for aurora spotting.

Even if you don't see Iceland's Northern Lights, you will surely see the stars, according to Valdís Björk Þorsteinsdóttir, chair of the Stjörnu-Oddi stargazing society. 'As soon as you get out of the light pollution you can find good conditions for stargazing. The constellation Cassiopeia is easy to find in the evening. Right above your head you'll see a "W". Ursa Major can easily be identified by its characteristic ladle shape, and it points towards Ursa Minor and Pole Star', she says.

'At certain times of the year it's almost guaranteed that you can see meteor showers. The Perseids are always in August and the Leonids in November. They're named after the constellations from which they seem to appear', she explains. 'You can also see the glow of the Milky Way, which extends from the east to the west. It's like a brighter stripe or lustre across the sky.'

Iceland lies in the path of a full solar eclipse in August 2026 and a penumbral lunar eclipse in February 2027. If you miss the eclipses? Valdís says the moon is always an interesting sight, as are the skies. 'In summer you can see amazing sunsets. When the midnight sun is shining you don't see much else, but it brings its own show in the evening.'

Medieval Astronomer

Oddi Helgason, or Stjörnu-Oddi, was an Icelandic astronomer who worked as a farmhand at Múli in Aðaldalur in

the 12th century. His observations of the summer solstice, the weekly change of the sun's declination and the varying arrival of twilight in North Iceland proved important for timekeeping and navigation. They were Iceland's most valuable contribution to natural sciences in the Middle Ages. Seafarers used the position of the sun to estimate their course, as well as the Pole Star after dark.

'It's incredible that Stjörnu-Oddi was given the scope to make these observations', says Valdís, whose society is named after the medieval astronomer. 'He timed the spring equinox much more accurately than others had done. He measured the diameter of the sun as a ratio of the entire arc across the sky. It's much more accurate than the church's official number at that time', she states. 'He used a method where he noted where the sunray hit the wall through a small crack on the door and made his calculations that way.'

Not much else is known about Stjörnu-Oddi or his methods, but he was likely self-educated and had no books to reference – he may even have been illiterate. He is known to have spent time on Flatey island where there is a mysterious circular construction called Arnargerði. Some believe that it served as Stjörnu-Oddi's observatory. There is a memorial to Stjörnu-Oddi at Grenjaðarstaður turf farm and museum in Aðaldalur.

> At certain times of the year it's almost guaranteed that you can see meteor showers.

Celestial Phenomena in Norse Mythology

Stars The sparks that flew from Múspellsheimur – the burning-hot world in Norse mythology – as stated in *Snorra-Edda*'s description of the creation of the world.

Sun and Moon The siblings Sól and Máni. Sól drives the sun's carriage across the sky and Máni leads the moon on its path. Both the sun and the moon are being chased by wolves, which is why they are constantly on the move. At Ragnarök – doomsday – wolves will swallow the heavenly bodies, blacken the sun and turn the night sky blood red.

Bifröst The bridge between heaven and earth, which connects the world of gods, Ásgarður, with the world of men, Miðgaður. In *Snorra-Edda* it is clearly stated that Bifröst is the rainbow, although it has also been described as the Northern Lights or the Milky Way.

27 Arctic Coast WAY

SEAFOOD | BEACHES | SLOW TRAVEL

Take your time when driving the Arctic Coast Way. It is close to the Ring Road, yet feels far from the beaten track, taking you between isolated headlands and remote communities where time seems to slow down. Locals live off the sea and the rhythms of daily life are shaped by the whims of the weather.

Trip Notes

Getting around Hire a car at Keflavík International Airport or in Akureyri. Make sure it's fit for gravel roads.

When to go The best driving conditions are in summer. Not all roads are cleared in winter, but there are **alternative routes** *(arcticcoastway.is)*. Go in September to May for Northern Lights; mid-June to mid-July for midnight sun.

Top tip For solitude, the westernmost and easternmost parts of the Arctic Coast Way are your best bet.

Bounty of the Sea

Dive into local culture and history through 'hero' experiences (see arcticcoastway. is). **Brimslóð Atelier** in Blönduós offers workshops on local seafood, wild herbs and other raw ingredients. The **Herring Era Museum** (p189) in Siglufjörður takes visitors back to the herring boom. In Hauganes, catch your own fish, learn about salt fish and enjoy a meal at **Baccalá Bar**.

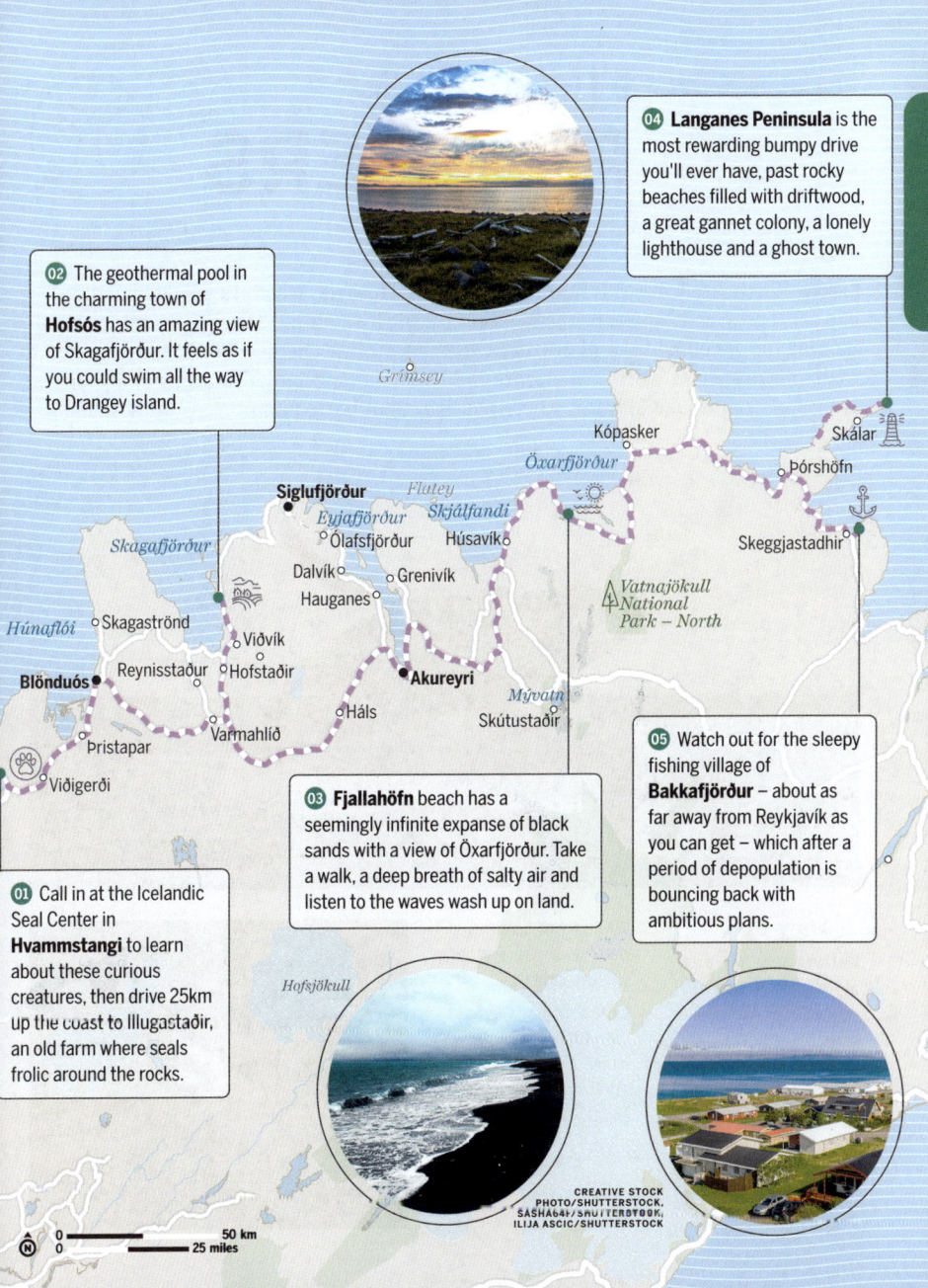

28 Flippers & FEATHERS

SAIL | WALK | WILDLIFE

Northeast Iceland is home to charming Húsavík, Iceland's whale-watching capital. The area is also a prime location for bird-watching. There are puffins nesting on the cliffsides and northern gannets around the headlands, but also many more species worthy of attention. Birding is especially rewarding south of Húsavík around lake Mývatn, where you may spot harlequin ducks and gyrfalcons.

How To

Getting here Hire a car at Keflavík International Airport or in Akureyri. Once in the north, a car is the most practical means of transport, although you can travel by bus from Akureyri to Húsavík, or to Skútustaðir on lake Mývatn's southwestern edge.

When to go Summer is peak season for watching whales and birds.

Expect to pay Guided two- to three-hour whale-watching tours per adult/child cost about 13,000/6500kr.

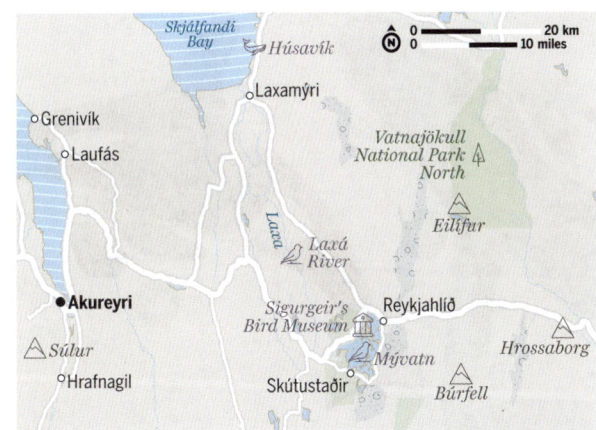

Top Humpback whale breaches near Húsavík Bottom Tufted duck

Whale-Watching Capital

A town of 2300 people, **Húsavík** overlooks Skjálfandi bay where around 11 species of whales and dolphins can be sighted. Humpbacks are the most common, but the elusive blue whale, the world's largest animal, sometimes makes an appearance. The season runs from April/May to October/November, with peak whale-watching months in July and August, when around 1000 people a day go whale watching with Húsavík's four whale-watching companies. The University of Iceland has a **research centre** on marine biology in town and the **Húsavík Whale Museum**, with its massive blue-whale skeleton, teaches visitors about these fascinating creatures. **Geosea Geothermal Sea Baths** has views of Skjálfandi, and sometimes whales can be seen from there.

Birds of Paradise

An hour's drive from Húsavík is lake **Mývatn**, a paradise for bird-watchers with more than a dozen species of nesting ducks, including the tufted duck, greater scaup, Eurasian wigeon and common scoter. The banks of the Laxá river (which flows from lake Mývatn) are a prime habitat for harlequin ducks and Barrow's goldeneye. Also watch for gyrfalcons on the hunt. Find **Sigurgeir's Bird Museum** in a beautiful building by the lake, with 280 taxidermied birds – nearly every species that nests in Iceland – and 300 eggs. Bird-watching enthusiasts can venture along the **Birding Trail of Northeast Iceland** (birdingtrail.is), which connects wetlands, rivers, lakes and ponds, sea cliffs and coastal areas, heaths and highlands.

🐋 Gratitude

Even though the daily probability of spotting whales in Húsavík's Skjálfandi Bay is high, it is not a marine park and they can choose to leave at any point. It's important to be aware of what a privilege it is to be out there and to approach the experience with gratitude above all. Whale watching should be passive – observing whales behaving like they would if we were not around, and never pushing for close encounters or interfering with their natural behaviour. In my experience, that's when the most amazing interactions happen.

By Madalena Gaspar, a marine biologist who works with **Friends of Moby Dick** (friendsofmobydick.is) in Húsavík.

WILD Things

01 Blue whale
One of the largest animals this world has ever seen, the blue whale can sometimes be sighted on whale-watching tours in North Iceland.

02 Orca
The world's largest dolphin species. These highly intelligent creatures hunt in groups and develop different techniques for different areas. Sightings in Iceland are rare.

03 Minke whale
Averaging 8m to 10m in length, minke whales are among the smallest of the baleen whales and are commonly seen in Iceland, including in shallower waters.

04 Humpback whale
Commonly sighted in North Iceland, humpbacks can be identified by the pattern on their flukes. They migrate some 25,000km each year, further than any other mammal.

05 White-beaked dolphin
One of the most northerly dolphin species, white-beaked dolphins are commonly seen year-round, sometimes in large pods.

06 Harlequin duck
This colourful bird is found in fast-flowing

streams in northeast Iceland year-round, primarily in the Laxá river near Mývatn.

07 Gyrfalcon
The majestic gyrfalcon is Iceland's national bird. Watch for them around Mývatn and in the Jökulsárgljúfur canyon.

08 Northern gannet
A large and elegant seabird known for its high-speed dives into the sea. There are large colonies around Melrakkaslétta and Langanes.

09 Ptarmigan
This bird has feathered claws and changes colour three times a year to blend in with the environment.

10 Arctic tern
Migrates further than any other bird on the planet, from the high Arctic to Antarctica. It nests by the coast, lakes and wetlands.

11 Bird eggs
The eggs of guillemots and other seabirds are collected from cliffs on Grímsey island. While an acquired taste, they're definitely eye candy.
Arctic Trip *(arctictrip.is)* offers egg-collecting tours.

01 ANTIKVA/SHUTTERSTOCK, 02 HAPPY WHALE/SHUTTERSTOCK, 03 COSMICANNA/SHUTTERSTOCK, 04 POLINAVYUN/SHUTTERSTOCK, 05 ALONA K/SHUTTERSTOCK, 06 JUKKA JANTUNEN/SHUTTERSTOCK, 07 STEVE BYLAND/SHUTTERSTOCK, 08 NICOLAS PRIMOLA/SHUTTERSTOCK, 09 ROCK PTARMIGAN/SHUTTERSTOCK, 10 LILIYA BUTENKO/SHUTTERSTOCK, 11 ARCTIC IMAGES/ALAMY

29 Journey Through **STORIES**

FOLKLORE | FILM | HISTORY

▬ Legends come to life and history looms large in North Iceland. Follow in the footsteps of legendary outlaw Grettir the Strong, see petrified trolls, take part virtually in ancient civil war battles, tour museums celebrating tradition and get your fortune told in the same village where a famous prophetess once lived. Stories, old and new, can add another dimension to your journey.

How To

Getting around Buses will get you to the major centres but you'll need to hire a car to reach most destinations, or book tours for specific experiences.

When to go Year-round, but most events take place in summer. Some museums close in winter, or are open by appointment only.

Top tip Tourist information centres can help you plan your trip – Sauðárkrókur Tourist Information is particularly helpful – as can online resources such as northiceland.is and sagatrail.is.

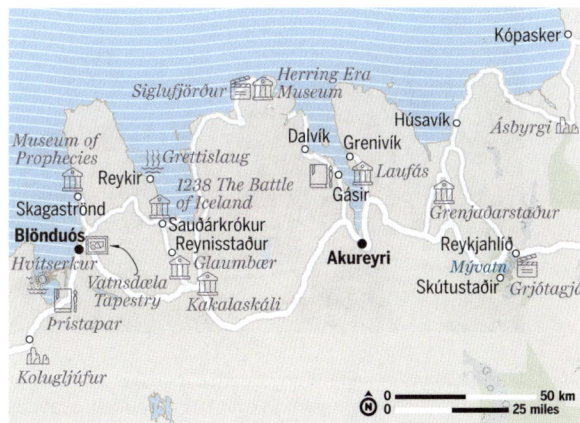

Top Hvítserkur
Bottom Glaumbær

Myths and legends These are often interwoven with nature and landscape. **Hvítserkur** sea stack was a troll that turned to stone, the falls in **Kolugljúfur** are named after the ogress who lived in the gorge and the horseshoe-shaped canyon **Ásbyrgi** was created when Sleipnir, Norse god Óðinn's eight-legged horse, stepped down from heaven.

Submerge in the sagas Bathe in **Grettislaug** where Grettir the Strong warmed up after his swim from Drangey island. Have your fortune told at the **Museum of Prophecies** in Skagaströnd, dedicated to settler Þórdís the Prophetess, and in Blönduós help stitch the **Vatnsdæla Tapestry**, documenting the *Vatnsdæla Saga*.

Sturlung Age This was the bloodiest period in Iceland's history, leading to the end of the Commonwealth era. Sites include **Kakalaskáli**, with an exhibition about the battle of Haugsnesbardagi in 1246, and **1238: The Battle of Iceland** in Sauðárkrókur, where you can become a warrior through virtual reality.

Turf farms These kept Icelanders warm and safe for centuries. **Glaumbær**, **Laufás** and **Grenjaðarstaður** are preserved as living museums, where you can step into history and experience traditional country life, haymaking and folk dancing.

Film and literature Visit **Þrístapar** and other sites connected with the last execution in Iceland in 1830, made famous in Hannah Kent's *Burial Rites*. Near **Mývatn** is Grjótagjá, the water-filled cave where Jon Snow and Ygritte from *Game of Thrones* had a steamy soak. Crime series *Trapped* was filmed in **Siglufjörður**.

Living History

Herring Era Museum
In its heyday, fishing boats crammed Siglufjörður's harbour unloading their catches of herring for waiting women to gut and salt. The award-winning Herring Era Museum does a stunning job of recreating this period and the struggles that followed. In summer, watch for salting exhibitions at the pier, with 'herring girls' salting herring in barrels to live accordion music.

Medieval Days
This late July festival brings the ancient trading centre of **Gásir** (14km north of Akureyri) to life. Watch a blacksmith beat metal or women dye wool with herbs, bake bread over an open fire or test your sharpshooting skills with a bow and arrow. (minjasafnid.is)

Modern Legends

QUIRKY TOWNS AND ALIEN ATMOSPHERE

Icelandic landscapes feature in medieval sagas and folk stories passed orally from generation to generation, and they also appear in modern murder mysteries, fantasy stories and sci-fi movies. Iceland has grown in popularity as a filming location and the North plays a big part.

Þór Kjartansson, supervising location manager at True North production company, is ever busy scouting locations for filmmakers from around the world. 'It's often a long process, especially with larger movies,' he says He explains that it takes a lot of back and forth before the right place is found. It needs to fulfil certain conditions; for example, be near the sea but not too remote and face the sun. 'The camera crews always fall for the light. They hate blue sky and sunlight – but that is rarely the condition in Iceland.'

Out of This World

Fast and Furious 8 which included a car race on lake Mývatn, is among Þór's most memorable projects. 'It was amazing to be able to carry out a Hollywood scene of that scale on the frozen lake,' he says. The landscape scenes for *Star Wars: The Mandalorian* at the site of the 2014–15 Holuhraun eruption in the northern highlands also stand out: 'It was a unique experience because it was so difficult to access and film the barren landscape all around the lava, the desert and untouched wilderness north of Vatnajökull glacier.' *Rogue One: A Star Wars Story* was filmed in various locations in Iceland, including the Krafla geothermal area near Mývatn. 'We shot scenes around Leirhnjúkur mountain in the snow,' reveals Þór.

North Icelandic nature also represents another planet in Ridley Scott's *Prometheus*. In the opening scene an extraterrestrial drinks a deadly potion and tumbles into a massive waterfall – Dettifoss, the most powerful in Europe. In post-apocalyptic *Oblivion*, ancient crater Hrossaborg serves as a devastated football stadium. Þór adds that in 2020, scenes for the *Welcome to Earth* TV series were shot at Jökulsárgljúfur canyon in Vatnajökull National Park.

Left Boats moored at Húsavík
Middle Dettifoss
Right Holuhraun eruption

Eurovision Town

Eurovision Song Contest: The Story of Fire Saga with Will Ferrell is of a totally different genre. 'The producers were looking for an Icelandic town to set the story in', says Þór. True North's first suggestion was Stykkishólmur and the producers loved it, but after they visited Húsavík, there was no turning back. 'Húsavík kind of stole the show', laughs Þór. In the comedy, main character Lars stubbornly pursues his dream of competing in the Eurovision Song Contest instead of becoming a fisherman like his father. At the 2021 Academy Awards, Húsavík stole the show again: the film's title song was nominated for an Oscar and True North recorded a music video with singer Molly Sandén and a local girls' choir in Húsavík.

> The region is so diverse, not only because of the varied landscapes but because they change from season to season.

'In North Iceland you find these special forces of nature in the shape of glaciers and lava, desert sands, canyons and waterfalls, from Kverkfjöll mountains to Dettifoss and Mývatn', states Þór. 'The region is so diverse, not only because of the varied landscapes but because they change from season to season. You can shoot at almost exactly the same location in summer, winter, autumn and spring and it looks totally different because of the changing light and colours, and whether it's covered in snow or not.'

🎬 North Iceland in Icelandic Films

The Last Fishing Trip (*Síðasta veiðiferðin*; 2020) A comedy about middle-aged friends who go fishing – and everything goes wrong! It was shot at Mýrarkvísl river.

The Swan (*Svanurinn*; 2017) Tells the story of a nine-year-old girl who is sent away to live at a farm and gets caught up in dramatic events. The film was shot in Svarfaðardalur valley.

Rams (*Hrútar*; 2015) Features two brothers who haven't spoken in 40 years despite living next to each other on sheep farms in Bárðardalur valley. When disaster strikes, they must stick together.

30 ISLAND Explorations

BIRDS | SEASCAPES | HIKING

North Iceland's islands are worlds of their own. In the past, residents had to be self-sufficient to survive when stormy weather cut off connections with the mainland. This isolation still marks the islands' present-day communities, with people attracted by the chance to wind down well off the grid, and to immerse themselves in landscapes defined by the sea and the ever-changing skies.

How To

Getting here Ferries go to Hrísey from Árskógssandur and to Grímsey from Dalvík. Flights connect Grímsey and Akureyri. Prearranged boat tours are required for Drangey and Flatey.

When to go Year-round for Hrísey and Grímsey. Summer for Drangey and Flatey. October to March for bird-watching.

Top tip For info on the islands and tours, check online at northiceland.is and arcticcoastway.is.

Doppelgänger Don't confuse North Iceland's Flatey with the Westfjords island of the same name.

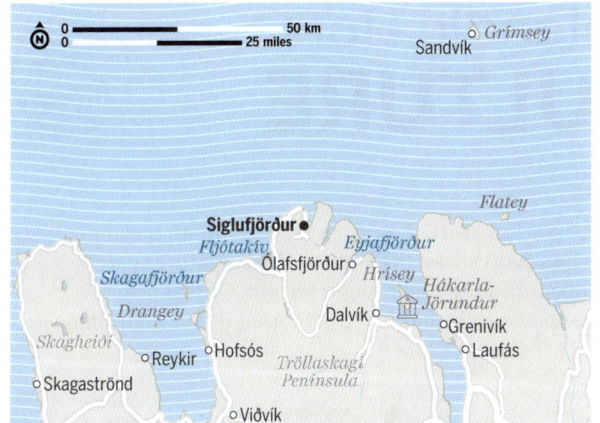

Top Drangey
Bottom Hrísey

Drangey This 180m-high rock is home to myriad birds but no people (although Grettir the Strong lived there as an outlaw). Farmers rowed over with their sheep for grazing, and hunted birds and collected eggs. The panoramic views of the fjord are worth the climb. Guided tours are offered June to August.

Hrísey This island has around 150 residents, many of whom live off the sea, as their ancestors did. The museum at the house of **Hákarla Jörundur** tells the story of shark fishing; shark oil was used for street lighting in Europe. The island is known for its rich birdlife and is a sanctuary for ptarmigans. Wild angelica is harvested for supplement production, and old tractors are used for transport rather than cars. The ferry from Árskógssandur runs daily, year-round, taking 15 minutes.

Grímsey The only place in Iceland that touches the Arctic Circle, its 50 residents live off fishing and, increasingly, tourism. People visit for the puffins and other seabirds, and quiet walks among friendly sheep. It's possible to snorkel or dive with the birds, collect guillemot eggs (a local delicacy) from cliffs, and go on fishing tours. The ferry from Dalvík goes several times weekly, takes three hours and is an adventure in itself.

Flatey This used to be a thriving community, but in 1967 all residents packed their things and left. The houses stood empty until the islanders' relatives and Húsavík locals saved them from decay. Some whale-watching companies include tours of Flatey.

Island Festivals

Sólstöðuhátíð Grímsey locals invite visitors to join them for a celebration of the summer solstice around 21 June each year. Enjoy fresh seafood, listen to live music, go sailing and watch the sun not set. (visitakureyri.is)

Hríseyjarhátíð The Hrísey family festival is held annually in July. Locals invite visitors to their gardens for coffee, and offer beach walks, tractor tours, games and entertainment for kids, traditional dances, live music and a sing-along event by the bonfire. Many visitors choose to camp. (hrisey.is)

31 Icelandic Horse CULTURE

RIDING | BONDING | NATURE

You will never feel closer to nature than from the back of an Icelandic horse. Purebred for more than 1000 years, these soft-gaited creatures carry travellers across streams, open meadows and rough terrain. Or just observe them from the roadsides as they nuzzle and frolic with each other, their manes flying in the wind.

How To

Getting here Hire a car in Reykjavík or Akureyri or take the bus, but you will need a car to reach most of the farms.

When to go Most tours are in summer. Early summer for newborn foals; autumn for horse roundups.

Tour operators Many companies offer horse-related experiences (see northiceland.is).

What to wear Warm, waterproof and comfortable clothing. For longer tours, proper riding clothing, sunscreen and lip balm.

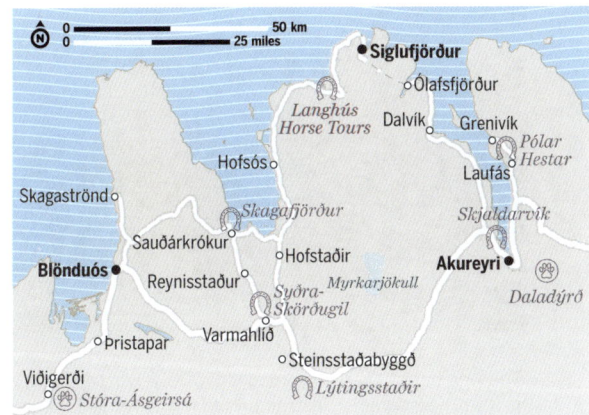

Top Icelandic horses, Skagafjörður
Bottom Mývatn Open

Choose Your Experience

Family-friendly Petting zoos include **Daladýrð** and **Stóra-Ásgeirsá**, while **Lýtingsstaðir** and **Langhús Horse Tours** offer special experiences for children too young for tours. Many horse farms have accommodation and some are open for drop-ins.

Shorter excursions If you're new to horses or don't ride regularly, book shorter excursions at the aforementioned farms or at **Pólar Hestar** and **Syðra-Skörðugil**. Tours are guided and sometimes include storytelling, with the experiences varying depending on the season and surrounding landscapes. Riding gear and safety equipment is included.

Multiday tours Experience the freedom of riding for days through wild nature or highland landscapes, along ancient routes and narrow sheep paths in smooth *tölt* or galloping with a herd of loose horses. These tours are magical, but are only for experienced riders. Operators include **Íslandshestar** and **Riding Iceland**. Midnight-sun tours, Diamond Circle tours and roundup tours are among the experiences on offer.

Skagafjörður This region, where horses outnumber people, is the centre of Icelandic horsemanship and home to many of the best-known breeding farms and horse roundups. **Hólar University** – which is renowned for its equine science programme – is located there, as well as the **Icelandic Horse History Centre** (open in summer and by appointment). **Landsmót Hestamanna** – the National Horse Competition – will be held at Hólar in July 2026.

Horse Festivals

Stóðréttir These horse roundups are true country festivals when farmers round up their horses from summer pastures in the mountains. Watch hundreds of loose horses being herded and sorted in a circular paddock called a *rétt*. There are food and local handicrafts for sale, and singing and dancing in the evening. Three of the best-known roundups are **Laufskálarétt**, **Víðidalstungurétt** and **Skrapatungurétt**. They take place in late September and early October (find the exact date on bbl.is).

Horses on Ice – Mývatn Open An annual riding competition on the frozen lake Mývatn (see visitmyvatn.is) in mid-March. Watch superb horses and riders 'fly' across the ice. **Saltvík** gives visitors the chance to ride on ice.

Tölting Through Time

FROM MOST INDISPENSABLE SERVANT TO MOST LOYAL COMPANION

When settlers arrived in Iceland in the 9th century CE, they brought domestic animals, including horses of different breeds. And these became the ancestors of today's Icelandic horse – a breed notable for its purity, ease of handling, friendly manner and unusual gaits.

'The land has shaped this breed for 1000 years', says Jelena Ohm, horse trainer, instructor and former project manager for Horses of Iceland, the official marketing initiative for the Icelandic horse. The small and sturdy breed was used for transport and farm work. It developed a double coat to keep warm in winter. Today horses are still kept outside except when they are being trained for riding, and in the summer large herds roam free in mountain valleys. 'They have a very strong connection with nature', says Jelena. 'Because they grow up in a natural environment, they are very smart and learn quickly, which makes them very fun to ride and train.' Due to better feed and selective breeding, the horse has grown taller over recent decades.

Five Different Gaits

The Icelandic horse has two extra gaits in addition to walk, trot and canter: The soft *tölt* for the comfort of riders, and the super-smooth and fast-flying pace for racing short distances. Other horse breeds have, or used to have, similar gaits. However, while in Europe there were roads and horses pulled carriages, in Iceland there were none and people rode their horses across rough terrain. Therefore, the *tölt* maintained its importance. 'What is special about the Icelandic horse is that it's one of the few breeds where all five gaits are trained and competed in', states Jelena. 'With the industrial revolution, roads and cars, the horse's role changed from being "the most indispensable servant," to a competition and hobby horse, and it's still a big part of today's culture.'

Left Icelandic horses graze near lake Mývatn
Middle Riders explore Iceland's landscapes
Right Man with Icelandic horse

Passion for the Horse

Horses are unusually common in Iceland. As of 2024, there were about 92,000 horses in the country, meaning about one horse for every four people. In comparison, recent statistics for Sweden, which has the highest ratio in the EU, show about one horse for every 32 people. Icelandic horses are also popular among travellers. From 2014 to 2018 the number of visitors enjoying horse-related tourism jumped from 120,000 to 287,000, and a 2018 survey on horse treks found that nine out of 10 tourists loved the experience.

> Because they grow up in a natural environment, they are very smart and learn quickly, which makes them very fun to ride and train.

Horse Legends

Sleipnir Óðinn's eight-legged horse is the most famous horse in Norse mythology. But there are many other mythological horses, including **Skinfaxi**, which Dagur (Day) rides across the sky; and **Hrímfaxi**, which is ridden by his mother Nótt (Night).

Fluga She is one of the four-legged settlers named in the *Book of Settlement* (Landnáma). The famous horse-breeding farm Flugumýri in Skagafjörður – which is also the site of the fateful arson in the *Sturlunga Saga* – was named after the mare.

Faxi This horse is important character in the ghost story *Djákninn á Myrká* (The Deacon of Dark River). Faxi's rider, the deacon, died when Faxi fell through the ice on a river they were crossing. The deacon came back to haunt his fiancé and took her for a ride on Faxi in the moonlight.

Icelandic Horses in Film & Literature

Of Horses and Men (*Hross í oss;* 2013) A multi-award-winning country romance by Benedikt Erlingsson, seen from the perspective of horses.

Nonni and Manni (*Nonni und Manni;* 1988–89) A children's TV series based on the books of Icelandic author Nonni (Jón Sveinsson). In one scene, Nonni's horse saves his life.

Skúlaskeið This poem by Grímur Thomsen celebrates Sörli, the horse that saved its owner Skúli, a murder convict, by pacing across rocky terrain in Kaldidalur, outrunning everyone and bringing Skúli home, only to then die from exhaustion.

Listings

BEST OF THE REST

Volcanoes, Lava & Geothermal Areas

Krafla

The last series of eruptions in the Krafla volcanic system occurred from 1975 to 1984. A colourful and steaming world of wonder featuring turquoise crater lake Víti, the area makes for an otherworldly hike, only 30 minutes from lake Mývatn.

Þeistareykir

These geothermal fields are as colourful and steamy as Hverir (Námafjall) by Mývatn but less frequented. The power station built there in 2017 can be reached on paved roads from Húsavík. You'll find hot springs, mud pools and fumaroles.

Mývatn area

All around lake Mývatn are spectacular craters and lava formations. At Dimmuborgir are dark and eerie lava fields. Lava paths lead past fascinating structures like Kirkjan (the Church) – a lava tube. Hverfjall is an easily accessible ancient crater.

Highland Destinations

The following ares only accessible in 4WD vehicles in summer, and tours are usually recommended.

Askja

This complex of calderas is surrounded by the Dyngjufjöll mountains. In the 1960s, the Apollo astronauts trained here for lunar missions. Other areas nearby include Drekagil canyon, Holuhraun (created in the 2014–15 eruption) and the green area of Herðubreiðalindir.

Kverkfjöll

On the northeastern border of Vatnajökull glacier lies the Kverkfjöll mountain range, made up of active volcanoes in one of the country's most powerful high-temperature geothermal areas. Go there for hiking and glacial exploration tours. Accommodation can be booked in Sigurðarskáli.

Hveravellir

Situated between glaciers Langjökull and Hofsjökull, Hveravellir Nature Reserve is a geothermal oasis on highland route Kjölur. It has a service centre, campsite, indoor accommodation, hiking trails and a natural pool.

Laugarfell

Off the highland route across Sprengisandur lies Laugarfell, an oasis in the desert between Hofsjökull and Vatnajökull. The area has mountain huts open in summer, a natural geothermal pool for bathing, and bubbling hot springs.

Dimmuborgir

Wondrous Waterfalls

Kolufoss
Kolugljúfur canyon with stunning Kolufoss has become one of Northwest Iceland's most popular destinations and a viewing platform was recently built there. The falls are in Víðidalur valley, a five-minute drive from the Ring Rd.

Reykjafoss
This beautiful waterfall in Skagafjörður is relatively unknown, perhaps because it is hidden from view until you're standing right next to it. At Vindheimamelar, about 7km from Varmahlíð, there's a small parking area by the walking path that leads to the falls.

Falls in Skjálfandafljót
Goðafoss is right on the Ring Rd and well known. An even more picturesque waterfall in glacial river Skjálfandafljót is Aldeyjarfoss, framed by columnar basalt. In summer it can be reached in regular cars by Rte 842 through Bárðardalur.

Falls in Jökulsá á Fjöllum
Dettifoss is the most powerful waterfall in Europe and one of the highlights of the Diamond Circle. Further upstream is the prettier Selfoss. For a complete series of falls, walk to Hafragilsfoss, too. A path leads between the three waterfalls.

 Small-Town Surprises

Sjávarborg €€€
Upmarket dining at the harbour in Hvammstangi, with seafood and meat dishes and views over the water.

Hótel Norðurljós Restaurant €€
The restaurant at this welcoming Raufarhöfn hotel serves up fresh, impeccably prepared seafood dishes and soups, with ocean views.

Kverkfjöll

Sauðárkróksbakarí €
This historic bakery is a local favourite, with delectable pastries, sandwiches and warm drinks.

Grettis Cafe €
The warm welcome, cakes and rustic ambience of this no-frills cafe, plus the chance for a hot soak afterwards, make the drive from Sauðárkrókur worth it.

 Soaking & Swimming

GeoSea Geothermal Sea Baths
These infinity pools in Húsavík offer views of Skjálfandi bay and the water contains mineral-rich seawater known to be good for the skin.

Hofsós Swimming Pool
This standard 25m lap pool could be anywhere, but it is elevated to new heights by its almost-infinity setting on a hillside overlooking Skagafjörður and the mountains beyond.

River Rafting

Viking Rafting & Bakkaflöt
These operators offer rafting tours on the glacial rivers of Skagafjörður: mellower for families and more extreme for adventurous types. There's also white-water kayaking.

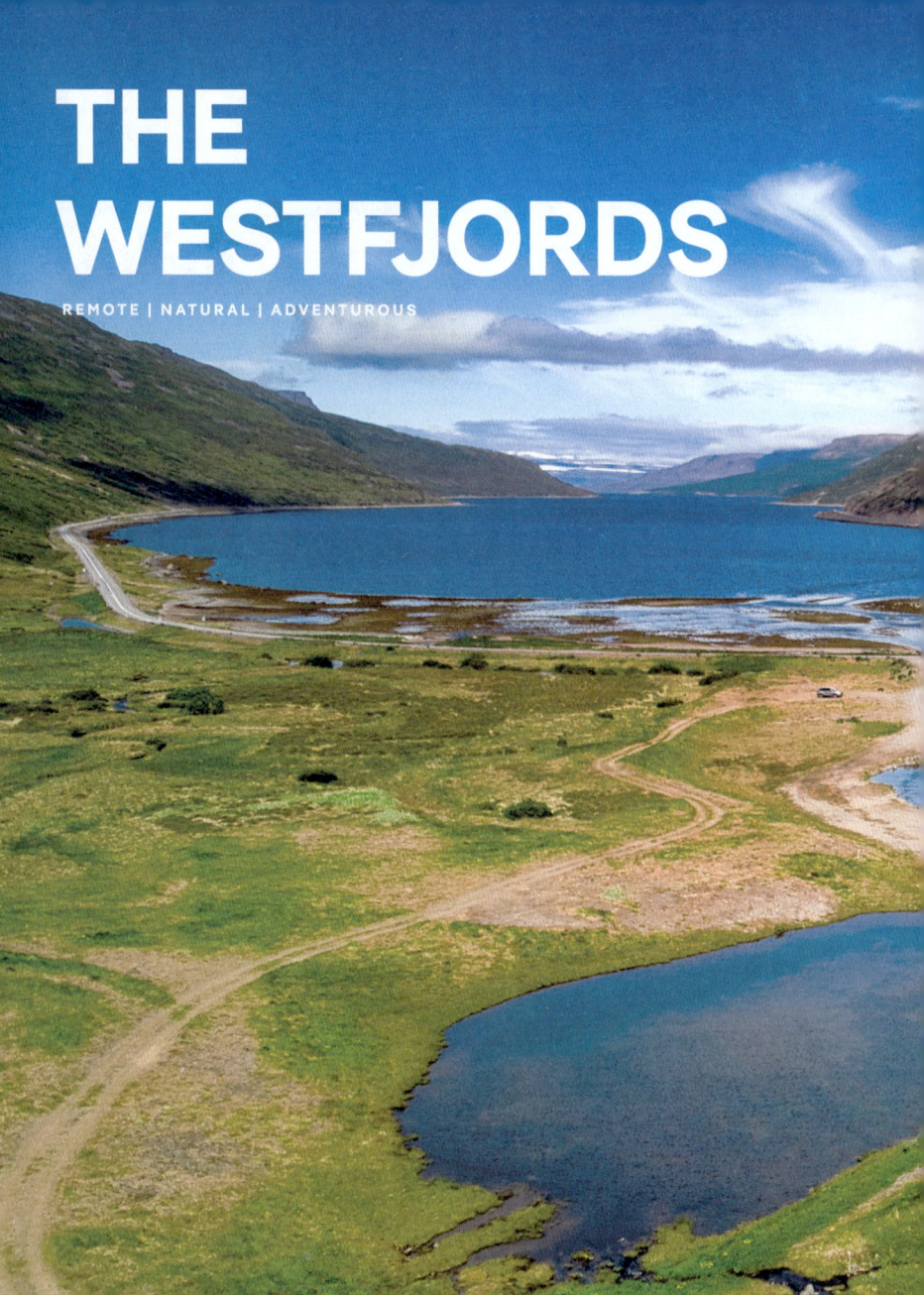

THE WESTFJORDS

REMOTE | NATURAL | ADVENTUROUS

- **Trip Builder** (p202)
- **Practicalities** (p204)
- **Westfjords on Water** (p206)
- **Westfjords Way of Life** (p208)
- **Road-Tripping Nirvana** (p210)
- **Fjords & Landscapes** (p212)
- **Hornstrandir Hikes** (p214)
- **Listings** (p216)

WESTFJORDS
Trip Builder

Fans of the outdoors are spoilt for choice in this Icelandic region, so allow enough time to take it all in. Roads in the remote Westfjords can be windy, bumpy and slow, but it's the journey that is part of the attraction. Mega tunnels, up to 9km long, make this untouched raw beauty easier to reach.

Observe puffins and other seabirds at one of Europe's largest bird cliffs, **Látrabjarg** (p212)
🚗 *3hrs from Ísafjörður*

Walk remote golden-red **Rauðasandur** beach (p212)
🚗 *2½hrs from Ísafjörður*

PREVIOUS SPREAD: PINYOLSTOCK/SHUTTERSTOCK
MENNO SCHAEFER/SHUTTERSTOCK, PALMI GUDMUNDSSON/SHUTTERSTOCK, , PEDRO CARRILHO/SHUTTERSTOCK, NICK FOX/SHUTTERSTOCK

- Join a seafood-themed walking tour through **Suðureyri** fishing village (p216)
  🚗 30min from Ísafjörður

- Challenge yourself with an adventure activity tour around **Ísafjörður** (p207)
  🚗 2¾hrs from Hólmavík

- Learn about the witch hunts of the Westfjords at Hólmavík's **Museum of Icelandic Sorcery & Witchcraft** (p217)
  🚗 2½hrs from Ísafjörður

- Learn about creatures of the deep at the **Icelandic Sea Monster Museum** (p209) in Bíldudalur
  🚗 2hrs from Ísafjörður

- Marvel at **Dynjandi**, the region's largest waterfall (p212)
  🚗 1hr from Ísafjörður

- Immerse yourself in the natural hot spring and pool in **Reykjafjörður** (p211)
  🚗 1½hrs from Ísafjörður

Practicalities

ARRIVING
Driving from Reykjavík to Ísafjörður is around 450km. For paved roads go via Hólmavík on the region's east coast, or via Dynjandi on partly gravel roads for the south. The ferry from Stykkishólmur to Brjánslækur is scenic, but won't save time. Carpool with samferda.is.

Flights from Reykjavík (see icelandair.com and norlandair.is) to Ísafjörður, Bíldudalur and Gjögur take 40 minutes. Bus journeys from Reykjavík (see westfjords.is) to Hólmavík and from Brjánslækur to Ísafjörður are infrequent and long.

HOW MUCH FOR A

Craft beer 600kr

Hot dog 500kr

Museum ticket from 1000kr

WHEN TO GO

NOV–MAR
Northern Lights, snowy landscapes, ski season December to April

APR–MAY
Cooler than summer, fewer visitors

JUN–AUG
Midnight sun for long days exploring, open attractions

SEP–OCT
Autumn colours, Northern Lights, some hotels and services closed

GETTING AROUND

Car Driving is the best way to get around to reach the more remote sights and attractions. Some roads are gravel. Check **online** (road.is) for information on road surfaces, conditions and weather, which can change at a moment's notice.

Bus Routes and connections exist but take time, plus many are infrequent and seasonal (see westfjords.is). Guided tours are possible from major towns to remote sites such as Látrabjarg for puffins and Rauðasandur for 10km of reddish beach (see wa.is).

Cycling Search **online** (cyclingiceland.is) and check out *The Biking Book of Iceland – Westfjords* by Ómar Smári Kristinsson. Bike hire is available in many towns. Plan your route, take emergency supplies and be prepared for changeable conditions.

EATING & DRINKING

This region has long survived through fishing – you'll find marine morsels on almost all restaurant menus. Cod and salmon (the latter is farmed here) are particularly prevalent, as is fish soup. Lamb and dairy are also everywhere. Protein-rich *skyr* yogurt is a great start to an adventurous day. Cafes and restaurants are few and far between. Pack a picnic if heading into the remote Westfjords.

Best craft beer Galdur Brewery *(galdurbrugghus.is/en)* in Holmavik serves witchcraft beer, made from Icelandic water.

Must-try restaurant Try the fish buffet at Tjöruhúsið *(facebook.com/Tjoruhusid)*, housed in a 1782 wooden building in Ísafjörður.

CONNECT & FIND YOUR WAY

Wi-fi Fast, free wi-fi is available at most accommodation and many bars, restaurants and tourist sites. Mobile coverage is good, but can be patchy in remoter areas.

Information There are a number of tourist information centres, including in Patreksfjörður, Þingeyri, Bolungarvík and Ísafjörður, but most have limited opening hours so check online first at westfjords.is.

WHERE TO STAY

Accommodation in the Westfjords is cheaper than in other parts of Iceland, on account of the area's remoteness, but book ahead in the summer months as towns have limited options.

Town	Pro/Con
Ísafjörður	Largest town in the Westfjords. Amenity-rich. Base for visiting the north.
Patreksfjörður	Base for visiting southern Westfjords. Hot pools.
Þingeyri	Village set on a spectacularly scenic fjord. Fewer services and accommodation options.
Hólmavík	Largest settlement in the Strandir region. Several guesthouses and good cafes.

HOT-POTS

The Westfjords have numerous stunning natural hot springs, many of which are open 24 hours and are entirely free to visit. Some have donation boxes to fund maintenance, so bring some coins.

MONEY

Almost everywhere accepts card/contactless payments. Car parks may require internet to use pay apps (these usually require a smartphone to scan a QR code).

32 Westfjords on WATER

ACTIVITIES | WILDLIFE | SEA

In a region strung together with fjords, you're never far from the sea. Exploring the Westfjords on the water offers a humbling sense of their grandeur. Kayaking, wildlife and whale-watching boat tours, sailing, diving and snorkelling are among the possibilities.

How To

When to go May to September is best for favourable weather and most tours, but check with operators as some run year-round with the right numbers.

Getting here Tour departure points include Ísafjörður, Ögur, Hólmavík, Heydalur and Norðurfjörður.

Tour tip Book tours at least a few weeks ahead in the summer months, as spaces are limited and fill up quickly.

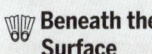

Top Kayaking, Ísafjörður
Bottom Sea urchin

Paddle the lengths of dramatic fjords and peninsulas for unforgettable panoramic views. **Tours** (adventures.is; 13,000–300,000kr per person) of different difficulty levels and lengths – from two hours to six days – are available. On your journey you might encounter seals, seabirds, dolphins and even whales. **Kayak** (westtours.is/kayaking, adult/child 16,000/12,000kr) around Ísafjörður on a half-day excursion paddling beneath the dramatic mountains or the seabird colony of Vigur, which is teeming with eider ducks, puffins and Arctic terns. Remote **Vigur** (vigurisland.com), situated in Ísafjarðardjúp, is a paradise for bird-watchers. The island is inhabited year-round by just one family, who harvest the island's eiderdown, used for luxury bedding and clothing, and run the accommodation and cafe housed in a wooden house from 1860. There are just two rooms with a kitchen for self-catering, and limited small-group camping with basic facilities, so this place doesn't get too crowded. Overnight stays certainly aren't cheap – especially for camping – but do include pick-up and drop-off to this unique location.

A range of whale species, including magnificent humpbacks, can be found in the waters off the Westfjord, including the waters near Hólmavík with **Láki Tours** (lakitours.com; adult/child 7-15/under-6s 12,000/6000kr/free). Whale- and bird-watching tours, including puffin tours to Grímsey island in Steingrímsfjörður, are available. Deep-sea angling trips, with cooking your catch encouraged, can also be booked from **Flateyri** (iceland protravel.com; eight-day fishing trips from 242,000kr).

Beneath the Surface

The water in the Westfjords is very clean. It's also colder year-round than in the rest of the country, but there's better visibility. The rich marine life of the area includes scallops, mussels, urchins, seals, diving birds (like guillemot and razorbill), coralline algae (often pink) and maerl. There are also kelp forests and whale bones on the ocean floor at a 19th-century Norwegian whaling site, plus shipwrecks to explore. It's a truly off-the-radar place to dive.

Erlendur Bogason from *Strýtan Dive Center, is a dive instructor and guide, who has explored some of the most remote and unusual dive sites in Iceland. He can take you on a customised dive to remember in the Westfjords if you book ahead.* @strytandivecenter

Westfjords Way of Life

FISHING CONTINUES TO DOMINATE LIFE IN RURAL VILLAGES

Iceland and fishing are inextricably linked, and the remote Westfjords produce around 36,000 tons of fish annually. You will see this all around: small boat harbours, seafood menus, fish drying racks, processing plants, open-sea fish farms, and even an old cemetery for French fishermen.

'When you travel to the Westfjords, you still really sense that it's bound to fisheries', says Dr Matthias Kokorsch, academic director of the Coastal Communities and Regional Development Master's programme at the University Centre of the Westfjords.

The rich fishing grounds have sustained rural communities here throughout history, but they have experienced difficult times over the past 25 years. 'Over the years, villages have lost fishing quotas and processing centres have been moved, so jobs have been lost', explains Matthias. The winter of 2019 was particularly tough, he says. There were avalanches and road closures, making it impossible for goods to be transported out. Avalanches in the village of Flateyri in January 2020 destroyed much of the fishing fleet. In 2023, the industry had further problems due to a severe infestation of sea lice in its salmon farms, resulting in the slaughter of thousands of fish. This affected the 2024 harvest and opened up debates on how to treat such infestations in the future.

Changing Demographics

Over the years, Westfjords communities, as with many other rural areas, have seen a downward population trend. 'It's really difficult to get young people to move back, especially when most of the opportunities are in fishing', says Matthias. Having said that, he remains optimistic for the future. 'Some places are actually seeing an increase and innovative projects are being realised. But I also think it's important to consider quality of life.'

Only around 10% of the tourists to Iceland visit the Westfjords. 'It's so tempting to just follow the Ring Rd. To

Left Ósvör Maritime Museum **Middle** Dried fish tails **Right** Icelandic Sea Monster Museum

get here, you have to deliberately go out of your way and you need time', explains Matthias. Tourists also mainly visit in the summer.

Creative Solutions

Although the economy has yet to really diversify beyond fishing, a number of creative projects aim to attract visitors and new residents to the region. Among them are innovation programmes, the international master's programmes in coastal studies, co-working spaces, art residencies, alternative high-school education programmes, and tourism initiatives like Suðureyri's **Seafood Trail** (fisherman.is). There's also sea-related innovation, such as Kerecis' tissue-transplant products made from fish skin. 'There's some work being done with seaweed', Matthias adds. Aquaculture has also grown rapidly in recent years, with fish farms now in several places. It's a contentious area due to concerns about potential environmental impacts. 'Aquaculture is a delicate topic. We must consider the environment, of course', Matthias says. 'On the issue of jobs, it's important to remember that even though it might not seem like many, in a small place like this, it can make a big difference.'

The state-run Regional Development Institute's Fragile Communities programme is among the innovation grants being offered to boost rural regions and halt depopulation. 'It just takes time,' Matthias comments.

> To get here, you have to deliberately go out of your way and you need time.

Learn More about Icelandic Fishing

There are plenty of places to delve further into the fishing history of the Westfjords. In Bolungarvík, the atmospheric **Ósvör Maritime Museum** (@ osvor_sjominjasafn; adult/under-16s 1700kr/free) displays a 19th-century replica fishing station, salt hut, fish-drying area and drying hut on the shore, plus old fishing gear. In Ísafjörður, located in a cluster of houses from the 18th century, the **Westfjords Heritage Museum** (nedsti.is; adult/child 1600kr/free) gives an insight into the rich culture of the area and the families who've lived here. Families should pit-stop in Bíldudalur for the terrific **Icelandic Sea Monster Museum** (skrimsll.is; adult/child 1500kr/free) for life-like monster recreations and creepy retellings of encounters through words, pictures and multimedia displays.

33 Road-Tripping NIRVANA

LANDSCAPES | HIKING | POOLS

The Westfjords Way (Vestfjarðaleiðin) is a scenic driving route (which can also be done on two wheels) that zigzags around beautiful fjords, dramatic landscapes, big mountain passes and long tunnels carved out of rock. It connects adventurous road-trippers to waterfalls, hot pools, expansive beaches and more, and is one of the best ways to see what the Westfjords has to offer.

How To

Getting here The beginning of the route is 111km from Reykjavík where you turn off the Ring Rd onto Vestfjarðavegur (Rd 60) towards Búðardalur and the Westfjords. To begin from the east and travel anticlockwise, continue on the Ring Rd, turning off onto Rd 68 just past the N1 petrol station at Staðarskáli.

When to go The route is open all year, but in winter some roads are not cleared of snow every day. The weather is unpredictable even in the summer, so follow forecasts and road conditions (see safetravel.is, road.is and vedur.is)

Left Switchback road on Bolafjall
Below Bathers in Hellulaug

Sensational Scenery

Take care not to get distracted: the dreamy landscapes here are gawk-worthy. Pull over if you want to snap a picture, but be sure it's in a space you can stop safely. Also be sure to allow enough time for your journey and factor in many stops. Shops and places to eat are very few and far between, so pack a picnic to enjoy the view. Among the many highlights is the view from the **Bolafjall platform** in Bolungarvík, made from 60 tonnes of steel. Drive to the top of the mountain for panoramic views of Ísafjarðardjúp and Jökulfirðir. Note that the road is typically only open in summer, from mid-June, when the snow has been plowed and will close around mid-September.

Hikers' Heaven

The region is a dream for nature enthusiasts, and you can easily add a few short hikes to your road trip. At 998m, **Kaldbakur** in the so-called Westfjords Alps is the tallest mountain in the region. The hike to its summit – which rewards you with views over Arnarfjörður and Dýrafjörður – takes around four hours, but you'll need a Jeep to reach the trailhead, which is 2km west of Þingeyri town.

While most views are of uninterrupted landscape in this sparsely populated region, those over the town of Ísafjörður and beyond are worth the steep climb. It takes roughly 30 minutes (and some strong quads) to climb to the superb giant crater-like **Naustahvilft** (the Troll Seat), from just northeast of Ísafjörður airport. For more information, check out vestfjarda leidin.is and @VisitWestfjords.

♨ Soaking It Up

What I love about the Westfjords is the emptiness and ruggedness – and there are so few people. It's like going back in time. There are also quite a few geothermal springs and pools. My favourite is **Hellulaug**. Taking a dip there is a good start or end to the long drive through the region. The water is also the perfect temperature. Another favourite is the pool and hot spring in **Reykjafjörður** near Bíldadalur. In the winter you can sit there in the hot water surrounded by snow and darkness.

Páll Stefánsson has been photographing Iceland for 40 years. He has published more than 35 books, is the recipient of numerous awards, and is a Sony Global Imaging Ambassador. He visits the Westfjords four to six times a year. @pallistef

FJORDS
& Landscapes

01 Rauðasandur (also spelt Rauðisandur)
Long golden-red beach home to birdlife and seals. Views of Snæfellsjökull to the south on a clear day.

02 Látrabjarg
Nesting puffins and other seabirds can be observed up close at the bird cliffs of Látrabjarg between May and August.

03 Reykjafjarðarlaug
Free swimming pool and natural hot spring in Reykjafjörður, with views of Arnarfjörður. Donations welcome.

04 Dynjandi
Known as the 'Jewel of the Westfjords, this waterfall drops 100m and has six other cascades below.

05 Dýrafjörður
Another truly breathtaking fjord. The harbour village of Þingeyri is located here.

06 Hringsdalur
Narrow, rough coastal road (Rte 619) that hugs the cliffside, and ventures past gorgeous white sandy beaches such as the one near Hringsdalur. Drivable in a regular car in summer, but only a 4WD in winter.

07 Önundarfjörður
Stunning fjord with steep cliffs and a golden-sand beach. The village of Flateyri, with its historical bookshop, is located here.

08 Valagil
Ravine created by layers of ancient lava with a towering waterfall at its centre; near Súðavík.

09 Vigur
Island in Ísafjarðardjúp with abundant seabirds. Reached by boat or kayak trip.

10 Grímsey
Another island rich in birdlife. Off Drangnes in Steingrímsfjörður. Scheduled boat trips are available.

11 Drangsnes Hot Pots
Hot tubs down at the shoreline in the town of Drangsnes with views into the fjord in front.

12 Krossneslaug
Shoreside geothermal pool at the end of the road on Strandir. Uninterrupted views of the North Atlantic.

13 Hornbjarg
Dramatic sea cliff and another popular bird-nesting area in remote Hornstrandir. Reached only by boat or multiday hike.

34 Hornstrandir HIKES

HIKING | TOURS | LANDSCAPES

Remote Hornstrandir has no roads, shops or permanent inhabitants, and can only be reached by boat or on foot. It also has limited phone connections and few marked hiking trails. But what it *does* have is remarkable hiking, tall bird cliffs, wildflowers and Arctic foxes. Our itinerary includes a 23km two-day guided hike from Hornvík to Veiðileysufjörður.

Trip Notes

Getting here The tour, guided by **Borea Adventures** *(borea.is; 125,000kr per person)*, leaves by boat from Ísafjörður.

When to go Early June to mid-September depending on weather.

Tour and ferry operators See westtours.is and hornstrandaferdir.is from Bolungarvík, and strandferdir.is from Norðurfjörður.

Safety Those embarking on unguided hiking should register a travel plan, bring GPS, compass and map, and consider a personal locator beacon (PLB; see safetravel.is).

Respecting Nature

Hornstrandir is a protected area, so stick to the hiking trails. The flora is delicate, and the wildlife needs to be left alone. Drones require a permit from the Environment Agency. You must take out everything that you bring into the area. Pitch your tent only at designated camping spots.

Ragúel Hagalínsson is a ranger and guide on Hornstrandir.

Listings

BEST OF THE REST

Backcountry Skiing

Borea Adventures

Traverse remote fjords for top skiing with panoramic views in Hornstrandir nature reserve, only reached by boat. Borea also runs tours from its ski lodge on Hornstrandir. If you've got the cash to splash, you won't want to miss this. Backcountry skiing tours with Borea are also available in the mountains around Ísafjörður.

Dalirnir Tveir

This ski resort, located 6km from Ísafjörður, is a more affordable option than a tour. Tungudalur has three lifts and 9km of slopes for beginners and advanced skiers. Seljalandsdalur is for cross-country skiing.

Adventure Tours

Cycling Westfjords

Mountain biking has a strong following, with paths for all difficulty levels. Cycling Westfjords runs private tours, or check out trails on the **Mountain Bike Ísafjörður** (mtbisafjordur.is) website. Bikes are available for rent at Borea Adventures, and they also offer guided cycling tours several times a week, suitable for beginners.

West Tours

The calm fjords make Ísafjörður and the wider Djúpið (shorthand for the fjord system known as Ísafjarðardjúp) especially popular for kayaking. Tours range from two hours to several days, sleeping on a remote beach somewhere in the company of seals and seabirds, where the mind switches gear and time spools slowly, one paddle at a time. West Tours also runs Hornstrandir history day trips, lasting about five hours between June and September, including ferry transfers.

Láki Tours

Whale-watching tours off the coast of Hólmavík offer the chance to see minke and pilot whales, white-beaked dolphins, and even orcas and sperm whales. Tours last roughly two to three hours. (lakitours.com)

Cultural & Artistic Discoveries

Seafood Trail

Guided walking tour in Suðureyri, with ultra-local craft-food tastings, while learning how the fishing industry has shaped the area and its people. (fisherman.is)

Aldrei fór ég suður

Held annually over Easter, the 'I never went south' music festival in Ísafjörður features home-grown Icelandic talent and attracts hundreds of people to town. (aldrei.is)

Jón Sigurðsson Museum

At Hrafnseyri in Arnarfjörður is a museum dedicated to the leader of Iceland's 19th-century independence movement, Jón

Sheep Farming Museum

Sigurðsson (1811–79). Enjoy coffee and waffles in the turf house, a replica of the home in which Jón grew up in on the farm. There's a special programme on 17 June, Iceland's National Day. (*hrafnseyri.is*)

Museum of Icelandic Sorcery & Witchcraft

Learn about the history of witch hunts in 17th-century Iceland at this museum in Hólmavík, and see the disturbing 'necropants', an old mystical practice that required making trousers from the skin of a dead man's legs and groin. (*galdrasyning.is*)

Sheep Farming Museum

Find out about traditional sheep farming in Iceland. Feed the lambs and check out the handicraft shop. Located 11km south of Hólmavík. (*saudfjarsetur.is*)

Factory

Check out the annual summer art exhibition in the old fish-oil factory in Djúpavík. The exhibition showcases local and international multidisciplinary artists. Djúpavík is a 75-minute (69km) drive on gravel road from Hólmavík, and a natural stop on the way to Krossneslaug. (*@thefactorydjupavik, djupavik.is*)

Samúel Jónsson's Art Museum

This colourful museum in Sélardalur overlooking Arnarfjörður consists mostly of quirky outdoor sculptures of people and animals, and a church built by artist Samúel Jónsson (1884–1969). It's a 40-minute (20km) drive on a rough gravel road from Bíldudalur.

Swims & Soaks

Krosslaug Hot Spring

The free rock-surrounded pool and a separate purpose-built pool on the coastline in Barðastrandarvegur, offer views over Breiðafjörður bay. (*sundlaugar.is*)

Pollurinn

Reykhólar Sea Baths

Soak in scenic, hot sea baths boosted with nurturing seaweed from Breiðafjörður bay. It also sells dry kelp powder, which can be used as a face mask or in your bath at home. (*sjavarsmidjan.is*)

Pollurinn

Another perfectly located set of hot tubs, this time in Tálknafjörður. As with many hot pools in the region, upkeep is funded through the visitor donation box. Respect the area, take all rubbish with you and leave the boombox at home.

Hellalaugur

Hellalaugur is distinctive for being right on the beach, offering a view of the freezing ocean while being shielded from the road. Hop in for a dip while watching the fjord waters. At high tide, do as the locals do and jump in the frigid sea, then run back to the big, toasty, rock hot pool (38°C) to warm up. About 500m east of Hótel Flókalundur on Rte 62.

WEST ICELAND

WINDSWEPT BEACHES | VOLCANIC TERRAIN | HISTORICAL VILLAGES

- **Trip Builder** (p220)
- **Practicalities** (p222)
- **Into the Earth** (p224)
- **On the Saga Trail** (p226)
- **Sagaland** (p228)
- **Wildlife of the West** (p230)
- **Hiking in the West** (p232)
- **Listings** (p234)

WEST ICELAND
Trip Builder

Often named 'Miniature Iceland', West Iceland is an impressive blend of Iceland's geographical features, but without the crowds. Snæfellsnes Peninsula is known for its glacier, while the area around its national park has terrific bird- and whale-watching, lava-field hikes and horse-riding opportunities. You'll also encounter lava tubes and remote highland glaciers, including enormous Langjökull with its unusual ice cave.

Wander past chocolate-box houses in the buzzy harbour town of **Stykkishólmur** (p223)
🚗 1¼hrs from Borgarnes

Wander crunchy lava fields in **Snæfellsjökull**, the icy heart of the West (p224)
🚗 2¼hrs from Borgarnes

Skarð

Stykkishólmur
Skjöldur
Hellissandur Búlandshöfði Vatnaleið
Ólafsvík Grundarfjörður
Vegamót
Búðir
Arnarstapi Hafffjörður

Go on a Jules Verne–style adventure, descending deep into a lava tube at **Vatnshellir** (p225)
🚗 2½hrs from Borgarnes

Garður

Bathe in **Guðrúnarlaug hot tub** (p227), which resembles the pool used by saga heroine Guðrún Ósvífursdóttir
🚗 1¼hrs from Borgarnes

Get cosy by the long-fire in **Eiríksstaðir** (p227), a longhouse replica in Haukadalur
🚗 1hr from Borgarnes

Learn about famous settler, Egil Skallagrímsson, at the **Settlement Centre** (p227)
🚗 1¼hrs from Reykjavík

In winter, explore Iceland's second-largest ice cap, **Langjökull** (p97), on a snowmobile
🚗 1¼hrs from Borgarnes

Hike out to Iceland's second-tallest waterfall, **Glymur** (p233), crashing down for 198m
🚗 1hr from Borgarnes

Practicalities

ARRIVING

It takes just over an hour to drive from Reykjavík to Borgarnes by car and an extra half hour to Keflavík International Airport. This is the quickest and most convenient route to the west, and the easiest way to explore the region. Bus 57 also goes from Reykjavík to Akureyri and runs through Borgarnes, Bifröst and Staðarskáli. Many routes to other villages can be picked up from Borgarnes. Check the **Strætó** *(straeto.is)* website for connections.

HOW MUCH FOR A

Burger 400kr

Hot-pot soak free

Adventure tour from 6000kr

GETTING AROUND

Car Roads are mostly excellent and easy to navigate in Western Iceland. The rugged dirt roads are few, with only a handful of F-roads off-limits to 2WDs. Most villages have petrol stations.

Bus Buses serve the region's main villages. From Borgarnes, you can reach many destinations in the West using local Strætó buses. Reykjavík to Akureyri routes run through Borgarnes, Bifröst and Staðarskáli, so it's simple to continue onwards towards the north.

WHEN TO GO

NOV–MAR
Long nights with likely Northern Lights viewings and ice activities.

APR–MAY
Iceland awakes from winter. Mountain roads become passable. Puffins arrive in May.

JUN–AUG
Almost endless daylight. All summer activities are open. This is hiking season.

SEP–OCT
Tourist season begins to wind down. The weather becomes breezier.

Ferry Baldur Car Ferry connects Stykkishólmur on Snæfellsnes Peninsula and Brjánslækur in the Westfjords, via Flatey Island. There's a ferry office in Stykkishólmur, but it's best to book ahead online at ferja.is/en.

EATING & DRINKING

Seafood is one thing the area has in abundance, and it is a good bet anywhere. Shark meat was once also a staple, and can still be tried on the north coast at the Bjarnarhöfn Shark Museum (pictured top). Small farms in the West also raise free-roaming lamb, which is herb-fed and full of flavour. Dairy is another must – fill up on protein-rich creamy *skyr* yogurt and local cheeses.

Best place for *skyr* Erpsstaðir dairy farm (p234) fuses the yogurt with delicious praline chocolate.

Best for lamb Englendingavík (p235) serves superb roast lamb from a traditional Borgarnes house.

CONNECT & FIND YOUR WAY

Wi-fi Free and fast wi-fi is available at most accommodation places and many bars, restaurants and tourist sites.

Information The Visitor Center at Malarrif has maps on the area, trails and sites, plus nature displays, from the plant life to birds that can be spotted locally. There's also a good selection of books (on local trolls to monsters).

WHERE TO STAY

With fewer visitors, accommodation here is cheaper than in other parts of Iceland, but there's not much of it – book ahead.

Town	Pro/Con
Hellnar	Tiny fishing village on the south coast with a several accommodation options but few restaurants. Good for exploring lava tubes and coastal walks.
Stykkishólmur	Largest town on the Snæfellsnes Peninsula, with lots of options for all budgets, some in brightly coloured buildings. Very sleepy.
Borgarnes	Medium-sized town loaded with history and acting as a gateway to the West with handy transport links.
Grundarfjörður	Very scenic area, set on a dramatic bay with ice-capped peaks and some accommodation options. Limited entertainment.

ENTERTAINMENT

Evening entertainment is almost non-existent in the West, aside from nights at the **Freezer Hostel** (*thefreezerhostel.com*), which doubles as a theatre and live-music venue.

MONEY

Almost everywhere accepts card/contactless payments. Take coins for donations at hot-pots. For car parks, you may need internet to use pay apps (these usually require a smartphone to scan a QR code).

35 Into the EARTH

LAVA TUBES | CRATERS | VOLCANIC FIELDS

West Iceland is a hive of volcanic activity. The 700,000-year-old glacier-capped Snæfellsjökull is still considered active, despite its last eruption being around 1800 years ago. Surrounding it is a wonderland of peculiar rock formations, fields of lava, underground lava tubes, and craters to explore.

Trip Notes

Getting around It's best to rent a car at Keflavík International Airport or in Reykjavík. Infrequent **public buses** *(straeto.is)* run from Reykjavík to the region. For off-roading, opt for a high-clearance 4WD.

When to go Some volcanic attractions are only open in summer, and others only in winter.

Top tip Book lava-tube and glacial-summit **tours** *(summitguides.is, troll.is, thecave.is)* ahead of time – these can book out in peak months.

Journey to the Centre of the Earth

Snæfell features in Jules Verne's epic sci-fi adventure *Journey to the Centre of the Earth*, fusing fiction with Iceland's real-world geology. The volcano serves as the gateway to the subterranean world explored by Professor Otto Lidenbrock, who descends through a crater and enters the lava tubes and caves, and similar features can be explored by travellers today.

02 Ascend the **Snæfellsjökull** glacier with a local guide and experience a 1446m-high volcano completely covered in ice. Views are mesmerising from the summit.

05 Descend into **Viðgelmir**, one of the best-preserved lava-tube caves in Iceland, running 1.6km underground, with lava formations, stalactites and stalagmites.

03 Step inside an 8000-year-old lava tube, **Vatnshellir** that lies 32m below the earth's surface, visited by guided tour only.

01 Wander the magnificent **Djúpalónssandur** beach, where an ancient lava field meets the sea. Find jet-black sand, smooth pebbles, and dramatic rock formations, which have been moulded by the elements.

04 Climb 170m to the top of the ancient **Grábrók** volcanic crater and admire the view of the surrounding lava field, and cone-shaped mountain Baula.

36 On the Saga TRAIL

HISTORY | SAGAS | PIONEERS

West Iceland is where some of the most famous explorers and saga heroes lived. This is where their stories were told, retold and written down. This is where saga author Snorri Sturluson lived, worked and met his bitter end. When touring the Sagaland, pay close attention for their stories are inscribed on stones and echo among the mountains.

How To

Getting around It's best to hire a car at Keflavík International Airport or in Reykjavík. Infrequent **public buses** *(straeto.is)* run from Reykjavík to the region.

When to go Year-round, but some museums are only open in summer.

Top tip Download the Locatify SmartGuide app. The GPS navigation system will detect your location and provide you with insights into your surroundings – like a personal guide. You can also listen to it before you arrive.

Top Eiríksstaðir
Bottom Guðrúnarlaug

Living history Get cosy by the long-fire in **Eiríksstaðir** (eiriks stadir.is; adult/under-12s 2800kr/free), a longhouse replica in Haukadalur, and listen to storytellers clad in Viking clothing tell tales of the people who lived there. This is where Eiríkur rauði (Erik the Red) and his wife Þjóðhildur built their farm and founded their family.

Viking voyages Dedicated to explorers Eiríkur and his son Leifur Heppni ('the Lucky'), the **Leif Eiriksson Center** (vin landssetur.is; entry 3000kr) in Búðardalur traces the story of Grænlendinga Saga, documenting their exploration of Greenland and North America. According to the saga, Leifur arrived in America in the year 1000 – almost 500 years before Columbus.

Lethal love triangle Visit **Laugar** in Sælingsdalur, the lush countryside where the Laxdæla Saga took place. Bathe in **Guðrúnarlaug** (free), built to resemble the pool where heroine Guðrún Ósvífursdóttir soaked with her suitors, neither of whom foresaw the bloody end to their love story.

Skaldic warrior The **Settlement Centre** (krlandnam.is; adult/child 3700/1200kr) in Borgarnes is dedicated to Egill Skallagrímsson, a poet, warrior and one of the most colourful characters of the Icelandic sagas. The exhibition recounts the magical and mythical storyline of Egils Saga with displays and an audio guide. Another exhibition explains how the Norse explorers navigated across open ocean. In the centre's loft, storytelling events and monologues are held. The restaurant offers scrumptious classics such as lamb and fish stew, and is built into a rock face.

Snorri's Home

In **Snorrastofa** (snorra stofa.is; adult/child 1200kr/free), about 90 minutes north of Reykjavík, learn about the career and political influence of Snorri Sturluson, one of the most famous Icelanders who ever lived. Not only did Snorri have a strong impact on the political and cultural life in Iceland while he was alive, but his literary masterpieces – Snorra-Edda, Heimskringla and (most likely) Egils Saga – also continue to shape the culture and self-image of Icelanders and Nordic people. Snorri's pool has been maintained, along with part of the tunnel that connected it to his house, which are some of the oldest preserved structures in Iceland.

Sagaland

WHERE HISTORY WAS MADE

During the Commonwealth, West Iceland was the richest and most populated region in Iceland. Most of the Icelandic sagas were written in the region, including *Egils Saga*, *Sturlunga Saga*, *Laxdæla Saga* and *Eyrarbyggja Saga*, and many of the most powerful chieftains and notable characters lived here.

Left Snorrastofa, next to church
Middle 14th-century manuscript of Snorri Sturluson's *Snorra-Edda*
Right Sculptor Gustav Vigeland's statue of Snorri Sturluson

'It's the cradle of the country's literary tradition. There are many theories as to why that was. Writing manuscripts was expensive and this was the wealthiest region, maybe because of trade with Greenland, among other reasons', says Sigrún Þormar, service director at Snorrastofa. This cultural and medieval centre is based in Reykholt where Snorri Sturluson lived and worked in the 13th century.

Poetry, Fantasy & Adventure

'He wrote *Snorra-Edda*, poetry about Norse mythology, which has had a great influence on Western culture. It's everywhere. For example, the TV series *Vikings* and *Game of Thrones*, the *Lord of the Rings* trilogy and Marvel cartoons are all under the influence of Norse mythology,' says Sigrún. Snorri was a Christian, but he was interested in pre-Christian religion, myths, world view and poetry. '*Snorra-Edda* is really about fantasy and adventure', continues Sigrún. Snorri based his writing on older manuscripts, ancient poetry and oral stories about the gods, and his own imagination. 'Nobody had written anything like this before.'

Snorri also chronicled the history of the Norwegian kings in the so-called *Heimskringla* and most likely wrote *Egils Saga*, the first major Icelandic saga. 'It was probably the last book that he wrote. It was the biography of Egill Skallagrímsson who lived at Borg in Borgarnes, and he was one of the very few real Icelandic Vikings. Egill went to Norway and England for raids, and he was in the service of the English king as a soldier. But he always returned to Iceland to his farm. He was also a loving father and husband – and extremely ugly!' laughs Sigrún.

Pioneer & Businessman

Snorri had his own pool to bathe in, channelling water 120m from a nearby hot spring. 'Maybe he sat in his hot-pot in Reykholt, looked at the stars, Northern Lights and Milky Way and fantasised about the gods above', suggests Sigrún. The original pool has been maintained and part of the tunnel that connected it to the house. Snorri also heated one room with the steam from the hot spring, possibly for brewing or to use as a sauna. Around the house was a fort, for defence, and perhaps also to show off his wealth and power. 'The money came from the women he married. He knew how to pick them! But he was also a clever businessman.' Snorri received some additional financial support from his family. He financed his own book production and could therefore write what he wanted.

> History is all around... It's fascinating. It makes the story so real – because it's not just a story.

In Snorrastofa, visitors can learn about the life and work of Snorri Sturluson. History is all around, says Sigrún: 'I once went riding along Hvítá river, past a turf house that dates back to the 9th or 10th century.' Sources and archaeological evidence indicate that this was where Skallagrímur, Egill's father, first settled after arriving from Norway. 'It's so adventurous to ride past those remains and consider this was where Skallagrímur came with all his belongings, wife, children, slaves and farmhands after the king had killed his son', Sigrún says. 'It makes the story so real – because it's not just a story.'

Inspirational Characters

Auður djúpúðga (the 'deep-minded') was the only woman to lead a settlement expedition to Iceland. Escaping the escalating conflict in Britain, she settled in Hvammur in Dalir. Auður was a Christian and freed all her slaves.

Guðríður víðförla (the 'far-travelled') was among the first Icelandic settlers in Greenland and she later went on an expedition to North America where her son Snorri was born. Late in life, she went on a pilgrimage to Rome.

Geirmundur heljarskinn (the 'black-skinned') was described as 'the most noble of all settlers', yet his story is largely unknown. Author and scholar Bergsveinn Birgisson reasons that he was of Siberian descent and that he built an empire around walrus hunting.

WILDLIFE
of the West

01 Arctic foxes
Iceland's only native land mammal is known for its thick change-colour fur: white in winter and blue or brown the rest of the year.

02 Seals
Both harbour seals and grey seals can be seen off Ytri Tunga beach in the south. See them basking on rocks.

03 Puffins
Look out for these iconic birds around the Snæfellsnes Peninsula, particularly during the summer months (May to August) when they are breeding. They enjoy the basalt columns in Lóndrangar.

04 Whales
Orcas and sperm whales are regularly spotted off the coast. Tours depart from Ólafsvík, usually running from February to September.

05 Seabirds
Some 330 species of seabirds have been spotted in Icelandic waters. Guillemots, razorbills, fulmars, kittiwakes and shags are commonly seen at the Þúfubjarg Bird Cliffs.

06 Birds of prey
Keep eyes peeled for Iceland's national bird, the gyrfalcon, plus white-tailed eagles and merlin.

07 Porpoises
Shy and elusive, porpoises can be spotted in calm waters off the coast of the Snæfellsnes Peninsula, especially during summer.

37 Hiking in THE WEST

MOUNTAINS | FORESTS | WATERFALLS

West Iceland has an abundance of hiking opportunities without the crowds of the country's more famous trails. Here the intrepid can discover everything from lava fields and mountain vistas to green hills and forests, and glacial landscapes and waterfalls. Just pack for all seasons, as the weather can change quickly.

How To

Getting around Hire a car at Keflavík International Airport or in Reykjavík, or join a tour. Infrequent **public buses** (*straeto.is*) run from Reykjavík to the region.

When to go Summer and autumn are the best and safest seasons for hiking.

What to bring Warm and waterproof clothing, good hiking boots, lip balm and sunscreen, plus water and food for longer walks.

Top tip Wapp (*wapp.is*) is a free app with GPS tracks for hiking, detailed maps and other information.

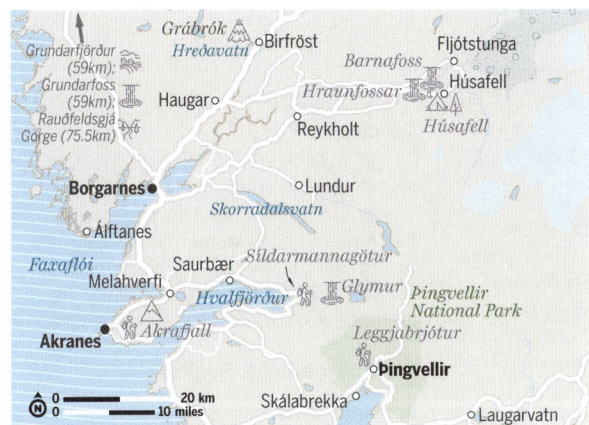

Top Rauðfeldsgjá Gorge
Bottom Hvalfjörður

Waterfalls & Wondrous Nature

Glymur The 198m Glymur waterfall in Hvalfjörður is Iceland's second highest. You'll go through a cave on the way up the steep path. For the best view, cross Botnsá river before moving up.
Distance 7km | Elevation 300m | Time 3hrs | Level Medium

Húsafell At the edge of Langjökull glacier lies the forested area of Húsafell, with a hotel, campsite and cottages. Find myriad marked hiking trails, of various lengths and levels, to natural attractions, such as the **Hraunfossar** and **Barnafoss** falls.

Grundarfoss East of Grundarfjörður, accessible from Road 54, is the mighty but lesser-visited Grundarfoss, a huge 70m cascade tumbling off mossy volcanic rock. It's a great flat hike for those who don't walk long distances.
Distance 3km | Elevation 50m | Time 40mins | Level Easy

Mountains & Canyons

Rauðfeldsgjá Gorge A terrific short hike, ideal for adventurous families, north of Arnarstapi and Stapafell, on Rte 574. A small track branches off to the stunning Rauðfeldsgjá, a steep, narrow cleft that mysteriously disappears into the cliff wall.
Distance 1km | Elevation 73m | Time 30mins | Level Easy/Medium

Akrafjall (643m) Head towards Akranes on Rd 51, but instead of driving into town, take a right and another right towards the mountain. From the top, there's a magnificent panoramic view.
Distance 5km | Elevation 500m | Time 3hrs | Level Medium

Ancient Routes

Síldarmannagötur connects Hvalfjörður and Skorradalur. The name comes from the time when herring was caught in Hvalfjörður. The route begins at a parking space in the innermost part of the fjord.
Distance 14km | Elevation 450m | Time 5hrs | Level Medium

Leggjabrjótur The name translates to 'leg breaker' but it's actually a pretty moderate hike. It leads from Hvalfjörður to the parliament in Þingvellir.
Distance 16km | Elevation 500m | Time 6hrs | Level Medium

Both routes lead from one area to another, so hikers will need someone to drop them off and pick them up.

Listings

BEST OF THE REST

Farm Visits & Family Fun

Hólar Petting Farm
Kids and adults alike delight in the close encounters with horses, dogs, rabbits, sheep and goats. The farm also has a cow and a pig, as well as some birds and even a raven! The locals show guests around the farm and introduce them to farm work. Open mid-June to mid-August.

Erpsstaðir
This dairy farm offers homemade ice cream, cheeses, *skyr* (a yogurt-like dessert) and *skyr* praline chocolates. You can also observe how the cows are milked by a robot and learn about milk production.

Bjarteyjarsandur
An authentic sheep farm with 600 sheep and other animals. Learn all about shearing, lambing and haymaking, and how farm work varies from season to season. In addition to free-range lamb, the farm produces free-range pork, poultry and organic vegetables.

Icelandic Goat Centre
Based at Háafell, the Icelandic Goat Centre was established to protect and maintain the Icelandic Settlement Goat – a special breed. Visit and pet the friendly goats; learn more about their qualities and goat-related products.

Sturlureykir Horse Farm
A horse-breeding farm with 60 horses, Sturlureykir offers horse-riding tours and stable visits. Meet the horses and learn more about the special Icelandic breed, including its five gaits. The farm has a hot spring where rye bread is baked.

Trollpark
Fossatún offers accommodation, a restaurant and an activity centre, and is located by the Tröllafoss falls. All around the park, find trolls that have turned to stone, at least according to proprietor Steinar Berg, who has written several books about them. Walk along the 'troll trail' and play 'troll games' in the park.

Swimming & Soaking

Borgarnes Swimming Pool
Right on Ring Rd 1, the geothermal pool in Borgarnes has great facilities for people who like to exercise, relax and play. It has a wading pool for kids and waterslides of various length – adults should also give them a try!

Akraneslaug & Guðlaug Baths
Jaðarsbakkalaug is a family-friendly 25m outdoor pool in Akranes with hot tubs, a steam bath and a waterslide. On Langisandur beach is the cleverly designed three-level Guðlaug Baths loved by sea swimmers and wonderful for relaxing. Entrance is free.

Guðlaug Baths

Lýsulaugar

This old country pool – which has been given a revamp – is filled with naturally hot mineral water rich in green algae and various minerals that are considered to have healing properties. From the pool, bathers can enjoy the view of Lýsuhyrna mountain.

Krauma

A mix of water from Deildartunguhver, Europe's most powerful hot spring, and glacial water is the recipe for a relaxing soak in Krauma. Additionally, it has a cold tub, two saunas and a relaxation room where guests can doze off by the fireplace to the sound of soothing music.

A Taste of West Iceland

Fjöruhúsið €
Renowned fish soup in a beautiful setting by the bird cliffs at the trailhead of the scenic Hellnar–Arnarstapi path.

Samkomuhúsið €€
Arnarstapi's tried-and-true old-school eatery for Icelandic specialities like lamb soup and fish and chips.

Sker Restaurant €€
Serves up reliable fish dishes, barbecue dishes and pasta in a cosy atmosphere in Ólafsvík.

Bjargarsteinn Mathús €€
Superb Grundarfjörður waterfront restaurant creating Icelandic dishes, with an emphasis on seafood and everything fresh.

Englendingavík €€
Casual, wonderful Borgarnes waterfront deck, serving tasty homemade dishes, from roast lamb to fresh fish.

Hotel Laxarárbakki Restaurant €€
In Akranes, at Hotel Laxarárbakki, with an emphasis on local produce and Icelandic classics including cod stew, meat soup, burgers and fish of the day.

Fjöruhúsið

Comfort Food in the West

Stapinn €
Laid-back Arnarstapi cafe serving burgers, fish and chips, vegetable soup and lamb soup, plus a selection of fried cheeses.

Kaffi 59 €
Cosy Grundarfjörður cafe serving burgers with patties made of local beef, plus pizzas, fish and chips, local lamb chops, and soup of the day.

Græna kompaníið €
A vegetarian Grundarfjörður coffee house serving soup of the day with vegan bread, plus cakes and coffee.

Valeria Coffee €
Who better than a friendly Colombian ex-pat and Icelandic partnership to import, roast and serve some of the best coffee in Iceland?

White Falcon Cafe €€
Inside the War & Peace Museum this is the place to try *kleinur* (Icelandic doughnuts) in a fun vintage setting. It also serves cakes, soups, tea, coffee and alcoholic drinks.

Practicalities

ARRIVING
238

GETTING AROUND
240

SAFE TRAVEL
242

MONEY
243

ACCOMMODATION
244

RESPONSIBLE TRAVEL
246

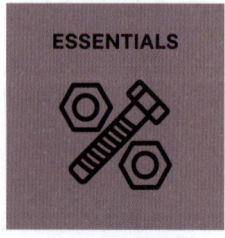
ESSENTIALS
248

LANGUAGE
250

Right Vatnajökull National Park (p138)

EASY STEPS FROM THE AIRPORT TO THE CITY CENTRE

Most travellers arrive in Iceland through Keflavík International Airport. It's approximately 50km from Reykjavík or a 45-minute drive. The airport is small and compact, with only one passenger terminal, but is being expanded. There are a variety of shops, restaurants and services, including ATMs and car-hire desks. There are also international flights into Akureyri Airport. Domestic flights go from Reykjavík Domestic Airport.

AT THE AIRPORT

SIM Cards
Tourists can purchase SIM cards in the convenience store in the arrivals hall. The largest telecom companies are Síminn, Vodafone and Nova, and SIM cards are also available in their shops. SIM cards from the EU/EEA work in Iceland.

International Currency Exchange
Available at the airport (look for the Change Group service desk), although note that the exchange rate is less favourable at the airport than in town.

Wi-fi
There is free, unlimited and open wi-fi at the airport (KEF FreeWifi), which reaches the taxi pick-up point but not the FlyBus departure point.

ATMs
The airport has ATMs scattered around the terminal, including several in the arrivals area.

Charging Stations
Available at numerous points around the airport.

CUSTOMS REGULATIONS
The maximum allowance of alcohol per person is six units (one unit is six large beers, one wine bottle or 0.25L of spirits) and one carton of cigarettes or 250g of other tobacco. Travellers may not import any meat and dairy products from outside the EEA. It is also prohibited to import used riding gear. For more, see skatturinn.is.

GETTING TO THE CITY CENTRE

Flybus *(re.is)* Offers airport transfers to central Reykjavík and some city-centre hotels in coordination with all flights. Tickets can be booked online (advance booking is recommended), together with any needed hotel connections. The pick-up points are outside the arrivals hall.

Public Buses Line 55, operated by **Strætó** *(straeto.is)*, runs throughout the day between Keflavík International Airport and Reykjavík's BSÍ bus terminal with a stop in Keflavík. Discounted tickets are available for children and seniors. The bus station is near the P1 parking area.

HOW MUCH FOR A

Taxi from 16,000kr — 45min

Airport transfer 3790kr — 45min

Public bus 2400kr — 75min

Taxi Taxis congregate outside the arrivals hall and can be booked on arrival or online in advance (try hreyfill.is). There are also apps *(hopp.bike/taxi)*.

Rental Cars & Domestic Flights

Several car-rental companies have service desks in the Keflavík International Airport arrivals hall. Reykjavík Domestic Airport (RKV), 45 minutes from Keflavík, is the hub for domestic travel. Flybus offers tickets (via a shuttle connection from BSÍ bus terminal) to RKV's Reykjavík terminal, from which Icelandair flies. Akureyri-based Norlandair also has a few flights from RKV. Find travel advice at visiticeland.com/plan-your-trip.

Plan Your Journey Useful contacts include Vedur (for weather), Straeto (for public buses), 112 Iceland (for emergencies), and road.is and safetravel.is for updated road conditions and volcanic activity.

OTHER POINTS OF ENTRY

Smyril Line Ferry Smyril Line's MS *Norröna* sails from Hirtshals (Denmark) to Seyðisfjörður in East Iceland via Tórshavn (Faroe Islands) from March to November. The journey takes from two to three days depending on the season and includes a stop of at least several hours in Tórshavn. For a family of four with one vehicle, a return trip costs from around 280,000kr, depending on what level of cabin accommodation you choose.

Akureyri Airport EasyJet (from London and seasonally from Manchester) and Edelweiss (seasonally from Zürich via Keflavík) have flights to/from Akureyri Airport, with more international connections planned. Icelandair (from Reykjavík) also services Akureyri Airport.

To/From Greenland Icelandair operates scheduled flights to destinations in west and south Greenland from Keflavík International Airport, while Norlandair flies to east Greenland from Akureyri Airport.

Cruise Ships Cruise lines sail to Iceland from Europe and North America, with Iceland ports of call including Reykjavík, Akureyri, Ísafjörður and Seyðisfjörður.

 **TRANSPORT TIPS TO HELP YOU GET AROUND**

The best way to explore Iceland is by car. Rentals and fuel are expensive, but a car allows you to travel at your own pace, make detours and visit more remote regions. It is also perfectly feasible to take a public bus between major hubs in each region and then arrange local tours from there. Domestic flights link major centres.

INSURANCE

Make sure you have insurance that covers damages to vehicles and personal injury from your insurance company or credit-card company at home. Car-rental companies offer additional insurance, including gravel protection.

CAR & CAMPERVAN HIRE

Car hire is available in larger towns, with the largest selections at Keflavík International Airport and in Reykjavík. Make sure your contract includes unlimited kilometres. Outside summer, it's best to hire a 4WD. If driving in the highlands, be sure the car is appropriately equipped.

AUTOMOBILE ASSOCIATIONS

FÍB *(Icelandic Automobile Association; fib.is/is/english)* is a non-profit NGO and a member of FIA, the worldwide organisation of touring clubs and automobile associations. Members are entitled to various benefits, such as emergency services, legal advice, and technical and travelling assistance.

CAR RENTAL PER DAY

 from 13,000kr

 Petrol approx 300kr/litre

 Charging station 30–70kr/min

DRIVING ESSENTIALS

 The speed limit is generally 90km/h on paved roads outside urban areas, 80km/h on gravel roads and 30km/h in towns.

 The car arriving first at single-lane bridges has the right of way. In single-lane tunnels, follow signs and use the pull-over spaces to your right.

 Slow down when crossing from paved roads to gravel to avoid skidding.

 The maximum legal blood-alcohol level for drivers is 0.02%.

 Watch out for sheep, birds and reindeer on the road.

Campsites

Many visitors to Iceland camp during the summer. There are campsites – for campervans as well as for tents – in practically every town and village, as well as in forests and national parks and near natural and historical sites. Most have excellent services and many have playgrounds. Visit tjalda.is for an overview.

FERRY
There are scheduled ferry services from Landeyjahöfn to Heimaey island (*Vestmannaeyjar; herjolfur.is/en*); from Reykjavík to Viðey island (*elding.is*); from Stykkishólmur to Brjánslækur in the Westfjords via Flatey island (*ferja.is/en*); from Dalvík to Grímsey island (*vegagerdin.is*); from Árskógssandur to Hrísey island (*vegagerdin.is*); and, from Neskaupstaður to Mjóifjörður (winter only; call 849 4797 or 849 4700).

PLANE
Icelandair flies from Reykjavík Domestic Airport to Akureyri, Ísafjörður, Egilsstaðir and Vestmannaeyjar. From Akureyri, there are connections on Norlandair to Grímsey, Þórshöfn and Vopnafjörður.

BUS
Strætó (*straeto.is*) has daily connections between Reykjavík and Akureyri with stops in main towns along the way and less frequent services to other areas. Pay fares with cash or card in the countryside. In Reykjavík, pay with card or the Klappið app.

KNOW YOUR CARBON FOOTPRINT
The **Iceland Carbon Fund** (*ICF; kolvidur.is*) offers carbon offsets through tree planting. Find their carbon calculator (*reiknivél*) online. As an example, one adult who travels three hours both ways by air would plant five trees. You can also support positive climate action through **Icelandair** (*icelandair.climate.site*).

ROAD DISTANCE CHART (KM)

	Reykjavík	Egilsstaðir	Ísafjörður	Blönduós	Selfoss	Húsavík	Stykkishólmur	Höfn	Vík	Akureyri
Reykjavík	–									
Egilsstaðir	636	–								
Ísafjörður	455	804	–							
Blönduós	244	391	412	–						
Selfoss	56	577	495	285	–					
Húsavík	463	219	631	219	503	–				
Stykkishólmur	172	600	152	209	213	430	–			
Höfn	456	254	895	576	400	404	613	–		
Vík	184	517	623	413	130	632	342	272	–	
Akureyri	388	248	558	144	428	75	353	502	556	–

ROAD CONDITIONS
Iceland's Ring Rd and most main roads are paved. On gravel roads, it is necessary to slow down. Also note that many gravel roads don't have winter service. F-roads are for larger 4WD vehicles in summer only. (*safetravel.is, road.is*)

DANGERS, ANNOYANCES & SAFETY

The weather is the biggest safety hazard for travellers in Iceland. It can be unpredictable, especially in winter, with high winds a particular risk. Remember to check the forecast and road conditions regularly and take weather warnings seriously.

SNOW & STORMS
Weather warnings are regularly issued because of gale-force winds. These are especially common in autumn and winter, but can occur in all seasons and are particularly hazardous when combined with snowfall. Blizzards block the visibility of drivers and make roads impassable, especially across mountain passes.

AVALANCHES, LANDSLIDES & ROCKFALL
In mountainous areas, certain weather conditions create a risk of avalanches, landslides and rockfall, sometimes causing damage or even fatalities. Barriers protect parts of roads and inhabited areas but pay attention to danger alerts and carry avalanche safety gear when skiing off-piste.

VOLCANIC & GEOTHERMAL ACTIVITY
Iceland has over 100 volcanoes, including several dozen that are active. Usually, eruptions occur outside inhabited areas and people are not in danger. While seismic activity is common, major earthquakes are rare. At geothermal areas, take care around hot springs and mud pools, and stay on defined paths to avoid suffering serious burns.

SAFETY OUTDOORS
When hiking, leave a travel plan or rent a personal locator beacon (PLB; see safetravel.is). Check the weather forecast. Bring suitable clothing, safety equipment, and a map, compass and GPS. In case of emergency, call 112.

SAFETRAVEL.IS
Run by the Icelandic Association for Search and Rescue, this site contains necessary information for travellers, including updates on weather and road conditions. Sign up for SMS updates and download the safety app **112 Iceland** *(112.is)*.

PERSONAL SAFETY
Iceland is one of the world's safest countries, with comparatively few violent crimes and murders. However, theft, sexual assaults and car accidents do sometimes occur. Use common sense and don't leave your drink unattended.

INSURANCE
Travellers from the European Economic Area should bring their EHIC card to be entitled to healthcare. Travellers from outside the EEA will need to pay for medical assistance in full and can seek reimbursement afterwards.

QUICK TIPS TO HELP YOU MANAGE YOUR MONEY

CREDIT CARDS
These are widely accepted and often preferred to cash. However, occasionally cash is necessary; for example, at public toilets or natural pools where bathers are asked to put money in a box for upkeep. There are ATMs in all towns. Visa and MasterCard are the most widely accepted cards. Travel money cards like Revolut and Wise are another option.

CURRENCY
Icelandic króna

HOW MUCH FOR A

Cappuccino 700kr

Pint of beer 1500kr

Dinner for two 16,000kr

BANKS & ATMS
Major banks have branches and ATMs in larger towns. Smaller towns have none but are usually fairly close to larger hubs.

VAT REFUNDS
Those with permanent residency outside Iceland may be refunded the VAT on purchases made in Iceland. Ask for a form at the counter and claim your VAT refund at the airport.

MONEY CHANGERS
Changing foreign currency is usually no problem at banks in Iceland and at the airport. Banks in towns are open weekdays from 9am to 4pm.

PAYING THE BILL
It's common to pay your bill at the counter in cafes, bars and restaurants, even when they offer table service.

TIPPING
Completely optional. The total on your bill is all you need to pay and you're not expected to tip your taxi driver or guide.

ON A BUDGET
Iceland is expensive, and to some people, shockingly so. If you're travelling on a budget, camping is an option, costing from about 1500kr to 3000kr per adult per night. The price for a dorm bed at a hostel is from about 6500kr. Hiking and DIY nature exploration are free. Buy your food at supermarkets and drink tap water. Admission to swimming pools costs approximately 1300kr per adult (multi-visit passes are often available) and to heritage museums about 2000kr per adult.

DISCOUNTS & SAVINGS
Most sights, activities and public-transport services are offered at reduced rates (or free) to seniors and young children, and accommodation is usually discounted for children. Useful passes and discount cards include the **Reykjavík Culture Card** (reykjavik.is), the Camping Card (p175) and the **Fishing Card** (vefverslun.veidikortid.is/product/fishingcard).

UNIQUE & LOCAL WAYS TO STAY

Sleeping outside in Iceland is a special experience – but it's not for everyone. From modest tents to caravans, glamping, cottages, farmstays and luxury lodges, Iceland has a range of options for an enjoyable holiday. In towns and villages, choose between classic hotels and guesthouses, self-service apartments, special-themed and boutique accommodation.

HOW MUCH FOR A NIGHT IN A
- Campsite from 1500kr per person
- Cottage 30,000kr
- Luxury lodge 60,000kr

NATURE RESERVES & NATIONAL PARKS

Experience nature with all your senses. Crawl into your sleeping bag, listen to the rustling stream and tweeting birds, and smell the wild vegetation. Prepare for bright but cool nights and bring thermal underclothes and a sleeping mask. Find epic hiking trails in Ásbyrgi, Vesturdalur and Skaftafell; historical sites at Þingvellir National Park; and geothermal wonders at Landmannalaugar. All campsites have good facilities. Prices average from 1500kr to 3000kr per adult per night. Note that biting midges can be a nuisance in South, West and North Iceland.

GLAMPING

The 'glamorous camping' hype has caught on in Iceland, too. There are igloos, domes and bubbles, luxury tents and Mongolian-style yurts in various secluded locations in South and North Iceland, adding more comfort and elegance to the camping experience. Prices vary, with one night for two people generally ranging from 20,000kr to 55,000kr.

CAMPERVANS

Campervans are increasingly popular. They often don't cost much more than a hire car and allow for flexibility, with some also suited for highland roads. They generally seat and sleep from two to five people, with average daily prices ranging from 20,000kr to 30,000kr. Campervan rentals are available at Keflavík International Airport and in Reykjavík, among other places.

FARMSTAY

Farmers all around Iceland welcome visitors to their homes. Accommodation is offered in cottages, farmhouses or even renovated stables and barns. The level of service and experience varies. Visitors are invited to observe or take part in farm work, pet the animals, go horse riding and taste food produced at the farm. The **Wilderness Centre** (wilderness.is) at the edge of the eastern highlands takes its guests on a journey through the past, as they can sleep in a 'museum'. Prices vary, but a double room at a farm usually costs from about 30,000kr per night.

SUMARBÚSTAÐUR

Icelanders love their *sumarbústaðir* (country cottages), preferably close enough to home so that they can go there on weekend breaks in all seasons. There they enjoy the peaceful countryside, sunbathe, pick wild berries and relax with a beer in their hot tub under the stars. Many families own a cottage, but they can also be rented from labour unions. Travellers can rent them, too, and experience a true Icelandic-style holiday. Prices vary greatly, but cottages are usually an affordable option for groups. For a twist on the *sumarbústaður* experience, try the huts in **Mjóeyri** (mjoeyri.is), 'beer barrels' in **Vestmannaeyjar** (glampingandcamping.is) or camping pods in **Fossatún** (fossatun.is/camping-pods).

BOOKING

Book well in advance for the peak tourist season in summer and around the Christmas to New Year holiday period.

Bungalo (bungalo.com) Cottage rentals in Iceland. Great for groups.
Hey Iceland (heyiceland.is) Countryside accommodation and adventure tours.
Tjalda (tjalda.is) Provides an overview of campgrounds in Iceland. Pre-booking isn't necessary.

HOSTELS

Operating 29 hostels around the country, **HI Iceland** (hostel.is) is one way of stretching your accommodation budget further. Prices for a dorm bed start at about 6500kr per night and for a private room from about 13,000kr. In addition to HI-operated hostels, there are also private hostels, including KEX Hostel in an old biscuit factory in Reykjavík and Akureyri's Hafnarstræti Hostel, which offers capsule sleeping pods in mixed dorm areas.

VAKINN

The official quality and environmental certification for Icelandic tourism, Vakinn offers certification for accommodation categories and star ratings for hotels. Criteria focus on access, environment, security, shared areas, room facilities, cleanliness, service, education and staff training.

POSITIVE-IMPACT TRAVEL

Tips to leave a lighter footprint, support local and have a positive impact on local communities.

ON THE ROAD

Minimise your carbon footprint. Hire electric or hybrid cars; there are charging stations around the country.

Public buses are generally more eco-friendly than private vehicles and often run on green energy. For carpooling, check samferda.is.

In Reykjavík you can hire a bike, e-bike or e-scooter.

Look out for the green Vakinn logo, the Nordic Swan logo and the European Environmental Label.

Leave no trace. Don't leave waste behind, don't removing anything from nature and use designated bathrooms.

Flying drones is forbidden in national parks. It can disturb wildlife and spoil the experience for others. The same applies to loud music.

Reusable bags, cups and cutlery make a handy eco-friendly travel kit. Bring your own bottle for tap water.

Infectious diseases can be transferred to Icelandic wildlife; for example, via used angling or riding clothes, which must be disinfected prior to arrival. *(mast.is)*

GIVE BACK

Volunteer with the **Iceland Conservation Volunteers** *(facebook.com/ICV.is)*, **Thórsmörk Trail Volunteers** *(trailteam.is)*, **Worldwide Friends** *(wf.is)* or **SEEDS** *(seeds.is)*, if you have time. But make sure that you are volunteering for a non-profit; see volunteering.is.

Plogging (called *plokka* in Iceland) is picking up rubbish while exercising. It's a good habit and more and more people are doing it, including tourists.

Eliminate food waste. Head-to-tail cooking is catching on in Iceland. Look out for dishes at restaurants that strive to make use of food that would otherwise have gone to waste.

Make a donation to **Landvernd** *(landvernd.is)*, Iceland's leading environmental NGO, or the **Icelandic Association for Search and Rescue** *(ICE-SAR; icesar.com)*, a non-profit, non-commercial, volunteer-based organisation.

DOS & DON'TS

Don't drive off-road, stray from marked trails, walk across sensitive vegetation or camp outside designated areas.

Do close all gates behind you. Otherwise farm animals might escape and get hurt in traffic, and cause damages to vehicles and injuries to people.

Don't attempt to pet or feed animals, wild or domestic, unless given permission.

LEAVE A SMALL FOOTPRINT

Build your own base camp. Consider picking a specific region to explore. Book a cottage or camp at a campground in your region of choice, and go on hikes and tours from there. Eat and shop locally.

When booking tours, consider the carbon footprint of horse riding, biking, hiking, skiing and kayaking compared to tours using motorised vehicles.

Take the Icelandic Pledge (pledge.visiticeland.com) before travelling and implement it while on the road.

SUPPORT LOCAL

Support local businesses in small towns by booking accommodation and tours run by locals, and buying products and handicrafts from the area.

Eat locally. Minimise your carbon footprint by eating as locally as possible. On **Slow Food Iceland** (slowfood.is/slow-food-guide) get tips on where to find good local food across the country.

CLIMATE CHANGE & TRAVEL

It's impossible to ignore the impact we have when travelling, and the importance of making changes where we can. Lonely Planet urges all travellers to engage with their travel carbon footprint. There are many carbon calculators online that allow travellers to estimate the carbon emissions generated by their journey; try *resurgence.org/resources/carbon-calculator.html*. Many airlines and booking sites offer travellers the option of offsetting the impact of greenhouse gas emissions by contributing to climate-friendly initiatives around the world. We continue to offset the carbon footprint of all Lonely Planet staff travel, while recognising this is a mitigation more than a solution.

RESOURCES
- landvernd.is/en
- pledge.visiticeland.com
- vakinn.is/en
- plantatreeiniceland.is
- hostel.is/en/moya/page/travel-slow

ESSENTIAL NUTS & BOLTS

POOL RULES
Everyone must shower and wash with soap without their swimsuits before entering the pool area (posters show the correct procedure; for more, see p106).

SHOES OFF
Remove your shoes before entering someone's home. For other buildings, best practice is to check whether there's a shoe rack in the entryway.

SMOKING
Smoking is forbidden inside public buildings; on rare occasions you may find designated, closed-off smoking areas.

FAST FACTS

Time Zone
GMT

Country Code
+354

Electricity
220V/50Hz

GOOD TO KNOW

Citizens from many countries do not need a visa to enter Iceland. Check your nationality online at utl.is.

Stay on the right when driving, cycling and standing on escalators.

The legal drinking age is 20 years. Alcohol is sold at state-run shops called Vínbúð.

Non-Icelandic residents are entitled to a VAT refund on purchases of more than 6000kr at a single point of sale (p243).

ACCESSIBLE TRAVEL

Iceland has made major strides in recent years to improve accessibility.

Hotels – mainly newer ones – often have wheelchair-friendly rooms (book in advance), accessible bathrooms and wheelchair ramps (thanks to the Ramp Up Iceland initiative).

Restaurants increasingly offer accessible dining, especially in larger towns, although accessibility can be tricky in rural areas.

Public buses in Reykjavík are wheelchair accessible, but users have to enter and exit the bus on their own. Buses outside Reykjavík are not as accessible. Blind travellers ride for free in the capital area.

Major natural attractions, like the Golden Circle, are wheelchair accessible. Consult with a specialist travel agent, such as **Iceland Unlimited** (icelandunlimited.is). For wheelchair-adapted transport contact **Stólabílar** (stolabilar.is) or **Hreyfill Taxi** (hreyfill.is).

Sjálfsbjörg – The **National Confederation of Physically Disabled People** (sjalfsbjorg.is) provides information and short-term mobility-equipment rental. Their accessibility list is in Icelandic, but they are helpful in responding to accessibility-related questions in English.

Accessibility information Check wheeltheworld.com and the Iceland pages on curbfreewithcorylee.com and wheelchairtraveling.com.

NO HONORIFICS
In Iceland everyone is on a first-name basis. Honorifics are hardly ever used.

GREETINGS
Shaking hands is the go-to greeting in Iceland. Friends (and very friendly strangers) hug. Kisses are for family.

BREASTFEEDING
Permitted in public and considered a natural thing. Mothers rarely cover up when feeding their babies.

FAMILY TRAVEL

Restaurants and cafes generally welcome families, offering high chairs and children's menus, child-friendly food like hot dogs and chicken nuggets, and sometimes even toys or children's corners.

Admission to museums, tours and swimming pools is usually free for children under six and discounted (often to 50% or more) for older children. Most hotels and campsites have child rates.

Child seats are often available in taxis, but should be ordered beforehand. Most car-hire companies rent child car seats.

GEOTHERMAL WATER
Geothermal water is used for heating in most regions. Icelanders like their homes toasty and take long showers. However, in some parts of the country, especially the East and Westfjords, the water is heated with electricity and visitors are encouraged to keep their showers short.

RELIGION
- Most Icelanders (just under 60%) are members of the Lutheran State Church.
- Another 10% are registered in other Christian denominations, including the Free Church of Iceland and the Roman Catholic Church.
- About 1.5% of Icelanders practise *ásatrú*, the traditional Norse religion.

LGBTIQ+ TRAVELLERS

Iceland is progressive when it comes equality and non-discrimination and is considered to be one of the most LGBTIQ+ friendly countries in the world.

Reykjavík has the largest gay and lesbian scene and Reykjavík Pride in early August is one of Iceland's most attended festivals. For a night on the town, head to Kiki. **Samtökin '78** *(samtokin78.is)* is the national queer organisation, with counselling and support groups and other programmes.

Pink Iceland specialises in gay wedding, travel and event management.

For tips and news, follow gayice.is and gayiceland.is.

LANGUAGE

Icelandic belongs to the Germanic language family, which includes German, English, Dutch and all the Scandinavian languages except Finnish. It's related to Old Norse, and retains the letters 'eth' (*ð*) and 'thorn' (*þ*), which also existed in Old English. Be aware, especially when you're trying to read bus timetables or road signs, that place names can be spelled in several different ways due to Icelandic grammar rules.

Most Icelanders speak English, so you'll have no problems if you don't know any Icelandic. However, any attempts to speak the local language will be much appreciated.

BASICS

Hello.	Halló.	*ha·loh*
Goodbye.	Bless.	*bles*
Yes.	Já.	*yow*
No.	Nei.	*nay*
Thank you	Takk./Takk fyrir.	*tak/tak fi·ri*
Excuse me.	Afsakið.	*af·sa·kidh*
Sorry.	Fyrirgefðu.	*fi·rir·gev·dhu*

What's your name?
Hvað heitir þú?   *kvadh hay·tir thoo*

My name is ...
Ég heiti ....   *yekh hay·ti ...*

Do you speak English?
Talarðu ensku?   *ta·lar dhoo ens·ku*

I don't understand.
Ég skil ekki.   *yekh skil e·ki*

DIRECTIONS & NUMBERS

Where's the (hotel)?
Hvar er (hótelið)?   *kvar er (hoh·te·lidh)*

Can you show me...?
Geturðu sýnt mér ...?   *ge·tur·dhu seent myer...?*

Is this the ...	Er þetta ...	*er the·ta ...*
to...?	til...?	*til...*
boat	ferjan	*fer·yan*
bus	rútan	*roo·tan*

I'm lost.
Ég er villtur/villt. (m/f)   *yekh er vil·tur/vilt*

1	einn	*aydn*	6	sex	*seks*
2	tveir	*tvayr*	7	sjö	*syeu*
3	þrír	*threer*	8	átta	*ow·ta*
4	fjórir	*fyoh·rir*	9	níu	*nee·u*
5	fimm	*fim*	10	tíu	*tee·u*

EMERGENCIES

Help!	Hjálp!	*hyowlp*
Call ...!	Hringdu á ...!	*hring·du ow ...*
a doctor	lækni	*laik·ni*
the police	lögregluna	*leukh·rekh·lu·na*

Where are the toilets?
Hvar er snyrtingin?   *kvar er snir·tin·gin*

Index

1238: The Battle of Iceland 189

A
accessible travel 248
accommodation 244-5, *see also individual regions*
  travel seasons 27
activities 6-25, 26-33, 96-7
air travel 241
airports 135, 238
AK Extreme 32
Akrafjall 233
Akranes 43, 234, 235
Akureyri 37, 158-69, **160**
  accommodation 161
  drinking 161, 168
  festivals 189
  food 161, 168
  hiking 169
  itineraries 160
  money 161
  navigation 161
  shopping 168
  travel seasons 161
  travel to Akureyri 161
  travel within Akureyri 161
Aldrei fór ég suður 32
Álfaborg 155
Almannagjá 89
alphabet 44
animals, *see individual species*
Annual Sheep & Horse Round-Ups 40
apps 239
Arctic Coast Way 182-3

000 Map pages

arctic foxes 230
Arctic Henge 176
arctic terns 187
arts 8-9
Ásbyrgi 189
Askja 198
astronomy 180-1
ATMs 238
automobile associations 240
avalanches 242

Æ
Ægissíða 79

B
Bæjarstaðarskógur Forest 141
Bakkafjörður 183
Bárðarbunga 113
beaches
  Djúpalónssandur 225
  Dyrhólaey 125
  Fjallahöfn 183
  Furðustrandir 177
  Grímsstaðavör 79
  Langisandur 234
  Nauthólsvík Geothermal Beach 83
  Önundarfjörður 213
  Rauðasandur 212
  Reynisfjara 125
beer 66-7, 80
Beluga Whale Sanctuary 117
berries 27, 58
Bifröst 181
bird-watching, *see also* puffins
  Hornvík 215
Hrísey 193

Húsavík 185
Ingólfshöfði 138
Langanes Peninsula 183
birds 89, 207, 231, *see also individual species*
Björk 46
Bláhnúkur 129
Blönduós 182, 189
boat trips 116-17, 143, 192-3, 241
books 46, 91, 197, 223, 234
border crossings 248
Borgarfjörður 43
Borgarfjörður Eystri 154-5
Borgarnes 223
Borgarvirki 177
breastfeeding 249
Breiðamerkurjökull 139
Brennisteinsalda 129
Brennivín 59
breweries 66-7, 80, 130
Bridge Between Two Continents 115
Brimketill 115
budgeting 19, 239, 240, 243, 244
bus travel 241

C
campervans 244
camping 23, 99, 127, 207, 244, 246
Cape Ingólfshöfði 138
car travel 18
  hire 239
  road rules 240
carbon footprints 247
cats 78
caves 131, 139, 149, 189, 225, *see also* ice caves, lava tubes
cell phones 238

chess 130
children, travel with 234, 243, 249
chocolate 57
Christmas 31
Christmas House 163
churches & cathedrals 74, 79, 89, 98, 146, 163
classical music 167
climate 26-33, 45, 95
climate change 44, 141, 144-5, 247
clothing 95, 96
coffee 59
constellations 178-9
costs 19, 239, 240, 243, 244
credit cards 243
culture 8-9, 72-5, 76-7, 208-9
Culture Night 68-71
currency 243
customs regulations 238
cycling 216

D

Dalvík 165
demographics 249
DesignMarch 32
Diamond Beach 143
Diamond Circle 41
Dimmuborgir 17, 198
discount cards 53, 73, 175, 243
distilleries 80
diving 169, 207
Djúpalónssandur 225
Djúpavík 217
Djúpavogskörin 156
dog sleds 165
dolphins 186
Drangey 193
Drangsnes 213
drinking, see individual regions
driving, see car travel

drones 214, 246
ducks 186
duty-free allowance 238
Dynjandi 212
Dýrafjörður 212
Dyrhólaey 125

E

earthquakes 83, 112-13
East & Southeast Iceland 132-57, **134**
  accommodation 135
  artworks 157
  drinking 135
  festivals 157
  food 135
  money 135
  navigation 135
  planning 134
  road trips 157
  travel seasons 135
  travel to East Iceland 135
  travel within East Iceland 135
Eastfjords 148-51
Eiriksson, Leif 9, 227
Eiríksstaðir 227
Eiríkur rauði 227
Eldborg 115
Eldfell 113
electricity 248
elves 114, 155, see also folklore
emergencies 250
environment 44
Esja 82
Eskifjörður 147, 149
etiquette 106-7, 248, 249
events, see festivals & events
Eyjafjallajökull 113
Eyjafjarðará estuary 169
Eyjafjarðarsveit 41
Eyjafjörður 162-3

F

Fagradalsfjall 111, 113
Falljökull 138
family travel 234, 249
Fardagafoss 151
farms 162-3, 167, 168, 189, 194-5, 217, 234, 245
Fáskrúðsfjörður 147
fermented shark 58, 61
ferries 135, 239
festivals & events 26-33, see also individual locations
  Aldrei fór ég suður 216
  Culture Night 68-71
  Gásir 189
  horse riding 195
  Hríseyjarhátíð 193
  Listasumar 167
  Mývatn Winter Festival 165
  Sólstöðuhátíð 193
  Víðidalstungurétt 40
filming locations 190-1
films 9, 47, 191, 197
Fimmvörðuháls 127
Fischer, Bobby 130
fishing 89, 129, 163, 208-9
Five-Summit Challenge 150
Fjallahöfn 183
Fjallsárlón lagoon 143
Fjarðabyggð 146
fjords 212-13
Flatey (North Iceland) 15, 181, 193
Flatey (Westfjords) 241
folklore 153, 188-9, see also elves, sagas, trolls
food 12-13, 58-9, 60-1, see also individual regions
  farm restaurants 61, 98, 130, 153, 156, 163
fortune telling 189

G

Game of Thrones 47, 189
gannets 183, 187, see also bird-watching, birds
gardens, see parks & gardens
Garðabær 75
Gásir 189
geothermal energy 44, 249
geothermal pools, see hot springs & geothermal pools
geysers 86, 95, 99
Geysir 95
glaciers 16-17, 144-5
  Breiðamerkurjökull 139
  Eyjafjallajökull 125, 126, 127, 131
  Falljökull 38, 138
  Langjökull 97
  Morsárjökull 138
  Mýrdalsjökull 127
  Snæfellsjökull 224-5
  Solheimajökull 131
  Svínafellsjökull 137
  Vatnajökull National Park 136-9
gin 80
glamping 244
Glerárdalur 169
Gljúfrabúi 123, 125
Glymur 23, 233
goats 234
Goðaborg 150
Golden Circle 39, 84-99, **86**
  accommodation 87, 99
  food 87, 98
  history 90-3
  hot springs 99
  itineraries 38-9, **38-9**
  planning 86
  travel seasons 87
  travel to the Golden Circle 87
  travel within the Golden Circle 87

golf 169
Grábrók 225
Grænavatn 115
Grandi 57
greetings 249
Grettislaug 189
Grímsey 187, 193, 213
Grímsstaðavör 79
Grímsvötn 113
Grindavík 114
Grjótagjá 189
Grótta 82
Grundarfjörður 223
Grundarfoss 233
Guðrúnarlaug 227
guided tours 111, 131, 224, see also caves, hiking, horse riding, wildlife-watching
Fjallsárlón lagoon 143
Hvannadalshnjúkur 137
Westfjords 216
Gullfoss 97
Gunnuhver 115
gyrfalcons 187

H

Hádegisfjall 150
Hafnarfjörður 75
Háleyjarbunga 115
Hallgrímskirkja 74, 79
Hallormsstaður Forest 152-3
Haukadalur 227
Heiðmörk 82
Heimaey 116-17
Helgason, Oddi 180
Helgustaðanáma 149
Hellalaugur 217
Hellisheiði eystri 157
Hellnar 223
Hellulaug 211
Hengifoss 153

hiking
  Borgarfjörður Eystri 154-5
  Five-Summit Challenge 150
  Hornstrandir 214-15
  Landmannalaugar 128-9
  Mt Súlur 163
  Skaftafell 141
  Vatnajökull National Park 136-9
  Víknaslóðir Trail 155
  West Iceland 232-3
  Westfjords, the 211
  Þórsmörk 126-7
history 8-9, 90-3, 189
Hjalteyri 166
Höfn 37
Hofsós 183
Hólmatindur 150
Hólmavík 33, 43, 203, 205, 216, 217
Hornbjarg 213, 215
Hornstrandir 213, 214-15
Hornvík 215
horse riding 97, 129, 163, 195
horses 194-7, 234
hostels 245
hot dogs 56
hot springs & geothermal pools 10-11, 25, 44
  east Iceland 147, 154
  Eastfjords 156
  etiquette 45
  Golden Circle 86, 99
  Landmannalaugar 129
  north Iceland 189, 198, 199
  south Iceland 131
  west Iceland 227, 234-5
  Westfjords 205, 211, 213, 217
Hraunsvatn 169
Hringsdalur 212
Hrísey 193
Hríseyjarhátíð 193

Húsafell 233
Húsavík 184-5, 191
Húsavíkurfjall 177
Hvammstangi 40, 175, 183, 199
Hvannadalshnjúkur 137
Hveravellir 41, 198
Hvítserkur 189

I

ice caves 139, *see also* caves
ice cream 57
Iceland Airwaves Music Festival 29
Icelandic language 44, 250
Icelandic Sorcery Festival 33
Illugastaðir 183
Imagine Peace Tower 28
insurance 240, 242
internet resources 47, 245, 247
  accommodation 245
  gigs 77
Ísafjörður 31, 32, 43, 205, 207, 209, 215, 216
itineraries 34-43, *see also individual regions*

J

jet-skis 169
Jökulsárlón glacier lagoon 142-3
Jólasveinabrekkan 165

K

Kakalaskáli 189
Kaldbakur 211
Kálfshamarsvík 177
kayaking 143, 150, 169, 207
Kerið 97
Kerling 169
Kistufell 150
Kjarnaskógur 168
Kolaportið 83
Kolugljúfur 189
Kópavogur 75
Krafla 198
Kristínartindar 141
Krossanesborgir 169
Krosslaug 217
Krossneslaug 213
Krýsuvík 115
Kverkfjöll 198
Kvernufoss 15, 123

L

Lagarfljót 153
Lagarfljót Wyrm 153
Lakagígar 138
Lake Kleifarvatn 115
Landmannalaugar 39, 128-9
Landsmót Hestamanna 195
Langanes Peninsula 183
Langisandur 234
Langjökull 97
language 44, 250
Látrabjarg 212
Laufás 167
Laugahringur 129
Laugar 227
Laugarfell 198
Laugavegurinn 129
lava 110-11
Lava Show 130
lava tubes 111, 224-5
LGBTIQ+ travellers 63, 65, 249
libraries 81
lighthouses 114
Listasumar 167
literature 189, 228-9, *see also* books
Litli-Hrútur 111
live music 63, 77, 83, 146, 167, 223
Lögberg 89
Lónsöræfi 138

M

markets 69, 83, 98
media 47
midnight sun 177
Midwinter Feast 30, 31
mines 149
Mjóifjörður 157
mobile phones 238
money 19, 53, 238, 243
Morsárjökull 138
Mt Kaldbakur 165
Mt Súlur 163
Mugison 46
Múlagöng 177
Múlakolla 165
museums & galleries 72-5
  Akureyri Art Museum 166
  Akureyri Museum 166
  Árbær Open Air Museum 81
  Bobby Fischer Center 130
  Centre for Contemporary Art 166
  Davíðshús 167
  Duushús 114
  Einar Jónsson Museum 74
  Eiríksstaðir 227
  Eldheimar Museum 116
  Factory 217
  French Museum 147
  Gerðarsafn Art Museum 75
  Glaumbær 189
  Grenjaðarstaður 189
  Hælið Museum 163
  Hafnarborg 75
  Hákarla Jörundur Museum 193
  Herring Era Museum 182, 189
  Horse History Centre 195
  Húsavík Whale Museum 185
  i8 81
  Icelandic Folk and Outsider Art

Museum 166
Icelandic Phallological Museum 79
Icelandic Punk Museum 81
Icelandic Sea Monster Museum 209
Icelandic Seal Center 183
Jón Sigurðsson Museum 216
Laufás 167, 189
Lava Centre 130
Leif Eiriksson Center 227
Maritime Museum 147
Museum of Design & Applied Art 75
Museum of Icelandic Sorcery & Witchcraft 217
Museum of Prophecies 189
National Gallery of Iceland 74
National Museum of Iceland 74
Nonnahús 166
Ósvör Maritime Museum 209
Petra's Mineral Collection 147
Reykjavík Art Museum 9, 73
Reykjavík Maritime Museum 55
Saga Museum 81
Samúel Jónsson's Art Museum 217
Settlement Centre 227
Settlement Exhibition 79
Sheep Farming Museum 217
Sigurgeir's Bird Museum 185
Skógar Museum 130
Smámunasafnið 163
Stekkjarkot 114
Sudurnes Science & Learning Center 114
Toy Museum 167
Viking World 114
Wartime Museum 147
Westfjords Heritage Museum 209
music 46, 76-7
Musterið Spa 154
Mývatn 32, 37, 165, 185, 195, 198

N
National Day 26
national parks 244
Naustahvilft 211
Neskaupstaður 147
New Nordic food 13
New Year's Eve 30
Nonni 197
Norse mythology 176, 181, 197
North Iceland 40-1, 170-99, **40-1, 172-3**
  accommodation 175
  bird watching 183
  costs 174
  drinking 175
  food 175, 199
  planning 172-3
  rafting 199
  travel seasons 174
  travel to/from North Iceland 174
  travel within North Iceland 174
  waterfalls 199
Northern Lights 6-7, 30, 45, 176-7, 178, 180-1

O
Of Monsters & Men 46, 76, 77
Ólafsfjörður 165, 169
Ólafsson, Ólafur Örn 56
Ono, Yoko 28
Önundarfjörður 213
Öskjuhlíð 82
Ósmann, Jón 177
outdoor activities 22-3, see also snow sports, individual activities

P
parks & gardens 82, 153, 168
parliament 86, 88-9, 90
Páskahellir 149
Patreksfjörður 42, 205
Perlan 83
plogging 246
poetry 228
Pollurinn 217
pool etiquette 45
pools 248
porpoises 231
ptarmigans 187
public art 74
puffins 26, 230
  Akureyri 169
  Grímsey 193
  Hafnarhólmi 155
  Ingólfshöfði 138
  Látrabjarg 212
  Vestmannaeyjar 117

R
rafting 97
Rauðasandur 212
Rauðfeldsgjá Gorge 233
Raufarhöfn 176
Raufarhólshellir 111
reindeer 149
responsible travel 44, 246-7
  carbon calculators 241
Reyðarfjörður 147
Reykhólar Sea Baths 217
Reykjadalur 131
Reykjafjarðarlaug 212
Reykjafjörður 211
Reykjanes Peninsula 38, see also Southwest Iceland & the Reykjanes Peninsula
Reykjanestá 115

Reykjavík 48-83, **34-5**, **50-1**
  accommodation 53
  budgeting 52
  discount cards 75
  drinking & nightlife 53, 62-5, 66-7, 83
  entertainment 83
  festivals & events 27, 68-71
  food 53, 54-61, 60-1, 80-1
  internet access 53
  itineraries 34-5, **34-5**
  museums & galleries 72-5, 81
  planning 50-1
  swimming pools 82
  travel seasons 52
  travel to Reykjavík 52
  travel within Reykjavík 52
  walking tour 78-9, **79**
Reynisfjara 120, 125
Ring Road 18, 36-7, 44, **36-7**
road conditions 241
road distances 241
road rules 240
road trips 18
  Arctic Circle 176-7
  Arctic Coast Way 182-3
  Coast Road to Vík 124
  Hringsdalur 212
  Westfjords 210-11
Rutshellir Cave 131

S

Sælingsdalur 227
safe travel 23, 242
sagas 81, 91, 226-7, 228-9
Sandgerði 114
Sauðárkrókur 165
scenic flights 111
sea stacks 125
sea swimming 11, see also swimming, beaches
seafood 182
seals 183, 230
Secret Lagoon 86
Selárdalslaug 156
Selfoss 36
Seljalandsfoss 123, 125
Seljavallalaug 131
Seltún 115
Seyðisfjörður 37, 135, 146-7, 151, 155, 157
sheep 217, 234
shoes 248
Siglufjörður 165, 189
Silfra 97
Skaftafell 136-9, 140-1
skiing, see snow sports
Skógafoss 123, 125
Skógar 123
Skúlaskeið 197
skyr 58, 234
sledding 165
Slow Food 13
smoking 248
Snæfellsjökull 224-5
Snæfellsnes 42
snorkelling 97, 169
Snorrastofa 227
snow sports 20-1, 97, 164-5, 216,
social media 47
solstices 7, 26, 30, 178-9, 193
Sólstöðuhátíð 193
South Coast & Southern Highlands 39, 118-31, **120-21**
  accommodation 121
  drinking 121
  food 121, 130
  money 121
  navigation 121
  planning 120
  travel seasons 121
  travel to South Coast 121
  travel within South Coast 121
Southeast Iceland, see East & Southeast Iceland
Southern Highlands, see South Coast & Southern Highlands
Southwest Iceland & the Reykjanes Peninsula 100-15, **102**
  accommodation 103
  money 103
  navigation 103
  planning 102
  travel seasons 103
  travel to Southwest Iceland 103
  travel within Southwest Iceland 103
spas, see hot springs & geothermal pools
Stampar 115
Star Wars 190
stargazing 6-7, 176-7, 178-9, 180-1
Stefánsson, Davíð 167
Stjörnu-Oddi 180-1
Stóðréttir 195
Stórurð 155
Stuðlagil canyon 150
Sturluson, Snorri 226-7, 228-9
Stykkishólmur 223
sumarbústaðir 245
Sundhnúksgígar 111, 113
Sundlaug Eskifjarðar 156
Sundlaug Hafnar 156
Svartafjall 150
Svartifoss 137, 141
Sveinsson, Jón 166, 197
Svínafellsjökull 137
swimming 11, 234-5
  etiquette 45
  Forest Lagoon 163
  Hofsós 199
  Hrafnagil 163
  Kópavogslaug 75
  Laugardalslaug 73, 82

Reykjafjarðarlaug 212
Reykjavík 82-3
Vesturbæjarlaug 79

T

taxis 239
tea 135
tectonic plates 89, 97
telephone codes 248
telephone services 238
Thomsen, Grímur 197
time zones 248
Tindfjöll Circle 127
tipping 243
tölting 196
Trapped 189
travel seasons 26-33, *see also individual regions*
travel to/from Iceland 238
travel within Iceland 239, 240-1
Tröllaskagi 41
trolls 114, 234, *see also* folklore
turf churches 163
turf farms & houses 131, 167, 181, 189
TV series 47, 189

V

Vaglaskógur 168
Valagil 213
Valahnúkur 127
VAT refunds 243
Vatnajökull National Park 136-9
Vatnsdæla Tapestry 189
Vatnshellir 225
Vattarnes 157
Veiðileysufjörður 215
Verne, Jules 224
Vestmannaeyjar 13, 116-17
Viðey 28, 35, 74, 81
Viðgelmir 225

Víðidalstungurétt 40
viewpoints 114, 211
Vigur 207, 213
Vík 37, 39
viking restaurants 114, 130
Víknaslóðir Trail 155
Vök Baths 147
volcanoes 16-17, 86, 110-13, 116, 198, 224-5
safety 242
volunteering 246

W

waffles 69, 115
walking tours 78-9, 203, 216, **79**, *see also* hiking
water therapy 25
waterfalls 94-5, 122-3
  Brúarfoss 95
  Fardagafoss 151
  Faxi 95
  Gljúfrabúi 123, 125
  Glymur 23, 233
  Grundarfoss 233
  Gullfoss 86, 95, 97
  Hengifoss 153
  Hlauptungufoss 95
  Húsafell 233
  Kvernufoss 15, 123
  Miðfoss 95
  Öxarárfoss 89
  Reykjafoss 199
  Seljalandsfoss 123, 125
  Skaftafell 141
  Skógafoss 123, 125
  Svartifoss 137
weather 26-33, 45
  safety 242
West Iceland 218-35, **220-1**
  accommodation 223
  food 223, 235

itineraries 42-3, 220-1, **42-3**
travel seasons 222
travel to/from West Iceland 222
travel within West Iceland 222
Westfjords 200-17, **202-3**
  accommodation 205
  drinking 205
  fjords 212-13
  food 205
  itineraries 202-3
  travel seasons 204
  travel to/from the Westfjords 204
  travel within the Westfjords 204
whale-watching 33, 117, 169, 184-5, 207, 216
whales 83, 186, 230
wi-fi 53, 238
wildlife 186-7, 230-1, *see also* bird-watching, whale-watching, *individual species*
wildlife-watching 89, 183, 207
winter solstice 30

Y

yoga 163
Yule Lads Bath 165

Þ

Þeistareykir 198
Þingeyri 42, 205, 212
Þingvallabær 89
Þingvellir National Park 86, 88-9
Þórsmörk 39, 123, 124, 126-7
Þríhnúkagígur 111
Þrístapar 189

Z

ziplining 131
zoos & animal sanctuaries 82, 117, 195

'The first time I walked the coast in the Vestmannaeyjar islands (p116) watching puffins teeter into the ocean and return to their burrows.'

ALEXIS AVERBUCK

'Standing at Raufarhöfn's Arctic Henge (p176) with views in all directions, imagining the ancient Icelandic sagas coming to life.'

MARY FITZPATRICK

'Sailing in Húsavík's Skjálfandi Bay (p185) on a brilliant, blue-sky day and spotting whales breaching against a backdrop of snowy mountainsides.'

MARY FITZPATRICK

Although the authors and Lonely Planet have taken all reasonable care in preparing this book, we make no warranty about the accuracy or completeness of its content and, to the maximum extent permitted, disclaim all liability arising from its use.

All rights reserved. No part of this publication may be copied, stored in a retrieval system, or transmitted in any form by any means, electronic, mechanical, recording or otherwise, except brief extracts for the purpose of review, and no part of this publication may be sold or hired, without the written permission of the publisher. Lonely Planet and the Lonely Planet logo are trademarks of Lonely Planet and are registered in the US Patent and Trademark Office and in other countries. Lonely Planet does not allow its name or logo to be appropriated by commercial establishments, such as retailers, restaurants or hotels. Please let us know of any misuses: lonelyplanet.com/legal/intellectual-property.

THIS BOOK

The 2nd edition of Lonely Planet's *Experience Iceland* guidebook was written and researched by Anthony Ham, Alexis Averbuck, Jade Bremner and Mary Fitzpatrick. The previous edition was written and researched by Zoë Robert, Eygló Svala Arnarsdóttir, Egill Bjarnason and Jeannie Riley.

This guidebook was produced by the following:

Destination editor
Amy Lynch

Production editor
Kate Chapman

Cartographer
Valentina Kremenchutskaya

Image Editor
Compton Sheldon

Coordinating editor
Mani Ramaswamy

Assisting editors
Imogen Bannister, Peter Cruttenden, Melanie Dankel, Kellie Langdon

Cover researcher
Stefanie Delgado

Thanks
Darren O'Connell, James Smart, Saralinda Turner

LONELY PLANET

ICELAND MAP

- Must-see Highlights
- Travel Tips
- Walking Tour

NEED TO KNOW

Weights & Measures
Iceland uses the metric system. Distances and speeds are measured in kilometres.

Opening Hours
Supermarkets 7am–midnight. Some open as late as 10am and close as early as 8pm.

Government-owned liquor stores (Vínbúðin) Typically 11am–6pm Monday to Saturday. Some remote stores only open between 4pm and 6pm.

Bars To 1am Sunday to Thursday, and as late as 5.30am on Friday and Saturday.

lonelyplanet.com

Images by Daniel Dorsa for Lonely Planet; alicina, Banana Images, endorphine, ImageBank4u, Kristvin Gudmundsso, Louise Kurir Neumann, Matt93, Megpier, pio3, Phailthun Anantaket, Thorsteinn Asgeirsson, VicPhotoria/Shutterstock

OUR PICKS

▼ If you're a beginner, go river rafting down the welcoming **Hvítá (G9)** or **West Glacial (H5)** rivers. If you're looking for more of an adventure, take on the **East Glacial River. J6**

▼ Feel the rich silica mud between your toes as you wade into the **Blue Lagoon** to soak in its iconic blue geothermal water. **D9**

◄ Get a close-up view of **Kirkjufell**, an iconic pyramid-shaped mountain on the Snæfellsnes Peninsula. **C6**

◄ Head to UNESCO World Heritage Site **Þingvellir National Park** to watch the Northern Lights. **F8**

◄ Look for gigantic blue whales on a whalewatching tour off the coast of **Húsavík**. Humpback and minke whales are most common, but blue whales have also been spotted. **L3**

▲ Depending on your timing, you may be able to fly over a volcanic eruption such as **Fagradalsfjall** on a helicopter tour and see bubbling, flowing lava. **D9**

▲ Visit during winter to explore natural ice caves like **Katla Ice Cave**. A human-made ice cave within **Langjökull** is open year-round. **J11**

▲ Take an hour-long hike around the lake **Víti crater** in the Krafla volcanic area near Lake Mývatn. **L4**

▲ Take a boat tour from Reykjavík's Old Harbour to **Akurey**, **Engey** or **Lundey**, where thousands of puffin pairs nest each summer. **E9**

▲ Dive into the glacial water of the **Silfra fissure**, the only place in the world where it's possible to swim between continents. **F8**

ICELAND

Towns/Cities

A
Akranes E8

B
Bakkafjörður O3
Bíldudalur C4
Blönduós G4
Bolungarvík C3
Borgarnes E8
Breiðdalsvík P7
Brjánslækur C5
Búðardalur E6

D
Djúpivogur P7

E
Egilsstaðir O5
Eskifjörður P6

F
Fáskrúðsfjörður P6

G
Geysir G8
Grindavík D10

H
Hella G10
Höfn O8
Hólmavík E4
Húsavík P5
Hvammstangi F5
Hvammsvík E8

Hvammsvík Hot Springs E8
Hveragerði F9
Hvolsvöllur G10

I
Ísafjörður D3

K
Keflavík D9
Kirkjubæjarklaustur K10

N
Neskaupstaður P6
Njarðvík P4
Norðurfjörður E3

O
Ólafsvík C6

P
Patreksfjörður B4

R
Reyðarfjörður P6
Reykjahlíð L4
REYKJAVÍK E9
Rif B6

S
Sauðárkrókur H4
Selfoss F9
Seyðisfjörður P5
Siglufjörður J3
Skagaströnd G4
Skógar H11
Stafafell O8
Stöðvarfjörður P7

Stykkishólmur D6
Suðureyri C3

Þ
Þingeyri C4

Sights
Akureyri K4
Blue Lagoon D9
East Glacial River J6
Engey E9
Fagradalsfjall Volcano D9
Heimaey G11
Húsavík L3
Hvítá River G9
Jökulsárlón M9
Katla Ice Cave J11
Kirkjufell C6
Langjökull G7
Silfra F8
Víti L4
West Glacial River H5

National Parks & Gardens
Fjallabak Nature Reserve H9
Hallormsstaðaskógur O6
Haukadalur G8
Hornstrandir Nature Reserve D2
Reykjanesfólkvangur E9
Skaftafell L9
Snæfellsjökull National Park B7
Þingvellir National Park F8

Vatnajökull National Park L8
Vatnajökull National Park – North M4
Vatnsfjörður Nature Reserve C4

Geographic Features
Askja (1514m) M6
Bárðarbunga (2009m) L7
Berserkjahraun C6
Breiðamerkurjökull M9
Buðahraun C7
Drangajökull D3
Dyngjujökull L7
Eiriksjökull (1675m) G7
Eyjabakkajökull N7
Eyjafjallajökull H10
Fláajökull N8
Grímsvötn (1719m) L8
Hallmundarhraun G7
Heinabergsjökull N8
Hoffellsjökull N8
Hofsjökull J7
Holuhraun L7
Hvannadalshnúkur (2110m) M9
Katla (1250m) J10
Kverkfjöll (1860m) M7
Mýrdalsjökull J10
Myrkarjökull J4
Neshraun B6
Öræfajökull M9
Síðujökull K9
Skaftafell L9
Skaftárjökull K9
Skálafellsjökull M8
Skeiðarárjökull L9
Snæfellsjökull B7
Sólheimajökull H10

Þrándarjökull O7
Tindfjallajökull H10

Water Features
Apavatn F9
ATLANTIC OCEAN B8
Austari-Jökulsá J5
Austura G6
Bjarnarfjorður E4
Blanda H5
Blöndulón Reservoir H6
Eyjafjarðará J5
Fnjóská K5
Geldalsa O6
Geithellnadalur N7
Grímsa F8
Hafralonsa N4
Hágöngulón K8
Hálslón Reservoir H5
Haukadalsá E6
Hjaltadalsa H4
Hólmsá J10
Hörgá J5
Hofsa N5
Hvíta H8
Hvítárvatn G7
Jokulsa N7
Jokulsá á Brú N6
Jokulsa á Fjollum M5-M7
Kaldakvist J8
Kreppa M6
Kverka M7-N3
Kvíslavatn J8
Langisjór J9
Lagarfljót O5
Laxa L4
Laxá E6
Markarfljót G10

Morilukvísl M4
Mývatn L5
Nordhura E7
Nordhlingafljot F7
Núpsá L10
Ölkjuvatn L6
Sandvatn G8
Sela E3
Selá N4
Skaftaros J10
Skidhadalsa J4
Skjálfandafljót K5-K6-L4
Skorradalsvatn E8
Stóra-Laxá G9
Svarta H5
Svinavatn G5
Tungnaa J9
Vestura F6
Þingvallavatn F9
Vatnsedalsa G5
Vestari-Jökulsá H5
Vidhidalsa G5
Vík J11
Vopnafjörður O4
Þjórsá H8
Þórisvatn J8
Þorlákshöfn E10

REYKJAVÍK

Streets
Aðalstræti P2-R10
Amtmannsst R3
Austurstræti Q2
Bankastræti R3
Fisch P2
Garðastræti P2
Geirsgata Q1

Grjótagata P2
Hafnarstræti Q2-Q9
Hverfisgata S3
Ingólfsstræti S3
Kalkofnsvegur S1
Kirkjustræti Q3
Kirkjutorg Q3
Lækjargata Q3-Q10
Laugavegur S3
Lindargata S2
Mjóstræti P2
Pósthússtræti Q2
Suðurgata P3
Þingholtsstræti Q3
Tjarnargata P3
Tryggvagata Q2
Túngata P2
Veltus Q2
Vesturgata P1
Vonarstræti Q3

Neighbourhoods
OLD REYKJAVÍK Q3

Plazas
Ingólfur Sq P2
Lækjartorg Sq R2

Parks and Gardens
Austurvöllur Q3

Water Features
Old Harbour R1
Tjörnin P3

Sights
Aðalstræti Settlement Exhibition P2
Alþingi Q3
Arnarhóll S2
Dómkirkja Q3
i8 P1
Icelandic Phallological Museum R2
Icelandic Punk Museum R3
Jón Sigurðsson Statue Q3
Raðhús P3
Reykjavík Art Museum Hafnarhús Q1
Reykjavík Museum of Photography Q1
Skúli Magnússon Statue P2

AKUREYRI

Streets
Aðalstræti R10
Álfabyggð Q10
Byggðavegur P10
Dalsbraut P10
Davíðshagi Q12
Drottningarbraut R10-R11
Eyjafjarðarbraut Q9
Hafnarstræti Q9
Hamarstígur P9
Hrafnagilsstræti Q9
Kjarnagata Q11
Kjarnavegur Q12
Lækjargata Q10
Mímisbraut Q10
Myrarvegur P9

Naustagata Q11
Naustavegur Q10
Skogarlundur P10
Spitalavegur Q9
Þingvallastræti P9
Þjóðvegur R10
Þórunnarstræti Q9

Transportation
Akureyri International Airport R11

Parks And Gardens
Hamarskotstún P9
Jaðarsvöllur P11
Lystigarður Q9

Water Features
Eyjafjörður R9

Sights
Akureyrakirkyja Q9
Akureyri Art Museum Q9
Akureyri Museum R11
Davíð Stefánsson Writers' Museum Q8
Hafnarstræti Q9
Icelandic Aviation Museum R12
Laxdalshús R10
Motorcycle Museum of Iceland R11
Nonnahús R11
Páðhústorgið Q9
Toy Museum R10

GETTING AROUND

Road Conditions
Major roads in Iceland, like the Ring Road (Rte 1), are well maintained throughout. Secondary roads may be gravel roads but are accessible to all types of vehicles. F roads are challenging roads, sometimes over mountains or through rivers, that should only be attempted by experienced 4WD drivers.

Trains & Buses
There's no public train system in Iceland. Reykjavík has an extensive bus system, but it's harder to get around by bus beyond Selfoss on the southern coast and Borgarnes to the north. Akureyri, Ísafjörður, Reykjanesbær and the Eastfjords also have local bus systems.

Ships & Ferries
Iceland is a popular cruise destination with several lines sailing to Iceland from North America and Europe. It's also getting easier to circumnavigate the island on a cruise ship. There's a weekly ferry service from Denmark via the Faroe Islands.

Planes
A domestic airport in Reykjavík connects the capital to three Icelandic cities: Akureyri, Egilsstaðir and Ísafjörður.

Ridesharing & Hitchhiking
Iceland has about as many cars as it has people. While it doesn't allow ridesharing services like Lyft and Uber, it does have a vibrant carpool scene. People submit routes they're driving on samferda.net, and passengers can request rides and offer to split costs. Because public transport is limited outside of Reykjavík, carpooling is a popular option for getting between cities. It's also not uncommon to see hitchhikers.

Cycling
Iceland's Ring Road is a major draw for cyclists, but there are no bike lanes. Cold, rain and wind can make for uncomfortable conditions and contingency planning is key. Bike rentals are available in Reykjavík and a handful of other towns. Off-road biking is also popular and many trails allow bikes.

HOW MUCH FOR

EV Charging
Around 420kr per 100km

Standard rental car
around 15,000kr/day

Bus
670kr per ride in Reykjavík

MONEY

Cash
Don't feel pressured to visit an ATM. Most places in Iceland accept credit cards and digital payments, even in remote towns and for small purchases. Some public restrooms require payment; coins can be useful here, but many also have card payment options.

Chip & Pin
A If you don't have a chip-based credit card, you'll need a pin to use your plastic in Iceland. Pins aren't required with chipbased cards, which are predominantly used for contactless payments.

Tipping
Taxes and service charges are always included in Iceland. Tipping is not expected, but rounding up restaurant bills or leaving an additional tip for exceptional service is always appreciated. Service charges may also be included in bills.

Taxes & Refunds
Iceland's standard VAT is 24%. Books, food and accommodation are taxed at a lower 11%. Visitors who live outside of Iceland can claim a tax refund on transactions of 6000kr or more – ask for a form to fill in and a receipt from the shop, and drop these off at the airport.

HOW MUCH FOR

Espresso 400kr

Beer 1050-1800kr

Golden Circle Tour 10000kr

Train seat reservation €5.50

Iceland for Free
If you're looking for a cheap holiday, Iceland isn't it. After flights, a large portion of budgets go on accommodation and eating out. Then fill your itinerary with free activities. Visit waterfalls, national parks and geothermal areas across the country. Go hiking. Take in epic views. Walk across the red lava fields, black beaches, visit glacial lakes and nature reserves. Check out Heiðmörk Nature Reserve, Harpa concert hall and the Reykjavík Botanic Garden. Set out in search of the Northern Lights. Believe it or not, the best things in Iceland are free.

Group up to Save
Skip the tours and self-drive with a group to save money – big attractions are easily accessible and mostly free (although watch out for parking fees). Smaller remote attractions usually don't charge for parking.

OCEANFRONT WALK IN SELTJARNARNES, REYKJAVÍK

Surrounded by wild ocean, Seltjarnarnes peninsula at Reykjavík's western edge is a place to escape for inspiring walks and abundant birdlife

Start Church of Seltjarnarnes
End Sundlaug Seltjarnarness
Length 7km; 2 hours

1 Church of Seltjarnarnes
Begin near the peaked **Church of Seltjarnarnes** and follow the coastal trail. As you go you'll see waves rushing in to lava-strewn beaches, fish-drying racks sitting by the shore, **Mt Esja** rising across the bay and **Arctic terns** screaming overhead.

2 Raðagerði Veitingahús
If you're feeling peckish, pop into one of Reykjavík's best Italian restaurants, cosy **Raðagerði Veitingahús**, with a menu of pizzas, bruschetta and great brunches.

3 Kvika Footbath
Stop at the tiny **Kvika Footbath**. Icelandic artist Ólöf Nordal carved the tiny pool out of a coastal rock, and it's fed by a warm geothermal spring. Soak your feet while taking in mountain and water views.

4 Grótta Lighthouse
Anchoring a nature reserve and surrounded by rugged coastline and black sand you'll find **Grótta Lighthouse**. On a clear day you can see as far as **Snæfellsnes Peninsula**. Arctic terns form a colony on the rocks (stick to marked paths) while tufted ducks hang out in an adjacent pond. You can only safely walk to the lighthouse's islet when tides are low.

5 Nesvöllur golf course
The trail curves around the flat expanse of the **Nesvöllur golf course**. At the golf club, the excellent restaurant Ness creates seasonally rotating menus featuring fresh fish, local produce and expansive views.

6 Sundlaug Seltjarnarness
Finish with a hot soak at the local pool, **Sundlaug Seltjarnarness**, with its mineralwater swimming pool, waterslide and steam bath.

GET PREPARED

Clothes

Layers The weather in Iceland is unpredictable, and layering is your best strategy regardless of when you're travelling. Pack a lightweight puffer jacket and sturdy waterproof hiking boots for summer travel.

Choose waterproof trousers over jeans for hiking, and leave the vest tops, sandals and shorts at home – you won't need them, even in July.

Winter gear Winter weather is milder than you might expect, with temperatures rarely dipping below freezing. Pack snow pants, snow boots, a warm coat, gloves, a hat and thermal base layers. Excursion operators provide heavy winter gear for activities like snowmobiling and glacial hiking.

Casual vs formal Icelanders dress casually, so you can leave the heels, sport coats and formalwear behind.

Words

Icelandic is a Germanic language of the same family as German, English and the Scandinavian languages (excluding Finnish). It stems from Old Norse and has changed remarkably little since the Saga Age. Most Icelanders and those who work in the tourist industry speak English. However, Icelanders do appreciate it when visitors make an effort.

Here are a few helpful words:

Halló (hah-lo) 'Hello'
Góðan daginn (go-thah-n die-in) 'Good day'
Vinsamlegast (vin-saamleh-gast) 'Please'
Takk (tak) 'Thank you'
Já (y-ow) 'Yes'
Nei (neigh) 'No'
Bless (bles) 'Goodbye'
Hvar er...? (kva-r-eh-r) 'Where is…?'
Klósett (k-low-seht) 'Toilet'
Skál (sk-owl) 'Cheers'

FOOD & DRINK

When to eat

Breakfast (9–11am) Most coffee shops don't open until 8am. Many cafes open at 10am or later.
Lunch (11am–2pm) Many restaurants close in the late afternoon. Expect limited dining options between 3pm and 5pm.
Dinner (7–9pm) Restaurant kitchens start closing before 10pm, and it's hard to find anything to eat after then.

Eat Skyr

Skyr is a rich, creamy dairy product that's packaged like a yoghurt but technically defined as a cheese, like ricotta or mascarpone. Icelanders have been eating skyr, which is made from cow's milk, for centuries. It's high in protein but low in fat and accompanied with calcium and B vitamins.

Skyr can be eaten for breakfast or as a snack, or is used to make desserts like cheesecake, crème brûlée or an Icelandic twist on tiramisu. It can also form the base for drinks and smoothies, and there's a type of runny skyr that's essentially a milk.

Skyr is often eaten on the go, with individual servings packaged with disposable spoons.

Pick up a carton at a shop or visit a skyr bar for a bowl topped with fruit, nuts, peanut butter and more. You may opt for a skyr and oatmeal breakfast like many Icelanders do.

You'll encounter skyr on lots of restaurant menus and a skyr bowl for breakfast is popular at many cafes in Reykjavík.
To try skyr from the source, head to Efstidalur II, a farm that makes skyr, feta and ice cream on-site. In Höfn, don't miss the skyr volcano at Pakkhús.

Land of Greenhouses

Icelandic countryside is dotted with greenhouses. These allow Icelandic farmers to grow cucumbers, strawberries, lettuces, peppers, mushrooms, herbs and flowers year-round. At Friðheimar in South Iceland, guests can dine inside a greenhouse on farm-fresh tomatoes grown on-site at the family-owned farm. Or head to Farmers Bistro where you can sample the bounty from Flúðasveppir, Iceland's only mushroom farm. It doesn't get any more farm-to-table than this.

Icelandic beer

Icelanders were beer drinkers from the time this island was settled until prohibition came into effect in 1915. Wine was legalised in 1922 and spirits followed in 1935, but beer remained illegal until 1989.

Nowadays you can find quality craft breweries across the country. Icelandic beer is made with Icelandic water, giving these lagers, pilsners, pale ales and stouts an exceptional taste that can't be matched. The two largest brewers in Iceland are Egill Skallagrímsson Brewery and Viking, but there are more than two dozen smaller beer brands.

HOW MUCH FOR A

Glass of wine 1500kr-1800kr

Main course (dinner) 3000-9000kr

Burger 2700-3300kr

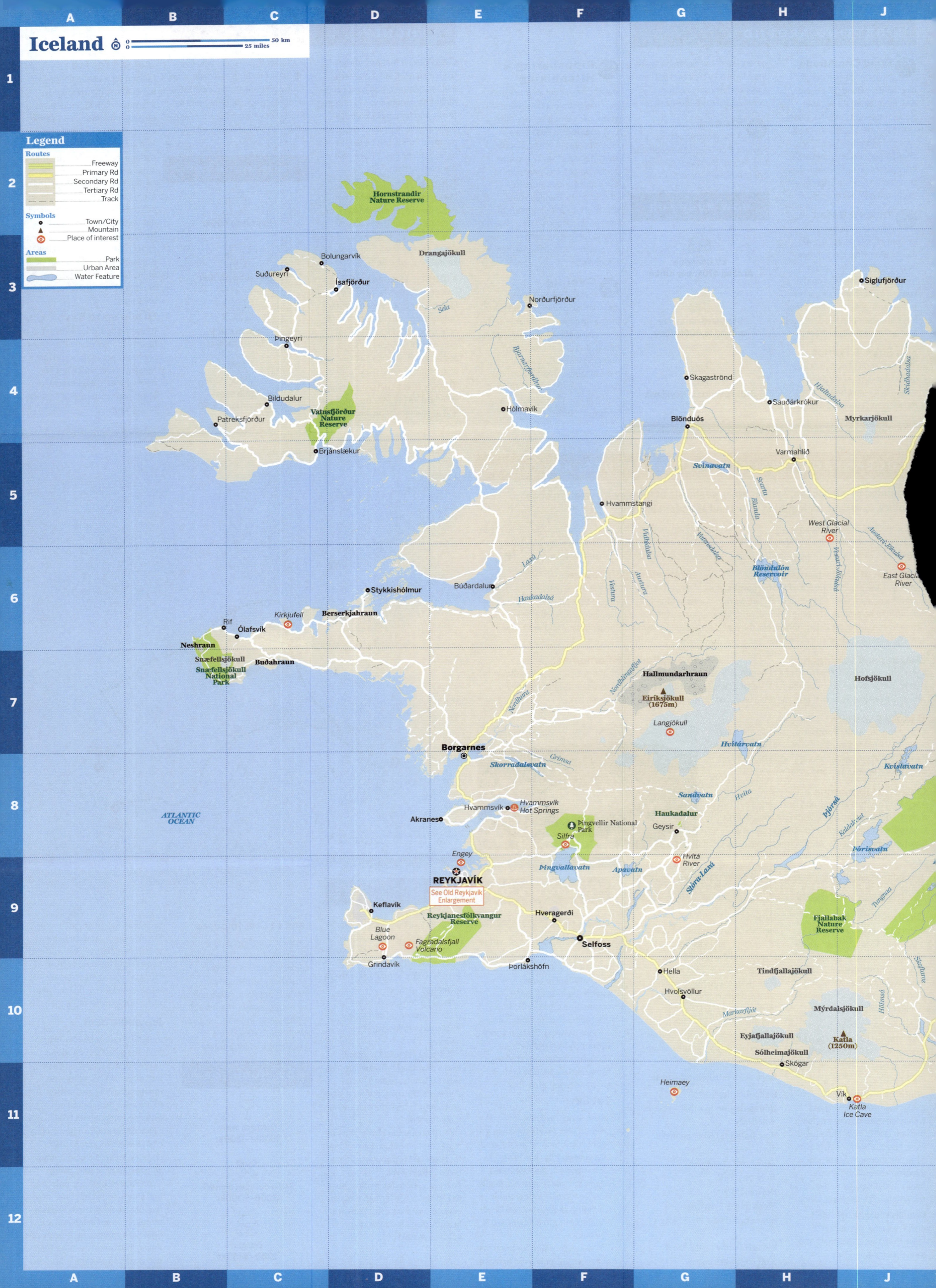

ICELAND

▬ Stare in wonder at lights dancing across the night sky. Climb glaciers and volcanoes. Circumnavigate the island by car. Snorkel where two continents meet. Hike into the highlands and pristine wilderness. Meet saga heroes and trace Viking voyages. Savour fresh flavours of the sea. Kayak along the coast or sail out in search of whales. Take a tractor to see puffins, or a boat between icebergs. Pamper yourself in hot springs and thermal pools. Explore snow fields and backcountry skiing.

This is Iceland.

Anthony Ham, Alexis Averbuck, Jade Bremner, Mary Fitzpatrick

TURN THE PAGE AND START PLANNING YOUR NEXT BEST TRIP →

Meet our writers

Anthony Ham
anthonyham.com; @AnthonyHamWrite

Every time I climb up into the mountains from Egilsstaðir, over the high passes, and down to Seyðisfjörður (p147), I can almost hear the earth exhale. Almost as far as you can get from Reykjavík without falling into the sea, this stunning village with its storybook blue church, thriving art scene and great food wraps around a narrow harbour and inspires in me a feeling of never wanting to leave.

Alexis Averbuck
alexisaverbuck.com

The highlands around Askja (p198) crack open my heart with their beauty. Undulating crater rows give way to iridescent volcanic pools and hidden oases, green with life. And the crater itself, with its magenta rocks and snow-studded rim, remind me of how vast and grand this earth is, beyond all human influence; a magnificent world to be protected and revered.

Jade Bremner
@jadeob

It's hard to beat the Westfjords Way (p210) – an empty stretch of tarmac that zigzags around beautiful fjords and runs through dramatic landscapes, big mountain passes, and long tunnels almost impossibly carved out of rock. It connects adventurous road-trippers to waterfalls, hot pools, expansive beaches and more. Following the route is humbling, yet few of Iceland's visitors even make it here.

Mary Fitzpatrick
@MaryFitzTravel

North Iceland's Arctic Coast Way (p182) is the journey of a lifetime, with its remote coastal villages, bird-filled headlands and unhindered views of the sky. Travelling here brings one spectacular vista after another – snow-covered mountains tumbling down into icy fjords, dramatic waterfalls, soaring gannets, cliffsides filled with nesting puffins and, everywhere, the sea.